Quarrier Press
Charleston, WV

Upper River

Skip Johnson
with Rob Johnson

Edited by
Peter & Elizabeth Silitch

Book Design and Layout by
Neal Gentry

Quarrier Press
Charleston, WV

10 9 8 7 6 5 4 3 2 1

Library of Congress Control Number: 93-86404

ISBN 13: 978-1891852-96-1
ISBN 10: 1-891852-96-5

Book and cover design: Neal Gentry, Wolfpen Digital

Printed in USA

Distributed by:

West Virginia Book Company
1125 Central Avenue
Charleston, WV 25302
www.wvbookco.com

To the memory
of my brother Bob,
whom I loved

Table of Contents

Illustrations

Preface

The high country that embraces the start of Elk River hadn't quite relinquished its hold on the winter of 2001-2002 when I made my first trip there in pursuit of inspiration for this book. It was May, but Kennison Mountain and Black Mountain, which I crossed on the way to the Elk drainage, were dusted with snow from the previous night.

Appalachian spring had truly arrived a month and a half later when I met Ed Maguire and his yellow lab, Abby, at the Cranberry Mountain Visitor Center, a delightful setting that I always enjoy. Then we drove over the parkway section of the Highland Scenic Highway to view the Crooked Fork of Elk Basin. It was there that I fully decided to spend three years of my life writing *Upper River*.

The view was persuasive, but so, in a quiet way, was Ed, the state director of The Nature Conservancy for eleven years and after that the founder and president of The Highlands Group, which has conceived and administered the combined sale and charitable donation to the government of 57,000 acres of mineral rights under the Monongahela National Forest, and initiated and coordinated the sale to the Monongahela of a package of eight privately owned, high altitude, and ecologically significant tracts of land totaling 1,480 acres. Most of the latter tracts are on the Elk drainage, including four hundred acres that corner on Elk at Elk Springs.

For a long time, I have thought of Elk as "West Virginia's river" because it flows through the center of the state, and because it presents such a wide variety of terrain and fish life along the way, from its mountain trout stream beginnings to its Great Kanawha Valley ending.

I chose the Crooked Fork Basin as the symbolic start of Elk for reasons that are given in the book, but I acknowledge that attempting to pinpoint the start of a river is difficult. The headwaters run here and there to greater or lesser degree. Perhaps it is best to say with assurance that Elk begins at Slatyfork where its two principal forks come together, and let it go at that. But writers are never satisfied with simple answers, so I leaped into the "origins" quagmire in Chapter One.

The four mountains that share unique positions in the Elk headwaters are easier to define. They are Thorny Triangulation Point near Snowshoe Mountain Resort, the highest elevation on the entire Elk watershed; Red Spruce Knob and Red Lick Mountain on the Crooked Fork drainage; and Gauley Mountain, which defines the start of Elk at Slatyfork and accompanies it all the way to Elk Springs.

I was disinclined from the beginning to contend that the fifty-five miles of untamed upper Elk from Slatyfork to Sutton Lake is the "real" Elk, separated forever from the rest of the river by five hundred thousand cubic yards of concrete known as Sutton Dam. But rarely does one river have two such distinct and totally different personalities.

Elk above Sutton Lake has a "canyon" personality, particularly in the Curtin area and again below Webster Springs. It takes on what I call a "muskie" personality after it begins the final one hundred mile distance run to Charleston as a broader, flatter river. Muskies are the big fish that inhabit Elk below Sutton. Choosing one personality over the other would be a subjective opinion if there ever was one.

But since I have opened the subjective door, and after spending three years appreciating all of Elk, I will argue its three most prominent components. One is geologic, one is geographic, and one is political. The geologic is the dry bed above Elk Springs where the river goes underground for six miles in dry weather. The geographic is where it flows through the center of the state at Centralia. The political is its ending in Charleston, the seat of state government.

None of that, however, addresses the people of Elk, and in the final analysis people define a river and its communities. Because of Elk's length and its journey through the heartland of the state, it has touched the lives of thousands of people, who have in turn left their imprint on Elk in ways that have become the fabric of folklore. Certainly the Hamricks of Webster County and the Carpenters of Braxton County come to mind, but there are many others who leave their footprints on the pages of *Upper River*. And two remarkable survivors of King Phillip's War were the first Europeans to describe its wonders, in 1675!

Rivers like Elk touch us in a spiritual way. Dave Teets, my neighbor, gave a talk on rivers at our 2004 church picnic. He said that rivers are important in the Bible, important to our soul and mind, and important to God. They also provide recreation, transportation, and natural boundaries. Then he made a less profound but equally important point: "Who hasn't spent at least a part of a day just watching a river roll on?"

Thousands of people see Elk daily from the interstates in Charleston. I hope this book will persuade those who see it *only* there to appreciate it for the diverse and historically significant river that it is, and one that helps to define us as West Virginians.

Upper River represents the contributions of a great many people who shared information or simply gave encouragement, and my thanks to all of them. I have lamented ever since four-wheelers came along that walking has become a lost art, and I am especially grateful, and in some instances offer my condolences, to those who were willing to walk with me and share their familiarity with a particular place or places on Elk.

Recognition is due also to the librarians at Marlinton, Webster Springs, Sutton, Gassaway, Clay, Clendenin, Big Chimney, and Charleston; to Esther Warner at the West Virginia Genealogical Society at Blue Creek; to the State Archives in Charleston; to courthouse personnel along the river's route; to Charleston City Hall; and to Jennifer Lynch, historian at the U.S. Postal Service in Washington, D.C.

My thanks to Ewell Ferguson and GTR, Inc. of Gassaway for the use of their Xerox Document Center.

I am pleased to introduce a young artist to readers of this book. He is Jordan Hudkins, son of Jeff and Molly Hudkins of Cowen. Jordan is a 2004 graduate of Webster County High School, and is attending Shepherd University. He has had five drawings published in the FlipSide section of *the Saturday Gazette-Mail.* One of those won second place in a national competition sponsored by the Newspaper Association of America Foundation. His drawing for this book appears in the Bergoo chapter.

Peter and Elizabeth Silitch did "double duty" this time around as editors, joining me in several adventures afield. One of those resulted in the formation of the mythical state of Middle of Nowhere, which in time may become the book's defining characteristic. If so, all three of us offer our sincere apologies here and now.

Well, we do live in the middle of nowhere, as does Neal Gentry, our neighbor and the design and layout person for this book and the previous one. Neal lives on Wolfpen Run, from where he operates his digital media production business, and certainly from my standpoint operates it quite well. It is nice to have him within walking distance, although I've never actually walked it.

My nephew, Rob Johnson, returns as photographer, which I know a little bit about, but perhaps just enough to be dangerous. Rob, like Peter and Elizabeth, does double duty. He is now the preeminent fisherman in the family, and the trips we have taken over six years and two river books have adequately confirmed that to everybody's satisfaction except mine.

"The river was slightly murky and running with a good flow as it came down from the headwater regions. Elk Springs was contributing most of the water, but the dry bed had a good flow too. They converged at the Mill Pool and raced through the right descending side, their milky hues of green and white very appealing, as was the thought of trout lurking where the water ebbed away from the swift currents of Upper River."

--- Skip Johnson

One

A Lofty Beginning

Elk's Origins on Red Lick Mountain

High up on the north side of Red Lick Mountain, at an elevation of four thousand feet, a tiny rivulet begins. In rainy times, it descends rather quickly to the valley of the Crooked Fork of Elk, and continues from there its inevitable downhill journey, like a racer on Snowshoe Mountain Resort's nearby Cupp Run ski slope. Charleston, the capital city of West Virginia, is one hundred and eighty four miles away.

Thus is born, at least in a symbolic way, the Elk River that we know and love, although it doesn't officially become Elk River until all its principal headwaters merge at the lower end of the Beckwith Lumber Company bottom in the Pocahontas County community of Slatyfork. From there, the river flows north and then ultimately west to Charleston.

Crooked Fork does not, by name, claim title to either of the two forks that come together at Slatyfork to form Elk River. Those are Old Field and Big Spring Forks. But Crooked Fork is a branch of Old Field, and, combined, the two drain an area of over thirty square miles and are almost twelve miles in length, larger on both counts than the Big Spring drainage.

The three prongs of Crooked Fork at its headwaters resemble, on a map, the track of a wild turkey as they imprint the side of Red Lick Mountain. The middle prong goes farther up the mountain, stopping just short of the Highland Scenic Highway. It is therefore crowned the "tiny rivulet" of the opening paragraph of this book.

One of the many grand vistas on the highway is that of the

Crooked Fork drainage, which lies near the highway's eastern terminus. On a bright day, Snowshoe can be seen on the farthest ridgeline to the left. In the broad basin below the highway the route can be traced in the trees where Crooked Fork bends like an elbow and soon joins Old Field Fork near U.S. 219. From that point, the stream is known only as Old Field Fork. It flows for almost nine miles through appropriately named Pleasant Valley to its place of destiny in the form of the start of Elk River.

Casting a giant topographical shadow over this Allegheny Highlands tableau is Red Spruce Knob, a four thousand seven hundred and three foot eminence that is the high point of the Highland Scenic Highway and one of the top ten elevations in West Virginia. The knob lies ten air miles southwest of Snowshoe. Rugged mountains, purplish in the summer haze and cold and stark in the winter, unfold between the two.

Whether Red Spruce Knob is a part of Red Lick Mountain is geographically debatable, although the White Low Place on the Scenic Highway at the intersection of the Friel Run Road is a distinct saddle that seems to separate the two. The low place is named for George White, who lived nearby and died in 1909. Friel Run is named for Uriah Friel, who lived near the head of the run prior to 1886.

When the Monongahela National Forest bought the tract that includes the White Low Place from the Davis Trust Company and Davis Elkins, son of Stephen B. Elkins, the survey plat identified the middle prong, which begins nearby, simply as Crooked Fork, thus lending substance to its role as the tiny rivulet of paragraph one.

The tract, consisting of 1,567 acres, was purchased on December 31, 1937, and is known as U.S. Tract 652. The significance of the purchase from an Elk River standpoint is that it preserves in public ownership the Crooked Fork drainage. It was in the 1920s and 1930s that the U.S. Forest Service began in a major way purchasing lands that had been logged over, including those on the head of Elk.

- - -

The parkway section of the Highland Scenic Highway was begun in 1965 and completed in 1980. The traffic on the highway is light, so light in fact that Peter Silitch spread his Scotch taped topographic maps on the pavement with impunity when we were there in October 2002 and viewed the Crooked Fork of Elk Basin. Peter and his wife, Elizabeth, are my neighbors and the editors of my 2001 book, *River on the Rocks*, as well as this one.

The breezes ruffled the maps. Elizabeth placed her foot on one corner, Peter held down another corner with his hand, and I donated my note pad to a third rebellious corner. The maverick fourth corner continued to ruffle, but it was only a minor irritant as we perused the wavy elevation lines, the place names, the triangulation points, the highway, the Forest Service roads, the cow paths, the rivulets, the drainages, the low places, and the level places, of which there weren't many.

Still there were no cars. During the time I worked on this book, I came to consider the highway my own personal domain. I traveled it many times, rarely saw a car, and hiked some of its trails. One early morning in August 2002, a bobcat ran across the highway as I traveled east toward Slatyfork. It was only the second bobcat I'd ever seen in the wild. The first sighting occurred on nearby Kennison Mountain many years ago. I saw hundreds of bobcat tracks in the snow when I deer hunted in the mountains, but no sightings of the largely nocturnal animals.

The bobcat may have been related to Miss Matilda, my calico cat who shows up early and unrepentant after a night of supposed debauchery. My brother Bob got along famously with Miss Matilda when not everybody did. He said the reason was that he told her the truth about herself, and she respected him for it.

The fall colors were not inspiring on our visit to Red Lick Mountain, the Crooked Fork of Elk, and White Low Place. The day was overcast, and fog hovered over the ridgetops. But visible or not, some of West Virginia's highest elevations lurked nearby:

Red Spruce Knob	4,703 feet
Red Lick Mountain	4,686 feet
Gauley Mountain	4,571 feet
Gay Knob	4,542 feet

We rolled up the maps, a laborious process, and drove the short distance to the low place. Peter unrolled the maps again, perused them, looked all around, and began striding purposefully through the weeds. He reached the ditch line on the upper side of Forest Service Road 184, and exclaimed "Ah! Ha!" He had found a ravine in the woods above us that seemed to feed into the middle prong. We looked for a culvert, found it, and "seemed" became fact. The middle prong extended higher than we had thought, not as a "blue line" but as an intermittent stream that added another two or three hundred feet to the tiny rivulet of history. In the late 1970s, highway construction had

Red Lick Mountain

remodeled the lay of the land at the low place, the result being that the culvert now connects the head of the rivulet with the rest of the middle prong.

But Peter, possessor of both a degree in physics and a restless mind, didn't completely accept the culvert-connected rivulet as the highest drainage within the domain we were viewing.

"What else *is* there?" I asked.

"Up there," he replied, pointing to Red Spruce Knob, which hovered over us like a mother hen guarding her chicks.

"But there are no rivulets on the north side of Red Spruce," I protested. "I've looked at the map and I've hiked it."

"Yes," Peter replied, "but the water has to go downhill, with or without a rivulet."

"Yes," I replied.

- - -

Later the maps were unfurled again, this time on the new asphalt surface of the parking area that was built in 2002 on Elk Mountain at the eastern end of the highway. The highest point of Red Lick Mountain loomed large to the west. Old Field Fork began nearby at an elevation of thirty three hundred and twenty feet.

The highway has been called "the road to nowhere" because it connects no towns and sits in the middle of nowhere, which makes it attractive to those of us who prefer the middle of nowhere. In fact, that day on Elk Mountain we created the state of Middle of Nowhere. Organization of the new state has proceeded well. There are no towns to name, and nobody to tax, although we somewhat regret not having taxable people.

The state song was born around a campfire on Birch River, where my nephew, Rob Johnson, parks his vehicle and plays Hank Williams Jr. tapes, and occasionally sings along as the night mellows. One night, for a change of pace, I requested the *1812 Overture* by Tchaikovsky. The next day my nephew's teenage son, Travis, commented on "the 1812 something or other by Shalosky." So there was our state song: the *1812 Something or Other*.

Peter, Elizabeth, and I then met in plenary session. We chose the state tree (crabapple), state bird (turkey vulture), state plant (skunk cabbage), state animal (weasel), state flower (multiflora rose), state insect (ladybug), and state parasite (wood tick). There were many nominations from a public that was clamoring to point an accusing finger at the appropriate state parasite, and we concede that our choice may not be the best one. There was some support for fried chicken as the state bird, but the turkey vulture's exemplary efforts in cleaning up roadsides gave it the edge.

The scenic highway was controversial in the planning stage because it was viewed by wilderness advocates as an unnecessary intrusion into roadless country, and indeed was eventually halted at U.S. 219 for environmental and cost reasons, and is now only a blip on the West Virginia highway map.

It was a "gift" from John F. Kennedy to West Virginia following the 1960 election in which this state played a major role. Kennedy's victory in the West Virginia primary disproved the political and social beliefs held at the time that a Catholic couldn't carry a rock-ribbed Protestant state, and therefore couldn't win the presidency.

Kennedy appointed a task force to identify ways in which the state might be rewarded, and a scenic highway was one of the suggestions. With the backing of West Virginia Senators Robert C. Byrd and Jennings Randolph, the highway became a reality.

But it remained controversial to the end. Had it turned north from U.S. 219, which was the original plan, it would have gone through additional remote areas, including the upper Shavers Fork River Basin. The U.S. Forest Service was not enthusiastic about further construction, and the price tag would have been astronomical, so the highway never went any farther than where it is today. But it went far enough to provide a magnificent platform from which to view the Crooked Fork headwaters of Elk River.

As we knelt over the maps at the parking area, my attention wandered to the top of Red Lick Mountain, and I wondered if bears were up there wallowing even as we spoke of more mundane matters. Larry Jarvinen, retired ranger on the Marlinton District of the Monongahela National Forest, compiled a dossier on the district in 1979 that includes many references to the headwaters of Elk, and he mentioned a buffalo and bear wallow on the top of Red Lick.

"There is a swamp-like area on top of the mountain approximately 1.5 miles east of the White Low Place," Jarvinen wrote. "It was believed to have been used by buffalo during the summer to keep the flies off."

Buffalo, of course, are long gone. But bears still wallow on Red Lick Mountain, although at the time of our visit the wallowing season had largely passed.

Elk Mountain, where we knelt, was the scene of one of the last Indian raids in West Virginia that resulted in the death of a settler. Jarvinen said that the wife of Thomas Drinnon, an early settler, was carried away from her home and killed by Indians in the late 1700s. According to most accounts, the eastern woodland Indians were gone by 1800.

Jarvinen added a splash of "treasure fever" to the history of Elk Mountain. He said that silver was believed to have existed on the mountain at a locality called Hickory Ridge, and that James Drinnon, son of Thomas, searched for the precious metal for a long time, but never found it.

- - -

Ten years had passed since Peter Silitch had last visited Snowshoe Mountain Resort, and Elizabeth had never been there. I had been there several times in the months prior to our visit, so I fit perfectly Ralph Beckwith's definition of an expert. "An expert," he once told me, "is someone who knows just a little bit about something talking to someone who knows nothing about it."

When we drove to the mountain for lunch, Peter and Elizabeth were astounded by the new construction. We were led to a table by the window at the Junction Restaurant in the middle of Snowshoe Village. The view was of a backhoe digging and workers engaged in putting up a building.

The transformation of Snowshoe into a year-round resort since Intrawest Corporation acquired "The Shoe" in 1995 was evident all around us. The most visible addition from where we sat was Allegheny Springs, a handsome brown and white five-level lodge opened in 2002. The clock in its tower is Snowshoe's version of Big Ben in the Tower of London.

Visible also was Rimfire Lodge, opened in 2001 and named for Rimfire Hamrick, the Webster County mountaineer. Tom Wallington, former director of the resort development group, suggested the name for the lodge. Rimfire was born on Leatherwood Creek of Elk River near the present community of Bergoo. He is often referred to as West Virginia's typical mountaineer.

Michael Ritter, director of mountain operations at Snowshoe, suggested the name Split Rock Pool for the resort's swimming complex. The name is derived from Split Rock of Big Spring Fork. In *Tale of the Elk*, Bill Byrne wrote about fishing there with Bearskin Bill Hamrick. After gaining permission from a reluctant landowner, they didn't catch a single fish. One hundred or so years later, Ed Hayne, a friend from Charleston, was driving past Split Rock, saw someone in a field nearby, and stopped to ask permission to fish. This landowner readily gave permission, but Ed didn't catch any fish either.

Byrne had a memorable line in his book about the difficulty

of a mere picture doing justice to Split Rock. He paraphrased from Sir Walter Scott's *The Lay of the Last Minstrel*: "If thou wouldst view fair Melrose aright, go see it for yourself." Those who do may be disappointed, although the rock is somewhat unusual in the size of the fissure, or split, that gives it its name.

Peter, Elizabeth, and I did a walking tour of Snowshoe Village after lunch, and then drove off the mountain to Slatyfork to visit Ralph Beckwith, who built one of West Virginia's largest individually owned lumber companies from scratch (see Slatyfork).

- - -

Red Lick Mountain and Snowshoe Mountain Resort hold special niches in the geographic origins of Elk. As we have seen, the largest headwaters drainage basin begins on Red Lick Mountain, while Snowshoe shares with a private landowner the highest elevation in the river's entire fifteen hundred square mile drainage.

The highest elevation is the Thorny triangulation point on the boundary between Snowshoe and a private tract owned by L.L. and Annabelle Burns of Charleston. L.L. Burns is retired from the coal business. He and his wife bought three hundred and twenty seven acres on Thorny in 1958 from Mower Lumber Company.

On Friday the 13th of June 2003, the West Virginia Association of Land Surveyors and the West Virginia Geological and Economic Survey sponsored a mapping of Spruce Knob, Bald Knob, and Thorny triangulation point, long thought to be the three highest elevations in the state, to determine their ranking. Don Teter, past president of the surveyors' association, called the endeavor "How High's the Mountain, Mama?" based loosely on a line in the song *Country Roads*.

The mapping was the outgrowth of a conversation held by Teter and Paul Liston of the Geological Survey. They discussed options to resolve the controversy over highest elevations. The option chosen was mapping with GPS (Global Positioning System) satellites, which are accurate to within a fraction of a foot, and save time over standard surveying methods.

Spruce Knob has long been considered the highest point, and Bald Knob, the destination of the popular Cass Scenic Railroad, was generally conceded to be second highest. Their elevations had been determined many years ago by the traditional method of leveling, or finding the heights of different points with a surveyor's level.

But questions remained, and Thorny was the huge unknown. Its elevation had never been surveyed, but it was thought to be the third highest point because topographical maps indicated that it was roughly 4,840 feet, which would place it third behind Bald Knob.

Snowshoe contended that Thorny was 4,848 feet, based on its reading of the topographical maps, and in fact the ski shop at Snowshoe Village is named "4848." Johnny Smith, who was part of the early Snowshoe management team, suggested the numerical designation. "It has a euphonious sound," he said.

The U.S. Geological Survey set a marker at Thorny in 1921, but assigned no elevation either on the marker or in any written record that could be found. Even the location of the marker had become somewhat of a mystery, but it was found prior to the GPS mapping by Teter, Liston, and William Dilley, the latter a Pocahontas County surveyor who has done boundary work for Snowshoe. They uncovered it underneath a decaying spruce log.

The precise spot is known as Thorny triangulation point, which differs from Thorny Flat, the generic name applied to the area. The USGS described the location of the marker as "on the highest part of the hill known as Thorny Flat." The flat itself lies slightly east of the triangulation point and is one hundred feet lower.

The day of the measurements was rainy and foggy. Water cascaded off Snowshoe buildings reminiscent of Blackwater Falls. Then fog rolled in, obscuring everything over ten feet away. But GPS isn't affected by weather, and quietly went about its work.

All that remained was for computers to download the data and provide the answer to the question, "How High's the Mountain, Mama?"

The GPS measurement, done with equipment furnished by Trimble Navigation Limited of Herndon, Virginia, stripped away the uncertainty that had always hovered over the elevation of Thorny triangulation point. It revealed an elevation of 4,848 feet, which moved it ahead of Bald Knob into second place, and earned Snowshoe an A-plus for map reading.

The GPS results:

> Spruce Knob: 4,862.64 feet
> Thorny: 4,848.38 feet
> Bald Knob: 4,841.98 feet

- - -

From Snowshoe's lofty perch on Cheat Mountain, its lands drain into the Shavers Fork of Cheat watershed on one side and Big Spring Fork of Elk on the other. Fifty percent goes to Elk, forty-five percent to Shavers, and the remaining five percent to the Tygart and Greenbrier Rivers.

Conceivably, droplets of water could slide off any of the highest roof lines of the buildings on the resort's western slope, find their way through the underground drainage system, trickle down to Big Spring Fork, and wind up in Charleston.

Jason Brown, a native of Peterstown, Monroe County, and director of engineering for Snowshoe, is very familiar with Snowshoe's divided drainage loyalties. Where the resort sits is the dividing line of two Army Corps of Engineer districts. Snowshoe projects that are located on the Shavers Fork side are under the jurisdiction of the Corps' Pittsburgh district, while projects on the Big Spring Fork side are under the jurisdiction of the Huntington district.

I searched for the highest man-assisted elevation in the entire Elk drainage and, with Ed Galford's considerable help, found it at the western corner of the Snowcrest condominium complex at Snowshoe. Ed, a native of Marlinton, is vice president of mountain operations at Snowshoe, and has been with the resort since 1974 when he was still a forestry student at West Virginia University.

In 1982, Ed, Joe Cummins, and Mike Cline lived at a higher elevation than anybody else in West Virginia. They shared a one-story apartment at Snowshoe and parked their vintage Harley Davidson motorcycles in the living room. The apartment was located near the site of the present General Store, which proudly displays its 4,760 foot elevation on the store front.

Ed parked near the western edge of Snowcrest, and I gazed in reverence at the roof line that pointed toward the Elk drainage like an artillery piece ready for firing. The ground level elevation at Snowcrest is 4,832 feet. Adding thirty feet for its three-story height, it tops out at 4,862 feet. The second highest man-assisted elevation is the top of the Snowshoe water tank at 4,850 feet. The third highest is Allegheny Springs Lodge at 4,816 feet, measured to the top of the chimney.

Those are the highest man-assisted points. The lowest natural point would be the belly of a carp or catfish lurking on the bottom underneath the Kanawha Boulevard Bridge where Elk enters Kanawha River at Charleston.

Almost a year earlier, Ed and I had gone to Thorny triangulation point looking for the 1921 marker. As it turned out, it was only

Ed Galford at Snowshoe Village

thirty feet away from where we stopped, but thirty feet might as well have been thirty miles in the thick stand of spruce.

I asked my inevitable question about drainage. Determining Elk River's exalted place in the grand scheme of things had become an obsession. "From where we sit," I asked, "where does the water go?"

"Well," Ed replied, "forgive me for not parking one foot to the west, but as we sit the vehicle is tilting ever so slightly toward Shavers Fork to the east." Then he mumbled something to the effect that if I was climbing Mount Everest, I would turn to my Sherpa guide one hundred feet from the summit and ask if we were on the Elk drainage. The Sherpa would shake his frostbitten head in the negative, and I would sadly begin my descent, leaving the final one hundred feet unclimbed.

I have nothing against Shavers Fork. It is a nice mountain stream of over three thousand feet elevation, it was host to the storied logging and pulp mill town of Spruce, Snowshoe founder Tom Brigham liked to fish its headwaters for native trout, and Ed saw a mountain lion there in 1993. But I was on the verge of asking him to move the vehicle one foot to the west so we would tilt toward Elk.

For me, the search for the Thorny marker achieved closure on the day of the GPS mapping when I accompanied Paul Liston and Leon Mallow, the latter a surveyor in Elkins, to the newly uncovered site. We walked through spruces dripping with rain, and I felt a sense of history revealed as we looked down at the little brass marker that signified the highest point in the Elk drainage.

- - -

Thorny is still covered with the red spruce that attracted the West Virginia Pulp and Paper Company to Cheat Mountain a century ago, but these aren't the large trees of that era. The trees of the present are of small to medium height, and more aesthetically appealing because of their "Christmas tree" look.

Christmas comes every day on Cheat Mountain for the snowshoe hare, which lives in the red spruce forests of the high elevations. Their large, well padded hind feet enable them to plow through deep snow as if they were wearing snowshoes, which in a way they are. Snowshoe Mountain Resort is named for the hare, and in the early days Snowshoe called its bus service "The Hare Line."

I saw a snowshoe hare in the Otter Creek Wilderness one early December when I was deer hunting and Army had just defeated Navy in football. The hare was in the molting stage, half brown and half white, and was certainly an inviting target for bobcats, foxes, and owls who might have been out shopping for *tenderloin de' hare*. I swung the bent front sight of my .300 Savage on the hare as it ran diagonally across a slight slope against a backdrop of brown leaves that had given up and curled up and awaited their winter fate.

I had no intention of shooting at the hare, which would have been a stupid thing to do anyway, but swinging on a moving target was a reflex action that was as natural as casting a fishing lure the right way with a quick back and then forward flip of the wrist. The bent sight came from an earlier hunt on Otter Creek when I fell and rolled with the rifle slung over my shoulder.

Later the same morning of the snowshoe sighting I skirted the edge of a rhododendron thicket and a bear came crashing out and ran down the hill. He was much higher on the food chain than the hare, and had nothing to fear from bobcats or anything else except man. He stopped, halfway hidden behind a hemlock tree, and looked at me, and I whispered the hare's location to him in case he hadn't had lunch.

I reserved the afternoon for getting lost. It was fully my intention to drop off the mountain to Otter Creek, but instead I wandered in a circle and came back to the log where I had sat to eat a late lunch two hours previously. I sat again and studied my situation, and then made what turned out to be the right choice. It was the right time, too, because the December sun was beginning to edge over McGowan Mountain to the west. I reached Otter Creek and walked the mile or so downstream to our deer camp on the Shavers Mountain Trail, arriving at dusk. I ate lightly and stretched out in my sleeping bag to dream of hares, bears, and Army football, the latter a childhood obsession that I've never outgrown.

- - -

Big Spring Fork, which begins on the slope below Thorny triangulation point at an elevation of 3,865 feet, has its backers as the fountainhead of Elk. Bill Byrne thought so. In *Tale of the Elk* he bestowed the fountainhead mantle on the large spring at "the old Colonel Gatewood place" which stood at the present intersection of U.S. 219 and West Virginia 66.

The two largest springs of Big Spring Fork are the Gatewood spring and another one about a half mile above the junction of Big Spring and Old Field Forks. "The upper, or Gatewood spring, is in fact the fountain source," Byrne wrote.

On a warm, dry day in late June 2002, at the beginning of a summer of drought, I came to Slatyfork with Ed Maguire and his saintly yellow Labrador retriever, Abby. Ed is former state director of The Nature Conservancy and current owner of The Highlands Group, Inc., a private land company that he founded in 1990. Abby travels with him, has probably gotten her feet wet in more trout streams than most hard-core fishermen, and once appeared on the front page of *the Charleston Daily Mail* accompanying an article written by outdoor editor John McCoy.

The three of us gathered at the sacred ground where Big Spring and Old Field Forks meet and Elk begins. For Big Spring, time and water stood still. It was making no discernible contribution to the flow of Elk that day. By contrast, there was enough flow in Old Field that we heard it before we saw it.

I mentioned this to Harry Mahoney, who is retired from the Monongahela National Forest. "But you must remember," he said, "that Big Spring's flow is there, it's just resting underground." Big Spring Fork is an "interrupted" stream in hydrological language, meaning it sinks and rises in its bed much like a sleepyheaded person who can't quite decide whether to get up or sleep some more.

Later I visited Clark Galford at his home on Stoney Creek near Woodrow, Pocahontas County. In the 1930s, he worked in the timber on the head of Gauley, on Tea Creek of Williams, and on Middle Mountain of Elk. In a June 2001 article in *the Pocahontas Times,* he described the early logging days on the head of Elk and more or less bestowed the fountainhead mantle on the Crooked Fork area:

> "The West Virginia Pulp and Paper Company came into existence about the year 1900. They began their operation on Cheat Mountain. After logging it out, they then moved to the area of Spruce Knob [Red Spruce Knob] where the Elk River heads up. Spruce Knob is at the head of Crooked Fork of Elk River. The railroad came up from Slatyfork and ran all the way around Spruce Knob and on around the head of the right fork of Tea Creek and Red Run, then on to Gauley Mountain. The Scenic Highway now comes around on the old railroad grade on the Elk Mountain side.

> "The town of Slatyfork was the center of the logging operation at that time. The original town of Slatyfork was up Slatyfork Run on some of the L.D. Sharp property. An old cement bridge still stands across the run up there. The road came out where the Old Country Store is still in operation.

> "There was a company store at the present location of Slatyfork and a big boarding house on the hill between Laurel Run and the Elk River. There was a boardwalk across the river, which led to the boarding house. Train crews and the 'wood hicks,' as we were called, stayed at the boarding house during the logging operations. It was a busy little town during those early days."

There are two Big Spring tributaries that come close to equaling Crooked Fork in elevation at their origins. The Cup Run and Hawthorne Run "blue lines" on the map end at slightly over three thousand six hundred feet, and continue upward to four thousand feet as intermittent streams.

The longest and most formidable of Snowshoe's ski slopes is named for Cup Run, although spelled Cupp. It is one and one-half miles long with a vertical drop of fifteen hundred feet. From the top of the slope, the skier sees Elk Mountain, where Old Field Fork begins, on the far ridgeline to the south.

This view was the favorite of Snowshoe founder Tom Brigham, who brought Jean-Claude Killy to Snowshoe to inaugurate Cupp Run. Killy won three gold medals for France in the Winter Olympics at Grenoble in 1968, and at the time of his visit to Pocahontas County was the most famous skier in the world. Later he won the Killy Cup Challenge, sailing down Cupp Run in a fraction over a minute and twenty one seconds.

I chose a warm day in August to visit Cupp Run. As I looked at the westward tableau, I thought of my introduction to Crooked Fork in May 1973 when I hunted turkey gobblers on two rainy and windy mornings. Twenty-nine years later, I had dried out enough to venture back to the Crooked Fork. I went there with Ed Maguire and Abby in their Mercedes SUV. The day was warm, sunny, and windless, and we viewed the drainage comfortably from the Highland Scenic Highway.

"Why," asked Ed idly, "do they call it Crooked Fork? There are hundreds of streams in West Virginia that are more crooked."

I wasn't sure if he was speaking to Abby, to a turkey vulture that was riding the currents over Red Spruce Knob, or, less likely, to me.

But all four of us agreed that Crooked Fork does qualify as crooked in at least one place. Coming off Red Lick Mountain, its three prongs gather and bend sharply east. Shortly thereafter an unnamed tributary enters near U.S. 219, contributing to the start of Old Field Fork. I proposed that it be named Maguire Run, and I heard no objections from any of us.

"Are there native trout in Crooked Fork?" I asked Abby.

Ed replied. "Yes," he said, "at least there were last Wednesday."

We drove down to Crooked Fork Road and headed up the lower reaches of the basin in the Mercedes, gliding to an elegant stop near a little pool below the road. Ed disembarked (one doesn't just "get out" of a Mercedes), unlimbered his seven and one-half foot Winston fly rod, and tied on an Adams, a tiny winged fly that resembled something I had once seen in the insect collection at the West Virginia Department of Agriculture's Guthrie Center near Charleston. There were insects on the wall, insects in cabinets, insects on the ceiling, insects on the floor, and insects in the ambient air.

The Adams is a popular dry fly pattern. Its dainty wings resemble the flight feathers of the wild turkeys that inhabit the Crooked Fork drainage. Ed began swishing the Adams behind great ever-unfurling coils of tapered and pampered

Ed Maguire and Abby

fly line, and soon the proud little fly settled on the water, barely dimpling the surface.

Abby and I watched breathlessly as a native brook trout came calling, but missed the fly. Three unfurling later, Ed had a brookie on and up to the road. The fish was seven feet shorter than the fly rod, but that's typical for native trout in small West Virginia headwater streams. We briefly admired the little fellow with his coat of many colors, and then Ed released him back into his natural element, in this case a small pool in a small mountain stream on the headwaters of Elk one hundred and eighty some blessed miles removed from where the West Virginia Legislature meets in "smoke-filled rooms" to chart the perilous and reef-strewn course of the Ship of State.

- - -

I was determined, in the manner of Lewis and Clark on the Missouri, to walk to the very head of Crooked Fork. I met Harry Mahoney, the U.S. Forest Service retiree, at Elihu's Restaurant at Linwood and explained my mission. He nodded and ordered a bacon, tomato, and cheese sandwich. I should have suspected that he envisioned a long day, but I was unsuspecting and ordered only coffee.

The Crooked Fork Road, where we began our uphill trek, was built by the Forest Service to haul timber out of Crooked Fork and Gauley Mountain. But around 1880, long before the Forest Service came on the scene, a sawmill existed on Crooked Fork, and the West Virginia Pulp and Paper Company built a logging railroad there in the early 1900s.

We followed an old railroad grade for a short distance, and came to a void where it had crossed a ravine. The little trestle had long since succumbed to the ravages of time, as I was about to do. I mentally commiserated with Clark, who at one point was described in Lewis' journal as being "still very languid and complains of a general soarness in all his limbs."

But there *were* diversions. Harry used the occasion to question the popularly held belief that the Dolly Sods Wilderness derives its name from a Dahle or Dolly family *that lived there* and grazed cattle or sheep in a cleared area known as a sods. He believes the name originated in 1929 when the Forest Service purchased five hundred acres from John Dolly, who grazed livestock on the windswept plateau *but didn't live there.*

After the 1929 purchase, the Forest Service managed the tract for grazing for a number of years. Harry believes the Forest Service gave it the name "sods," meaning a grass-covered area, and in this case "Dolly Sods" for John Dolly. Subsequently, other cleared areas on the Monongahela National Forest were also called "sods," including the former McAllister Sods on Crooked Fork, which was why the subject came up in the first place.

McAllister Sods was named for William McAllister, who cleared four hundred acres of land in the 1800s and grazed cattle. In 1899, he sold the tract to Henry G. Davis, who in turn sold it to the West Virginia Pulp and Paper Company in 1913.

We continued to climb and a light rain began. The skies and the National Weather Service had been threatening rain all morning, but they waited until we were halfway up the mountain before they made good on their threat.

It was puzzling. Not the rain but the appearance of fresh cow manure. I suggested that the cows were escapees from the Shearer Grazing Allotment, which is named for Royal Shearer, a previous owner of the tract. The cows may have thought the proverbial greener grass grew on Red Lick Mountain. Harry chuckled but had no better explanation.

The rain continued.

I asked about the origin of the name Red Lick Mountain. Harry replied that the "red" part may come from the reddish soil and layered reddish shale rock, and the "lick" part from salt licks on the mountain where deer come for their daily "fix."

The rain continued.

"Are there rattlesnakes here?" I asked Harry. "I don't know," he replied, leaving the door wide open.

We came to a steep slope that was covered with loose rocks, piled there carelessly by nature. "If we're going to find rattlesnakes, we'll find them here," Harry assured me. But I learned later that James Shearer, a former Monongahela National Forest employee who grew up at the Shearer Grazing Allotment, said he'd never seen a poisonous snake on Red Lick Mountain.

Harry told me about his son, Jon, being bitten by a rattler when he was twelve years old. They were hiking on Backbone Mountain in Tucker County, and Jon was wearing short pants.

"Hey, dad," he cried, "I've been bitten by a snake."

"Oh, I don't think so," Harry replied.

But he looked and sure enough there were the fang marks. Blood trickled from the wounds. Further proof, if required, came when Harry saw the rattler slithering away.

He carried Jon to the car and took him to the hospital at Parsons. The hospital had no antivenin, but they treated the bite as best they could, and Jon suffered no ill effects. He now lives in Belington, and works for Abenaki Timber Corporation.

The rain continued, but harder.

I don't recall which one of us first suggested that we seriously discuss our situation, but I do remember that the discussion was a brief one. We agreed unanimously to chart a course downhill to the car. I wondered what Lewis and Clark would have thought.

Later, back in the cozy dryness of Elihu's, I proposed a toast to the lost cows of Red Lick Mountain and implored the gods to be with them as they roamed the Elysian fields in their eternal and doomed quest for greener pastures.

One of the cows may have been a man from Marlinton who believed in reincarnation. Jo Debra Galford Gandee, a former administrative secretary at Snowshoe and the daughter of restaurant owner Pauline Galford, told us the story.

The man, now deceased, or so we think, was convinced that he had been an Eskimo in an earlier life, and had an Eskimo wife and son. One day when the three of them were on an ice floe his part broke off and he floated away and drowned in the frigid Arctic water. In his new life in Pocahontas County he composed songs of love and devotion to his Eskimo wife, and played the guitar and sang to her. He worried not at all about death, because he knew he would return somewhere sometime as something.

- - -

Prior to heading down Elk to meet whatever fate awaits us all in the dark recesses of Webster County, I hiked two trails on the headwaters. One was the Gauley Mountain Trail, which is slightly over five miles long and follows an old railroad grade the entire distance. The grade is gentle, ranging from 4,240 feet elevation at the Highland Scenic Highway to 4,299 feet at the Mine Road.

The trail runs through Tract 51-A, which is the designation given to the landmark purchase of 23,687 acres by the U.S. Government on December 10, 1936, from West Virginia Pulp and Paper Company. It preserves in public ownership a large chunk of the Elk and Gauley headwaters.

I met Tim Henry, recreation officer on the Marlinton District of the Monongahela National Forest, at the trailhead, where we left one car, drove to the Mine Road, and walked "downhill" back to the highway on a marvelous fall day in late September 2003.

The sun shone, and the temperature was mild enough that I felt comfortable wearing my favorite homemade forest green wool sweater with the tear down the seam on the right shoulder. Actually, it isn't homemade, unless it was homemade in Taiwan. And actually it isn't wool. It's acrylic. But it is forest green, and I love to wear it to formal dinners, weddings, coronations, church socials, and Kenny Chesney concerts.

We both carried rain jackets but never needed them. Heading out the Gauley Mountain Trail, I tied my yellow Appalachian Power Company jacket around my waist, where it remained for five miles. My nephew Rob, who works for the power company, gave me the jacket, and it was a faithful companion Up Elk, Down Elk, Thorny Flat, The Big Railroad Cut, Slatyfork Run, Point Mountain, Blackhole Run, and other places that my memory has misplaced.

Tim Henry is a Wisconsin native who came to the Monongahela in 1989. He'd never heard of gob, as mining refuse is called, nor had he heard of Bergoo, the upper Elk community, so it was a puzzle when he heard a secretary in the office say on the phone something about "hauling the gob to Bergoo." He thought they were conversing in a foreign tongue.

When we hiked, he was fresh from encounters with the two most dangerous wild animals on the North American continent. He went to Montana in early September 2003 to help fight fires on the Flathead National Forest, and one day, rounding a bend in the trail, he and his partner came upon a mother grizzly with cub. The mother bear rose up and looked at them, and then walked away. Such is the proverbial arrogance of grizzlies that she didn't run away, she walked away.

Another time they came upon a cow moose, which didn't have a calf with it, at least not that they could see. Fate was on their side again, because the moose trotted off. A group of Zuni Indians, who were there fighting the fires, said they would rather face a grizzly than a moose, although that's like preferring fire over brimstone.

The Gauley Mountain Trail is devoid of grizzlies and moose, as far as I know, but we did see fresh black bear tracks in the swampy ground near where the trail to Tea Creek branches off on a railroad spur. In the soft ground, they were very good replicas of human footprints.

At the start of our hike, the forest canopy was dominated by red spruce. I revere the cathedral effect of a spruce forest, especially the sound of the wind sighing through the tree tops and sounding like the concluding notes of the pipe organ at the Mormon Tabernacle.

Near the Scenic Highway, the canopy becomes dominated by birch, beech, and maple, the combination that produces the vibrant colors of autumn in West Virginia. But the resilient spruce is regenerating itself, and eventually will push its way through to become the canopy tree again. At some point it will say, "I was here first."

- - -

My other headwater hike was on the Red Spruce Knob Trail. The name has a nice ring to it, and I'd wanted to walk it ever since I learned that many people do. A tried and true rule of thumb for moderate hikers like myself is never choose a trail that has an untrodden look.

The Red Spruce trailhead is located on the Scenic Highway just east of the Gauley Mountain Trail. After an initial switchback climb, the trail levels off and meanders through a broad and pleasant plateau of ferns and small spruce. There is a slight climb at the approach to the knob, and then the trail forks and circles the knob. I thought of Yogi Berra's advice: "When you come to a fork in the road, take it."

The view from the knob is of the Crooked Fork drainage. It is a nice view but a narrow one because the trees are slowly crowding in. By far the better view is from the Scenic Highway, which lies almost four hundred feet below the knob.

I sat on a rock where a previous hiker had built a small fire and then covered the ashes with the rock I now sat on. I rested my chin in my hand, deep in thought, my reverie so deep that I've completely forgotten what I thought about. When I consulted my notes later, they were of no help. They said briefly and eloquently: "Sat on a rock in deep thought."

Years ago the Red Spruce fire tower was located near where I sat. Foundation stones remain, but the site is easy to miss. It is a small clearing, partially grown up in blackberry briers and goldenrod. From the former tower site, the drainage is to Elk toward the north and Williams River toward the south.

The first "tower" was quite basic. It was a tree, probably a red spruce, that the spotter climbed. A regular tower was built by the Civilian Conservation Corps (CCC) in the late 1930s, and served until 1963 when the Forest Service began using airplanes for fire patrols. The tower was torn down in the 1970s.

It came down with a crash. "Its timbers were deteriorating," said retired Monongahela employee Junior Hamons, "and we determined that it wasn't salvageable. Jack Bowen and I hooked a bulldozer to it, pulled it down, and burned it." I thought of the irony of a fire tower being burned.

The lookout in the final two years was Wade Rogers, who retired from the Forest Service in 1994 and lives in Bridgewater, Virginia. Rogers told me that the tower was made of ponderosa pine from Oregon because this species has strong straight-grained wood that is needed for a forty-five foot structure on top of a 4,703-foot knob. "There were some pretty wild winds up there," said Rogers. "The tower would tremble and water would splash out of a half-full bucket."

The furnishings inside the tiny lookout cabin included a wood stove and a bed. Spruce trees brushed against the catwalk underneath the cabin. Rogers closed the tower for the final time in the week prior to the 1963 West Virginia deer season. "I mopped the floor," he said, "and it was so cold that the water immediately froze and I skated across the cabin and locked the door."

- - -

On the return to my car, I startled two grouse who in turn startled me with their whirring takeoff, removing ten years from my life which I couldn't afford to be without, since there were many more Red Spruce Knobs to climb. Grouse don't just take off. They "explode" in a wild rush of beating wings, flying feathers, and swirling leaves.

Another ten years were removed from my life the next day after I had returned home, and was taking a morning walk. I caught a glimpse of something large and black out of the corner of my eye. It was a bear, just above the road bank, heading in the same direction I was headed, and it seemed to be keeping pace with me as it planted its furry paws on the forest floor with great dignity and firmness of purpose.

But it never looked at me, and I suspect that in the dimness of early morning it never saw me. When I last saw the bear it had stopped and was looking uphill, apparently having seen or heard something that had caught its attention. I took advantage of this lull in our shared morning walk to move out briskly, and I didn't see the bear again.

I know the old adage that black bears will run from you every time, with the possible exception of a mother bear with cubs. But there is another old adage that says bears are unpredictable, and I wasn't sure which old adage this bear subscribed to.

I certainly concede him the right to *his* morning walks, and in fact I have granted him diplomatic immunity. My nephew has a saying, "It's all good." I have no idea what it means, but I believe it may cover such things as granting diplomatic immunity to bears, and allowing them to live happily to the extent possible for any of us.

Two

Slatyfork

The Community

If pronounced as one word, the name Slatyfork slides easily off the tongue. If pronounced as two, it still sounds like one because everybody runs the two together. So for purposes of this book, and with apologies to the U.S. Postal Service and Ralph Beckwith, Slatyfork it will be. One word, forever joined, sliding easily off the tongue.

Ralph is the owner of Beckwith Lumber Company at Slatyfork, where Elk begins. One day in his office in the former Slatyfork Elementary School, I asked him the question: One word or two? "Two," he said without a moment's hesitation and in an emphatic tone of voice that left me agreeing with him even though I didn't.

He sealed the matter by handing me a paperweight that commemorates the company's fortieth anniversary. It is a very serious paperweight that spells Slatyfork as two words and was heavy enough to withstand the assaults of my large male cat, Avilar (named for reasons that are too complicated to explain in a book of only three hundred pages), who would jump onto the computer table and plop down on my manuscripts as I wrote this book. But he was never able to move the papers or the paperweight in any substantial way.

The post office was less emphatic about the spelling. The woman who answered the phone when I called with the "one word or two" question replied "Either way," and seemed busy so I accepted either way without further discussion. But the building front says Slaty Fork in two bold and distinct words.

In his 1990 book, *Sketches of Elk*, Raymond Mace was just as emphatic as Ralph Beckwith, except in the other direction. Mace, who was born on the upper reaches of Elk, said that Slatyfork is "one word, no space."

The Geographic Names Book, a publication of the U.S. Forest Service, says the official spelling is two words, but that one word is acceptable as a variant, which means that everybody is right and brings us to a very peaceful solution, and peaceful solutions are to be cherished more than gold, frankincense, and myrrh in the shadowy and often contentious world of writing in which I operate with one eye always on the back door.

The community of Slatyfork is named for Slatyfork Run, which enters Old Field Fork across U.S. 219 from the Elk River Touring Center. Proprietor Gil Willis, an Alexandria, Virginia, native, came to West Virginia in 1977 and opened a bed and breakfast. The touring center followed in 1982, featuring mountain biking. A restaurant was added in 1988. In recent years, Gil has branched out into fishing, with a fly shop and guided trips.

Slatyfork Run is named for the slate rock that is very evident in its lower section. Ed Maguire calls Slatyfork Run "the real Slatyfork," as opposed to the present community, because the original post office, established in 1901, was located about a half mile above the mouth of the run where the Marlinton-Huttonsville Turnpike crossed. A relic of the turnpike is a concrete arch bridge.

The first postmaster, L.D. Sharp, moved from Slatyfork Run to the present Slatyfork community around the time U.S. 219 was built. His home, a stately two-story farmhouse of the kind that can still be seen in Pocahontas County, remains in the family, as does his store, which is now the Country Store and Museum.

The Sharp cemetery is located near the old homestead on a pleasant knoll that divides the drainages of Slatyfork Run and Big Spring Fork.

William Sharp homestead

Lowell Gibson, who lives on Old Field Fork, and Ernie Shaw, a retired Marlinton dentist who grew up on Big Spring Fork, accompanied me on a visit there in May 2004.

The earliest marked grave is that of William Sharp, father of L.D., who died in 1888. The inscription on his tombstone says: *"Stop and think as you pass by, who in their graves here doth lie."* One of William's grandsons, Si Sharp, whom I interviewed for my 1993 book, *Woods & Waters*, died in 2002 and is buried there, as is L.D., who died in 1963.

Larry Jarvinen wrote that an unmarked grave in the Sharp Cemetery is the final resting place of a bank robber, who, along with his partner, lived in a cabin on Laurel Run of Elk. "They lived there for about two years and came to town only about once every two months," said Jarvinen. "One day the two men got into an argument and one shot the other."

Sharp Cemetery

- - -

Slatyfork Run is 4.66 miles long. The left fork heads on Slaty Ridge, and the right fork "rests with the buzzards" on Buzzard Ridge, both at over four thousand feet elevation. If I was ever compelled to visit anything, it was Buzzard Ridge, because I consider buzzards, or, properly, turkey vultures, to be both compelling and repelling, a rare combination worthy of respect. They are compelling in flight, soaring gracefully over the highest mountain ridges, holding their large wings tilted slightly above horizontal, and they are repelling on the ground with their grotesque naked red heads picking and slashing at road kills. They are a heavy bird, ponderous in getting off the ground like a fully loaded C-130 cargo plane.

The state of West Virginia, the one from which the state of Middle of Nowhere was formed, recognized the virtues of "turkey buzzards," as it called them, when it placed them on the protected list in 1882. In turn, the state of Middle of Nowhere chose them as its official state bird.

It is possible that Buzzard Ridge was named for people with the surname Buzzard who may have lived there. There are still Buzzards living in Pocahontas County. But Larry Jarvinen said it was named for the large number of turkey buzzards that once roosted in the dead trees.

Peter and Elizabeth Silitch and I went there on a very warm day in June 2003. We drove as far as the U.S. Forest Service road mutely told us was possible, which was to around the four thousand foot level, and then walked the final distance to Barlow Top, the highest point of the ridge at 4,313 feet.

Barlow Top is named for Asa Barlow, a previous owner. The top is elusive, especially on a hot day. We reached what had appeared from below to be the top, but a higher level of ground rose before us like a gentle ocean swell. We reached the "ocean swell" but there was still another higher level. That third level proved to be Barlow Top, a high alpine-like meadow that I immediately fell in love with, forsaking all other tops, ridges, crowns, crests, eminences, prominences, backbones, elevations, ranges, mountains, and promontories, until death do us part.

The meadow grass waved in the breezes that blew at that eleva-tion, and tall yellow and reddish orange wildflowers grew among the grass and at close inspection lent a touch of color that van Gogh would have liked to paint. Although we were on top, the ground still rolled, and it resembled pictures I've seen of the Custer Battlefield in Montana where the Indians concealed themselves in the folds of the ground until the moment of attack. Coincidentally, we visited Barlow Top on the one hundred and twenty seventh anniversary of Custer's demise.

A raucous bird of unknown identity, speaking from the woods that bordered the meadow, interrupted my train of thought as I thought of Custer's fate and looked at the rolls and folds with a strange feeling of being watched. But the feeling passed in the bright sunshine.

From where we stood, the headwaters of Slatyfork Run lay just to the southeast, and later we drove to where the right fork reaches its zenith in the vicinity of the Beale Hacking, a field that was cleared by slaves belonging to Robert Beale, a man who lived on Old Field Fork and died in 1833.

But my heart belonged to Barlow Top, and there in the rippling knee deep grass and refreshing breezes I nominated it for the capital of the new state of Middle of Nowhere. The vote was unanimous in the affirmative. Future plenary sessions will be held there, but never in the winter when the waving meadow grass would lie motionless under three or more feet of snow.

We concluded a busy and historic day by naming Pocahontas County High School as the new state's official Seat of Learning. It is located at Dunmore, which is located, well, we weren't quite able to locate Dunmore, which made it the perfect choice. But we do know that West Virginia Mountain Radio is located near the school, so while we were at it we named it the official voice of the new state.

- - -

According to William Price's *History of Pocahontas County*, the first permanent settler in the Slatyfork area was Joseph Hannah. Larry Jarvinen includes David Hannah on that list. He said that Joseph and David Hannah settled on Mill Run, a tributary of Old Field Fork, in

1820.

Another early settler was David Gibson, who came to Old Field Fork in 1823. A descendant, James Gibson, was most likely the namesake of Gibson Knob, a forty four hundred and forty foot prominence in the area. Jarvinen said the knob was named for him, and so did Andy Gibson when I visited him at his home on Old Field Fork.

In more recent years, Kyle Hannah owned Gibson Knob and pastured sheep there. The high pasture, reminiscent of a scene from the movie *Sound of Music*, is rounded and naturally bald, and has a very nice view of Snowshoe Mountain Resort. At one time, former West Virginia Governor Gaston Caperton expressed an interest in buying the property, but that never came about.

The present owner of the highest part of the knob is Ralph Beckwith, although the Forest Service and others also own property nearby. Hannah, who died in 1995, lived in a large white farmhouse on Big Spring Fork. There is a spring on the property that is one of the largest of several springs on this major contributor to the start of Elk.

Old Field Fork supposedly got its name from a bare patch of ground that was an Indian camp where all the trees had been cut for firewood. Joseph Hannah planted his first crop on this ground, and it became "the old field."

Old Field Fork flows through Pleasant Valley, which in its middle and lower sections is indeed pleasant farmland. An enduring mystery is the crop circle that was located in a large field presently owned by the heirs of Forrest and Allie Gibson. The legend began in the 1860s when William Gibson cleared a meadow, cutting the laurel and alder, and afterwards the large circle appeared. It was said to consist of a grass that wasn't known to grow anywhere else in the area, and it survived until recent years when the field was plowed.

"It was a big green circle, greener than the rest of the grass," said Kathleen Mace, who lives nearby.

- - -

From the end of July to late September 1861, the Slatyfork area had a visitor who was destined to become forever famous. He was Robert E. Lee, first the coordinator and then the commander of Confederate forces who were sent there to regain control of the Staunton-Parkersburg Turnpike that led south into Virginia, and to contest with Union troops for the divided loyalties of northwestern Virginia, later to become West Virginia.

In his 2004 book, *Rebels At the Gate*, Hunter Lesser of Elkins wrote that Lee camped at two places during his stay of approximately two months. First he camped on a knoll across U.S. 219 from a familiar historical marker at Linwood.

The marker reads: "On this knoll, General Robert E. Lee maintained headquarters from July to September 1861, after taking command of the Confederate forces in West Virginia. His army on Valley Mountain guarded the road leading south into Virginia." But Lesser thinks that Lee may have been at Linwood only a short time, perhaps for only a few days.

During this brief stay, according to Sharp family tradition, Lee rode to supper at Slatyfork. It isn't certain who lived there in 1861, but two possibilities are Hugh Sharp or Silas Sharp, both uncles of the Si Sharp that I interviewed in 1993. Lee's hosts lived in a log cabin that is still there, although the logs have been boarded over.

In early August, Lee moved to Valley Mountain, which straddles Pocahontas and Randolph Counties near Mace and Mingo, and from there, on September 12, 1861, launched his first battle as a senior commander, a foray against Union forces at Elkwater on the Tygart Valley River. The attack was not successful, and Lee was gone from the area by late September, the Cheat Mountain campaign behind him.

There is a monument on the Mingo Flats Road near Valley Head that is a reminder of the Confederate presence in the area. It is not of Lee, as many think and as a sign on the Mingo Flats Road says, but rather a generic monument "to the memory of the Confederate soldiers of Randolph County and vicinity and all soldiers who died on Valley Mountain in 1861." The biggest enemy of Confederate soldiers at Linwood and Valley Mountain was the cold, rainy August of 1861. Camp diseases such as typhoid fever, measles, and malaria took a heavy toll.

On a humid June day in 2004, Dudley Dodrill and I visited both the Confederate monument and a cross-shaped marker near Mingo that marks the site of Lee's Valley Mountain camp. The marker was erected in 1901 and is dedicated to the memory of Confederate soldiers on Valley Mountain.

The Lee campsite is on private property, the owners of which graciously consented to our visit. From the marker, a meadow slopes gently in the direction of the nearby mountains, which at the time of our visit were clothed in the bluish haze of approaching summer. Lee chose the site for military reasons, but he obviously had a "tent with a view."

- - -

In November 2002, I drove through a steady rain to visit Ernie Shaw and his wife, Bobbie, at their Marlinton home. They were still on a "high" after staying up late to watch a West Virginia University football win over Virginia Tech the previous night. We talked about the game, mutual acquaintances, and the approaching deer season, which Ernie would spend at his camp on Elk Mountain.

His wife, Bobbie Blackhurst Shaw, is a Cass native. Her uncle, Warren "Tweard" Blackhurst, was well known for his books on the Cheat Mountain logging era, including *Riders of the Flood* and *Men and a Mighty Mountain*. A few months after my visit, the Shaws planned to see an out-door play based on *Riders of the Flood*. The theater was located on Island Park in the Greenbrier River at Ronceverte. In one of life's little ironies, the river raised and flooded the stage before *Riders of the Flood* could be presented that night.

Ernie grew up in the vicinity of Split Rock pool and the present Slaty Ridge housing development. Later the family moved to Crooked Fork of Elk. He graduated from the West Virginia University School of Dentistry in 1966, and practiced for thirty-six years in Marlinton before retiring in 2002. His brother, Dave Shaw, still lives on the Crooked Fork farm.

When Big Spring Fork almost dried up in the drought of 1933, their father, Keith Shaw, filled washtubs with trout from parched pools and put them in Split Rock. "Some of them," said Ernie, "were twenty-two to twenty-four inch rainbows."

Over seventy years after Lee rode to supper from Linwood to Slatyfork, Ernie walked the same four miles delivering Grit, a homespun family-oriented newspaper that began in 1882. Ernie had eight customers between the L.D. Sharp store and Linwood. The paper cost ten cents, of which Ernie received two cents.

One of his Grit customers was Eugene Gatewood, a farmer and the last postmaster at Linwood, a community located at the intersection of U.S. 219 and West Virginia 66, commonly known as "the Snowshoe turn-off." Ernie recalled Eugene Gatewood as "a large and pleasant man given to wearing bib overalls, and a porch sitter." He remembers the Gatewood home as "a glorious big old house with cherry stairways."

Across U.S. 219 is the Colonel Gatewood spring. Colonel Gate-wood was Andrew C.L. Gatewood, father of Eugene and a Confederate colonel who came to the Slatyfork area after the Civil War and became Linwood postmaster in 1894. The post office was originally established as Split Rock, and was located in the home of Samuel Varner, the first post-master in 1875.

There was once a post office called Yelk that was located in Pleasant Valley near the Gibson Cemetery in the George Hannah home. Supposedly it was originally named Elk, but either because of a misprint or conflict with another post office named Elk, it became Yelk.

Pauline Galford, who died in April 2004, lived where the Gatewood house stood. She and her husband, Wallace, a logger and sawmill operator, bought the Gatewood house after their marriage in 1941, and lived there for several years, but eventually built a new house.

Over 300 acres of Galford property at Linwood is now part of Snowshoe, including the entrance at the foot of the mountain. Snowshoe's largest single acquisition was 7,000 acres from Mower Lumber Company that includes the upper Shavers Fork Basin, the Snowshoe Village site, and the West Ridge townhouse development that faces the start of Elk River.

The resort developers also bought 1,000 acres from Ralph Beckwith that embraced much of the present golf course. Ralph and developer Tom Brigham became good friends, and Brigham referred to the sawmill man as "quite the country philosopher."

Snowshoe's other major acquisition was approximately 2,600 acres from a group of Elkins investors that became the Silver Creek ski area.

Brigham left Snowshoe in 1991 and returned to Birmingham, Alabama, where he was a dentist before he started developing ski resorts. He and his wife, Marye, still live in Birmingham, and a son, Tommy, is chief executive officer of Realty South, the state's largest realtor. Another son, Peter, is a carpentry contractor at Sunlight, Colorado. A daughter, Anne, is a nurse in Birmingham.

Brigham first saw the southern end of Cheat Mountain in 1971 in the company of Charlie Bryant, a forester for Mower who is now retired and lives in Surprise, Arizona, twenty miles west of Phoenix. "I got really excited when we turned up the Cass Road and saw the big spruce trees on top of the mountain, and I envisioned ski trails snaking through them," Brigham recalled.

He was a fisherman as well as a skier. He fished Shavers Fork from its headwaters downstream to U.S. 250, the Slaty section of Elk, and Big Spring Fork. One day on the latter stream his visit coincided with an insect hatch, and he caught six brook trout and six rainbows in about thirty minutes.

- - -

Beckwith Lumber Company and the start of Elk are inseparable. Old Field Fork borders one side of the mill bottom, Big Spring Fork borders the other side, and the county road that provides access to Elk runs through the middle. The company office sits on U.S. 219 in the former Slatyfork Elementary School, which

First mill at the Sugar Camp

was closed in 1960. Ralph Beckwith bought the building in 1991.

Beckwith, who grew up at Barton, Webster County, founded Beckwith Lumber in 1961 when he bought two hundred and forty five acres near the head of Big Spring Fork. Now he owns 62,000 acres in fourteen counties. He set up his first mill just inside the gate where he and his wife, Glenda, still live, and first logged at the site of a former sugar camp where sap was collected from sugar maples.

He entered the lumber mill business with less than a ringing endorsement from a contemporary. "There's no use for Ralph to start in the lumber business," said another sawmill owner. "He'll never make it."

That prophesy was almost fulfilled after he moved his mill to Slatyfork in 1964, because fire struck in 1965, 1982, and 1993. The 1982 fire was especially disastrous. "Times were tough then," he said, "and I had laid off the night watchman, plus the loss was not covered by insurance." But a group of employees approached him and offered to work without pay to help rebuild the mill, and Beckwith Lumber rose, Phoenix-like, from the ashes.

Ralph was born at Wendell, Taylor County, and was six weeks old when his parents, Watson and Lola Beckwith, moved to Barton (now Curtin) on Elk above Webster Springs. His father was a coal miner for Pardee and Curtin. Barton was formerly called Ralph. "They named a town after me, and I hadn't even been born yet," Ralph Beckwith likes to say.

He recalls Barton as a typical coal mining town of about one hundred houses, with Friday night movies for only twenty cents in the community building. "Looking back," he says, "it seems it was always a Tarzan movie. I suppose it was a continuing series."

Most coal towns in West Virginia in the 1920s and 1930s had

a baseball team, and Ralph was a catcher on the Barton team. Once he "beaned" George Gillespie, who played for Webster Springs. "George tried to steal second base," Ralph explained, "and my throw hit him in the head."

But George, who now lives in Princeton and is an optometrist at Bluefield, Virginia, "got even" in a later game. He was a pitcher with a good fastball, and he plunked Ralph between the shoulders with a possibly errant pitch.

"I remember the beaning," said George when I contacted him, "but this is the first time anybody has asked me about it in fifty years."

Ralph played football at Webster Springs High School, but claims no great accomplishments on the gridiron. "Mostly the first team ran over me in practice," he said.

His high school graduation gift in 1952 was two red Tamsworth sows which he kept in a pen at the present site of the J.C. Hamer lumber mill at Curtin. He sold pigs to the Pardee and Curtin store and to local residents for fifteen dollars a pig. One time he sold a porker with a mashed tail to a woman at Bolair. "I think I ought to get a whole pig for fifteen dollars," she complained.

He worked a year and a half at Pardee and Curtin's 2-C mine on Gauley River, and eight years for Maust Coal and Coke at Sharp's Knob on Gauley Mountain, primarily operating a coal cutting machine. He left Maust when he bought the Big Spring Fork property and set up a sawmill. A 1957 picture of Maust employees hangs in the hallway of his schoolhouse office as a memento of his underground mining days.

- - -

Ralph's desk is large and curving, and he rarely sits at it. He is more likely to be found bouncing around the mill or at a logging site in his familiar, well-traveled red Chevy truck, frequently talking with employees. I think of him as the Slatyfork version of Sam Walton, the Wal-Mart founder who also drove a truck and would visit stores and lead employees in a Wal-Mart cheer.

Although Ralph is often a stranger to his office, his occasional

Ralph Beckwith

presence is indicated by Post-It notes pasted in multi-colored profusion around the desk, giving it the appearance of a flower garden in bloom. "People ask me if the different colors have any significance," he said, "and the answer is no. It's just whatever color I happen to pick up."

One day I asked him a question and he wrote it down on a Post-It note and placed it among the glittering array. On a subsequent visit I was curious to know if he remembered where it was. He immediately and impressively pointed it out, and just as decisively said he hadn't found the answer.

Well, no matter, because I couldn't remember the question.

Ralph believes that everybody should work at least fifteen hours a day and sleep a short time, perhaps even waking up feeling guilty about sleeping. His hobby is farming, which he finds therapeutic. "I can have a bad day at the mill and go home and relax by working on the farm," he told me one day when I was feeling especially trifling.

Ralph's three sons, Ralph W., Ronnie, and Ricky, son-in-law Charles Wood, and grandson Danny Wood all work at the mill. Another grandson, Bradley Beckwith, works on the farm, helping tend two hundred head of Black Angus cattle.

Ralph doesn't hunt or fish. "I don't like deer," he said, "but I couldn't shoot one." If he ever fishes, I would envision the Post-It notes being tied into trout flies of dazzling colors patterned after Joseph's coat of many colors and cast upon the sacred waters of upper Elk.

- - -

The Slatyfork community was on the railroad line to down Elk. Trains came through the Big Cut near Spruce to the Tygart River drainage, and then to the Elk drainage near Mount Airy, where the railroad crosses U.S. 219. The nearest train to Slatyfork today is the Cheat Mountain Salamander, an excursion train that goes only as far as the Big Cut. Beyond that, the track is out of service.

West Virginia Pulp and Paper began cutting timber on the Elk headwaters in 1913, and gradually worked its way downriver. Logging down Elk was completed by the late 1930s, by which time the track had been sold to the Western Maryland Railway, and the company's lands on the headwaters had been sold to the U.S. Government as part of the Monongahela National Forest.

Trains once ran to the Bergoo area, hauling out timber and, later, coal. The number of mines gradually dwindled until, by 1994, only one mine remained, and CSX, the final track owner, abandoned the line. The present owner is the State Rail Authority.

I visited the Big Cut in October 2002 with Ed Galford. From the end of Snowshoe land near Black Run, the first major tributary of Shavers Fork, we walked to the old logging town of Spruce and then a mile and a half up the track to the cut. The autumn color was nice at the higher elevations, and the day, although rainy, was pleasant for walking.

The concrete foundations and walls of the pulp mill are all that remain of Spruce, the West Virginia Pulp and Paper town whose heyday was from 1904 until 1925. Spruce was a ghost town by 1951. It once held the distinction of being the highest inhabited town in the state at 3,863 feet, a title now held by Snowshoe Village.

Construction on the Big Cut was started in 1910 by West Virginia Pulp and Paper and completed in 1914, thus opening the way to its Elk timber. The cut is almost 2,000 feet long and 100 feet deep. George Deike III wrote in his superb book, *Logging South Cheat*: "It was an unprecedented project for a lumber railroad."

The Big Cut is bounded by Snowshoe and Monongahela National Forest lands. It sits at an elevation of 4,066 feet, but there are higher elevations nearby. One of them is Fool's Knob in the national forest. I asked Ed why it's called that. "I think it must mean you're a fool to go there," he replied, "because of its steepness and the thick stands of spruce that survived the logging era. I went turkey hunting there once, and vowed I'd never go back."

On our return from the Big Cut, we sat on a stack of crossties near Spruce and ate a lunch of ham sandwiches and apples. I thought of all the trains that had rolled past over the years, many of them coming from as far down Elk as Bergoo. That day we heard only silence, if silence can be heard. At the very least, it can be experienced and appreciated.

~ Three ~

The Slaty Section

Where Elk Begins

Elk River begins in an abyss, and continues in one for the next fifty-five miles until the river reaches Centralia and escapes into gentler terrain. The start of the abyss is best appreciated by viewing it, as I did one hot day in August 2003, from the upper end of the road that runs through the Beckwith Lumber Company mill.

From that vantage point, the imposing ridgeline of Gauley Mountain towers over the abyss and in fact creates it. At first glance, the mountain appears to be on the right or north side of the river, but is really on the left, an illusion created by the topography. Framing the right side of the river, in actuality, is Middle Mountain, which, although forty four hundred feet high, is less visible at that point.

Gauley Mountain rises to over forty five hundred feet and accompanies Elk to Cowger's Mill, a distance of ten miles. From there, a spur ridge goes on to Whittaker Falls, followed by additional spur ridges below that. Geographically, therefore, this mountain that divides the Elk and Gauley River drainages for a considerable distance also defines the start of Elk River.

Its most prominent feature is Sharp's Knob, which lies in a westerly direction 2.036 air miles from the start of Elk and is forty five hundred and thirty two feet in elevation. The headwaters of Gauley begin in the vicinity of Sharp's Knob. From where I viewed the ridgeline, the knob can be identified on a clear day by the presence of three communications towers, which seem small at that distance.

The knob is named for William Sharp, who acquired the land

through a grant from the Commonwealth of Virginia in the 1800s. Today, Sharp's Knob and virtually all of Gauley Mountain on the Elk side is part of the Monongahela National Forest.

Squarely in the middle of the large swath of forest green on the map, near Sharp's Knob, is an arrow shaped parcel known as the Natwick tract. It was named for Natwick Lumber Company, which once owned it, had a sawmill at the mouth of Big Run, and used the West Virginia Pulp and Paper Company railroad to haul its logs out.

Ralph Beckwith bought the tract from Mildred Natwick, a well known actress in her day who performed on the Broadway stage and in movies. She was nominated for an Academy Award for her role in the 1949 John Wayne movie, *She Wore a Yellow Ribbon*. Beckwith, in turn, sold the tract and other properties totaling 1,480 acres to The Nature Conservancy in early 2004.

Another geographic feature at the start of Elk is Flat Ridge, which slopes down from Gauley Mountain in the manner of a very large finger that seems to point, godlike, to the abyss where Big Spring and Old Field Forks combine to form Elk. I always expect a voice to boom out, as it did to Moses on Mount Horeb: *"Put off thy shoes from off thy feet, for the place whereon thou standest is holy ground."*

The holy ground was overgrown in weeds and briers when I was there in August 2003, but the following summer the State Rail Authority cut the brush and graveled the approach to the spur line railroad bridge over Big Spring Fork that gives fishermen access to the path that follows the track downriver. There are no trains running anymore, but the possibility of a scenic run was being talked about by spring 2005.

From its beginning at Slatyfork, Elk flows not quite five miles before leaving the Pocahontas County motherland at Blackhole Run, which comes off Gauley Mountain near where Elk goes underground (see Disappearing Act). Elk enters Randolph County at Blackhole Run and continues in Randolph for eight miles to Whittaker Falls and the Webster County line.

Linguistically speaking, Elk starts at several places. Most people say it starts at Slatyfork, which is the name of the community; occasionally fishermen will refer to the start of the river as "the lower end of the Beckwith Lumber Company bottom"; a diminishing handful call the beginning point the Forks of Elk, because Big Spring and Old Field Forks meet there; and even fewer call it Laurel Bank, the former railroad designation.

The first catch and release trout fishing section on upper Elk begins with the start of the river and continues 4.6 miles downstream to the mouth of Dry Branch. Fishermen call this part of Elk the Slaty section.

I fished the first mile of Elk in June 2003 with Ray Menendez, a retired fisheries biologist with the Division of Natural Resources and a longtime friend. The third member of our party that day was rain.

Ray began fishing Elk from Bergoo upriver in the 1950s, and it has been a love affair ever since. The river rewarded him in the 1980s, perhaps grudgingly, when it yielded a twenty-two inch brown trout. He almost duplicated that feat on the day of our visit, but the river takes away as often as it gives.

We walked down the weedy railroad track to where a railroad car, abandoned like the track that runs down Elk, sits forlornly below Laurel Run and Props Run, the first two tributaries of Elk. Laurel Run is named for the shrub, and Props Run is named for the long ago Propst family that lived there. Props Run is one of the most popular mountain bike trails on the Monongahela National Forest.

Despite its forlorn look, the railroad car was to become a beloved haven of refuge when the first hard rain shower descended upon us without mercy and with only one or two small rumbles of thunder down-river as unfair warning.

We waded through tall weeds to reach the river. Splashes of color were sprinkled here and there in the form of a lavender phlox that is common on upper Elk.

The forlorn railroad car

The trout were feeding on the surface of the pool that unfolded before us, although only sporadically.

My first several hundred casts were made with a Green Drake mayfly, which I chose for the occasion because it is large enough that I could see it floating on the water even though the river was running higher than normal for the time of year. Light conditions were changing constantly, and sometimes Polaroid glasses helped and sometimes I could see the fly better without them.

The calendar said the Green Drake hatch was over. Charlie Heartwell, retired DNR fisheries biologist and fly tying and hatch guru, had put an arbitrary date of June 10 on the end of the revered Green Drake hatch in West Virginia streams when I posed the question to him during my newspaper days.

Ray and I came to the Railroad Car Hole, as I named it, on June 11. On my fourth cast, I raised a very robust brown trout which seemed to covet the Green Drake, but perhaps reluctantly, considering the royal decree that was in place. That was the only action of the day on that particular fly pattern. It is possible, in retrospect, that my trout was the last of the year 2003 to rise to a Green Drake on upper Elk.

I removed the handsome fellow from the leader with a sense of profound sadness and placed him in my plastic fly box as one would carefully lead a champion race horse into the stall. His once proud hair was damp and drooping from hours of tumbling down the swift currents, with only an occasional dusting of fly conditioner to soothe his frayed nerves. I took one last look before closing the lid, and closing the lid is a fitting term because the Green Drake in its sub-adult stage is also known as the Coffin Fly.

- - -

The Railroad Car Hole is the first large body of water on the Slaty section. In the spring, it is swift and adventuresome where it straightens out from a small curve at the upper end, and then it tames down to become placid in the lower end, and is a great place for trout to cruise.

But regardless of size or temperament, all of the water from the start of Elk down to the Railroad Car Hole is marvelous trout water, and quite possibly is underrated by anglers who believe that the farther they walk downstream the fewer fishermen they will encounter, when the reverse may be true.

A very faint rumble of thunder was heard.

"Was that thunder?" I asked, knowing full well that it was.

"I think so," replied Ray, who also knew full well.

Never have I known two people, who knew full well, to be so equivocal.

Within minutes it was raining hard. Someone who works at Snowshoe Mountain Resort once told me that the rain there always comes slanting down, but at the Railroad Car Hole it was coming straight down, as serious and decent rain should. Ray unfurled a green rain jacket, which he said did little good, seeing as how it was flimsy enough to fit in his fishing vest. But I suspected he was only trying to make me feel better, because soon I was soaked to the skin through my fishing vest and red Colonial Williamsburg T-shirt.

Wearing bright clothing tends to violate the Best Management Practices of fishing for wild trout, but that was what I put on that morning, half asleep, and anyway my fishing vest mostly obscured the flaming color of the T-shirt.

I have never minded being the first fisherman to seek shelter from rain, and I headed straight for the railroad car, Ray following. We tentatively stepped on the floor, which was sagging in places, and found that it was it sturdy enough to support the hundreds of pounds that my wet T-shirt weighed. We stared out at the rain and talked about this and that. I told the story from *Tale of the Elk* about Bill Byrne sleeping on the ground through a hard rainstorm. That had occurred ninety-five years ago almost within sight of where we were taking shelter in the railroad car.

Ray told about his and his son's sighting of a mountain lion crossing the highway a few years ago as they drove south on U.S. 219 paralleling Cheat Mountain near Beverly. In my walled-in world there are only two classes of people: those who have seen mountain lions in the wild and those who haven't, and I, being a founding member of those who haven't, listened with envy.

When it comes to mountain lion stories, wildlife biologists would make Doubting Thomas of the Bible look like the consummate true believer. But many, not just Ray and his son, have seen them. The only question is where they're coming from. They might be truly wild animals, but they might also be animals released from captivity. Officially, the

last wild cougar in West Virginia was killed in 1887 on Tea Creek in Pocahontas County. The last verified tracks were found on Kennison Mountain, also in Pocahontas County, in 1936.

- - -

The rain slackened and then stopped, and Ray and I returned to the Railroad Car Hole. It soon became evident that the trout were no longer rising to the surface for reasons apparently having to do with the rain, although I don't know why people who live underwater would let that influence them.

The Railroad Car Hole

We moved upstream, and at Ray's suggestion I tried a Sulfur emerger, which is the early or emerging stage of the Sulfur Dun mayfly and is usually created in a pale yellow or creamy color. Two weeks before our trip, and below where we were fishing, Ken Yufer caught a twenty-three inch brown trout, one of three browns he caught that day of over twenty inches. Ken is a Pennsylvania native who now lives in Newton, West Virginia, but whose real "home" is on upper Elk.

When Ray opened his fly box to change his offering to a nymph, I gasped in disbelief. There seemed to be hundreds of thousands of flies of all shapes, colors, and sizes arrayed in a two-sided compartment. Charlie Heartwell once told me that fly fishermen are gatherer/hunters, as were the Sioux Indians, and there unveiled before me on a glistening and slippery bank of Elk River was the undeniable proof.

I tried the emerger at the next hole above the Railroad Car. A hemlock had uprooted at the head of the pool, lending character to the setting. All trout pools should have at least one fallen tree somewhere. Ray, fishing below me, had just caught two brown trout on a Hare's Ear nymph in what he calls "pocket water," or swift flowing water with small pockets of cover. The largest of the two was about sixteen inches long, a very nice trout.

A nymph precedes the emerger in the development stage of aquatic insects, and is "fished wet," usually with a small sinker attached about a foot down the leader. The nymph tumbles down through the current, and it is a tribute to the athletic ability of trout that they can see it and then catch up with it, all in a blur of motion. My nephew's teenage son, Travis, who is athletically gifted (see Down Elk), is the only other living being I know who could do that.

It began to rain again, and my interest in Sulfur emergers and nymphs waned and then disappeared completely. I wished I was safe and dry in the fly box with the Green Drake.

Just below the Harmon Sharp Hole, where Bill Byrne slept in the rain, Ray hooked onto a trout that from the start announced that it was going to be belligerent. I watched, wet and cold, as Ray gradually gave ground down through the swift flowing current, unable to turn the fish. I was reminded in every respect of the classic scene in the movie *A River Runs Through It* where Paul, the maverick son played by Brad Pitt, battled and landed a large trout.

In real life on upper Elk, the big fish got into very swift current and broke the leader. Ray held up his arms in dismay, the empty line dangling lifelessly in the water. A picture would have been worth a thousand words, assuming the lens wasn't splotched with rain. Ray had gotten a good look at the fish, a brown trout, and estimated it to be well over twenty inches long.

We did not see any rainbow trout that day on upper Elk, which was puzzling because this import from the Western United States has become the dominant fish in the Slaty section, supplanting native brook trout. Perhaps it was the cloudiness. Charlie Nichols, an upper Elk fisherman, keeps a diary, and has found that rainbows prefer sunny days, while browns like overcast skies and milky water. The water was milky on the day that Ray and I fished, but sunshine was definitely lacking.

We fished the Harmon Sharp Hole before heading back to the car. Harmon was the son of William Sharp, an early Slatyfork settler. I visited Ralph Beckwith in my wet clothes, and then drove out onto the Highland Scenic Highway, still wet. On Black Mountain, at an elevation of forty five hundred and forty five feet, a wind and rainstorm descended with the fury of a brown trout that had been fooled by an imitation nymph. I pulled over, and there in the car, surrounded by pelting rain and swaying red spruce, changed to dry clothes, dumping my soggy fishing apparel in a soggy heap on the floor on the passenger side. The flaming red Colonial Williamsburg T-shirt seemed to glare at me. My favorite destination, then as always, was home.

- - -

I returned to the Slaty section in May 2004 to fish with Mike Cumashot, owner of Elk Mountain Construction Company at Snowshoe. It was raining. It thundered. Pleasantly jagged streaks of lightning flashed over Gauley Mountain. There was no need to ask the question I had posed to Ray Menendez almost a year earlier: "Was that thunder I heard?"

We met at the upper parking lot where the river begins. Ken Yufer, who defines the upper Elk fisherman because of the amount of time he spends on the river, was there too. Ken fishes upper Elk in spring, summer, fall, and winter, and perhaps in a fifth season if there is one.

We stood and talked, oblivious, or at least Ken and Mike were, to the rain and lightning. Later, between peals of thunder, Mike suggested that he and I drive to the lower end of the catch and release section.

The suggestion had nothing to do with the storm. There were several cars in the parking lot, indicating several fishermen downstream, and Mike is a lone wolf fisherman. As it turned out, we had to share the lower end too.

Mike lives near Split Rock of Big Spring Fork. Because of his close proximity to upper Elk, he fishes the river as much as anybody, and has done so for thirty years. He is a native of the Pittsburgh area, later lived

Mike Cumashot on the Slaty section

in Richmond, and then gravitated to Elk. He is regarded by his peers as maybe the best fisherman on the river. I use the qualifying adverb "maybe" so as not to offend anyone who might possibly consider themselves the best.

On a higher spiritual plane, the Father Confessor is Charlie Heartwell, whom I once described as "the definer of the shadowy world of mayfly hatches." I fantasize that each year at the somber End of the Mayfly Festival he receives confessions from fly fishermen who have sinned. Their sins may range from a probably forgivable failure to dust the fly after every third cast, to using cheese eggs when nobody is looking, which is the unpardonable sin.

From his home at Beverly, in the shadow of Cheat Mountain, Charlie ties a line of flies called Charlie's Charmers that are in great demand, and his West Virginia Mayfly Hatch Chart is the bible of fly fishermen.

But I know him for falling down twice in the same hole on the Slaty section, both times injuring the same knee. I'm ashamed that I find humor in other people falling. It's a sickness, I know, but I become hysterical and there's nothing I can do about it. Don't feel bad, Charlie told me, his son is the same way.

His falls occurred just above the Lower Bait Hole, where, going downstream, the railroad tracks narrow to just one after the four or five parallel tracks of the old switch yard. Fifteen years ago, as he was entering the river, the bank gave way and down he went. In summer 2003, directly across the river from the earlier fall, he tried to step over a fallen tree, and down he went again. Both times he hobbled back to the car on a very painful knee.

"Yes," Father Confessor replied in a forgiving tone when I confessed to him that I found humor in his falls. "I suppose it is funny, except to me."

- - -

The gateway to the lower end of the Slaty section begins above Elk Springs. A well beaten path has been chiseled down to the river by countless fishermen carrying or wearing their dreams, aspirations, flies, landing nets, magnifying glasses, tapered leaders, sunglasses, fishing vests, and waders. Mike Cumashot and I carried or wore the same luggage, waded the same river, in my case very shakily on the same slick rocks, and walked up the same railroad track to begin fishing.

We sat on a soggy log near the entrance to Harry Mahoney's cave (see Disappearing Act) , and tied on flies called The Usual. If I had envisioned a Gray Fox, March Brown, Green Drake or other familiar mayfly imitation, I would have been disappointed. But it was raining and I had only envisioned being wet and miserable.

The Usual has a more interesting history anyway. It is made of the furry padding on the large hind feet of snowshoe hares. Mike first heard of the fly in his native Pennsylvania. The story goes that two fishermen were on one of that state's fine trout streams. One was catching fish and the other wasn't, which can create animosity you wouldn't believe.

"What are you catching them on?" asked Envious Fisherman.

"The usual," replied Successful One.

The usual to which he referred was the fly made of the snowshoe hare padding. I learned later that its creator was Fran Betters, a New York fisherman who fished, among other of that state's famous trout streams, the Ausable, or probably more specifically the West Branch Ausable.

The Usual doesn't imitate any particular bug that hatches on a stream. In that respect, it joins the Snowshoe Rabbit Foot, the Adams Parachute, and other flies that come under the heading of "general attractors." Fly fishermen who feel good about their ability to match the hatch will concede the existence of general attractors only under torture, and perhaps not then.

Credibility can be stretched only so far, I know, but those who create The Usual don't stop with the snowshoe hare's hind feet padding. They also take the hair *between the toenails* to create tiny patterns. The toenail hair is kinkier, I am told, and therefore floats better.

About a month later, I had The Usual for lunch at the bar and grill at the Elk Springs Fly Shop. Their sandwich offerings are named for popular fly patterns, and the hot dog is called The Usual. Quite good, too, although next time for variety's sake I may try the March Brown breaded chicken, the Royal Coachman barbeque, the Adams barbequed ribs, or, well, you get the picture.

Joe Messinger Sr. probably never tied The Usual, but he *was* a fly tying legend on Elk. He drove a 1926 Hudson with the back seat removed and a work bench installed, and with the dome light rigged for extra brightness. He parked along the river, collected insects that were attracted to a light, and imitated them on the spot with soft downy feathers plucked from chickens that he kept in the car. But his first love was fishing for smallmouth, and his Messinger Frog, made from deer hair, was a favorite of bass fishermen.

- - -

Mike and I began fishing in the rain, and I quickly, which was unusual, caught a fish on The Usual. It was a brown trout of modest but energetic size. He or she was living temporarily, perhaps just renting, in a pool of water which, in the dry months, is part of the dry bed of Elk.

A short distance above where I caught the brown is where Black-hole Run enters Elk from the south. It is in this section that the river goes underground in the porous limestone strata, and it is where Boonie Sommerville's coon dogs got into a fight with a bear and then with each other (see Disappearing Act).

There is a long straight stretch of railroad track below Blackhole Run where immense beds of skunk cabbage grow between the track and the river. Fishermen often see bears there in early spring when the plants are young and succulent. Bears not only like to eat skunk cabbage, they also like to wallow in it.

It was just above Blackhole Run that I discovered the fourth Blue Hole on Elk. It is a very attractive pool of water, and I felt sad when Mike told me that it dries up, or almost so, during the disappearing season. On the day of our visit it undoubtedly held trout, although we didn't catch any there.

There is a pool farther upstream that Mike calls "the Smart Hole" because, for some reason, it contains fish that are a cut above the rest in intelligence. I have thought about this, but an explanation eludes me. Certainly they aren't smart for taking up residence in a stream that goes dry.

We walked farther up the track, crossed the river on the railroad trestle to the north side, and viewed a small pool of water near the track that resembles a goldfish pond. The story told by railroaders is that they disposed of dynamite by burying it, or igniting it there, and deer loved the residue so much that they created a "dynamite lick."

Above that is Rip Rap Hole, which is a name given it for the blasted out rock that railroaders used to build up the river bank. Rip Rap Hole is announced by two or three large hemlocks at the upper end, and then swift flowing water of moderate depth with underwater rocks for cover. Upper Elk stakes its reputation as a fine trout stream on such places.

But the fishing is far from easy to master, especially in the Slaty section. Max Robertson, one of the state's fine fly fishermen, calls it "technical water," meaning in layman's terms that it helps to know what you're doing.

Mike Cumashot was inspired by Rip Rap Hole, or perhaps it was just that the rain had ended and the late afternoon sun had come out. He caught three rainbows and two browns there. Rainbows, especially, are a fish of swift flowing water and sunshine.

Mike told me his theory concerning the pedigree of rainbows on upper Elk. "They originally came from the McCloud River in California," he said, "probably first to a federal hatchery and then to Elk." He detects red slashes on the lower jaws of rainbows he catches in the Slaty section, which tells him they are descendants of cutthroat trout of the west.

We returned down the track. It was a long walk. I was tired. My back hurt. Mike's back hurt. We felt unbridled animosity toward the people who place railroad ties so close together that the stepping distance between them represents cruel and unusual punishment.

- - -

Driving to Cowger's Mill on the Dry Branch Road, I encountered a great cloud of insects, and then I met Ken Yufer, who looked pleased. "I didn't get a nibble on the upper section," he said, "but returning to my cabin I saw the hatch. I immediately headed for the Mill Pool, and caught ten or twelve trout in a short time."

The Mill Pool (see Cowger's Mill) is a melting pot of hatches in late evening, not to mention a melting pot of fishermen. Ken once wrote that "trout are feeding on different insects, or on different stages of the same insect. The cry of success [from another fisherman] ten yards away may not help you at all."

Inside the Elk Springs Fly Shop, Bill Harkness showed me a vase filled with the same insects I had encountered. His collection exceeded the number of stars that are visible on a clear night in January from a high mountain. I was too tired and hungry to ask for further details, but I wondered if they would go well with cheese and mayonnaise on whole wheat bread.

The fly shop owners are Daron and Lisa Dean, who live in Kentucky near Huntington. They offer guide service, cabins, campground, and the bar and grill where I had The Usual. A pond on the property is called Fitzpatrick Pond in memory of Coy Fitzpatrick, who lived nearby. Outdoor writer John McCoy called him "the last of the mountain men."

He slept in a sleeping bag on the porch of his home at Cowger's Mill, usually regardless of the weather. He once said he hadn't slept inside in seven years. He was a fisherman in his younger days, and was an avid reader, especially of history.

Glen Barnes, the West Virginia artist, painted Coy twice. One painting is a portrait and the other depicts him and his dog on a rock ledge. Coy always had a dog. Glen went to a rendezvous of the Appalachian Rangers of Clarksburg, hoping to find a mountain man model, and saw Coy sleeping behind a tent. He later discussed Coy's modeling for him, visited him at his cabin, and made the two paintings which are familiar to patrons of West Virginia outdoor art.

Coy died in 2002 at age ninety-three, a longevity which could be attributed to sleeping outside in the fresh air. His friends erected a stone memorial at the intersection of Valley Fork and Elk River Roads and inscribed on it: "Coy Fitzpatrick. Elk River Mountain Man."

- - -

Driving across foggy Point Mountain that night, I thought of the day's fishing and recalled a story told by Ernie Nester. If Charlie Heartwell is the Father Confessor of West Virginia fly fishermen, Ernie is the Founding Father. He came to West Virginia in 1966 from Carroll County, Virginia, and was instrumental in getting Trout Unlimited started here.

He helped form the first chapter, the Kanawha Valley chapter, in 1972, and was its first president. He was also the first president of the West Virginia Council of TU, and for several years was on TU's national board of directors.

The story he told me was about breaking the 13-inch barrier on brown trout in the Slaty section above the Rip Rap Hole, where Mike and I had fished. I invited him to write about it, and his account follows:

"Slaty Fork [the Slaty section of upper Elk] is an excellent trout stream that I have fished since about 1972, although I only get to fish the stream once or twice each year. As far as catching trout goes, I have had some good days and some very slow days. I usually catch more of the reproducing rainbows than browns.

"Up until 2002, I had not caught a brown in Slaty that was over 13 inches long. I had never seen a big brown while fishing Slaty and I had never seen anyone else catch a good sized brown on Slaty.

"I fish a lot of streams in West Virginia that have reproducing browns or a wild brown population from fingerling stockings. Every year I manage to catch several good browns in the 16-20 inch range in several different streams, including a few streams that are not much more than 10 feet wide. However, I do not go out of my way to try to catch big trout and I am perfectly happy if I can catch a few 8-10 inch natives or reproducing wild trout.

"I have heard many stories about friends or their buddies catching big browns of 18-24 inches in the Slaty section when the water was up and sometimes when it was muddy. I have looked at photos on the internet of big browns caught in Slaty. I am not fond of fishing when the water is high and will not fish muddy water.

"On May 28, 2002, Ken Yufer, Charlie Nichols and I drove to the upper end from Yufer's camp on Point Mountain. We parked below Beckwith's lumber mill and walked downstream. I started fishing about 0.4 miles below the twin tubes and worked upstream. There was a good flow of water and it rained for about an hour that afternoon. I used a tandem rig consisting of a large yellow caddis (dry) with a trailing nymph. The trout really liked the yellow caddis, but I could not find a nymph that they liked. I caught several rainbows up to 14 inches and a few browns up to 13 inches.

"Around 8:30 p.m. I came to a long pool with a limestone cliff running the length of the pool on the right side. There were a few green drake spinners flying around and there were a few gray fox type spinners around. A couple of trout rose about five feet off the cliff near where a few rhododendron limbs were hanging from the cliff, and then a large trout rose. Usually the smallest trout in the area will be the first one to a fly, but I was lucky and the largest trout took the yellow caddis. With the help of my net I was able to land and release unharmed the 18-inch female brown.

"It was a good day."

- - -

On a warm and gorgeously sunny day in late June 2004, I walked down the Slaty section to photograph the forlorn railroad car where Ray Menendez and I had taken shelter from the rain. I also wanted a generic picture in the Slaty section, and, since I was there, to fish a short while. I was still hampered by a bruised leg from a fall at home, which I didn't find nearly as funny as Charlie Heartwell's falls, and wading in or along the river was painful.

My fall was a spectacular one. I went off the porch roof and fell about fifteen feet through a rhododendron. The rhododendron is the largest single specimen I've ever seen. I'd carried it from across Birch River thirty years ago, and obviously it was pleased with where I replanted it. In a way, I thought, it repaid me by cushioning my fall and perhaps preventing more serious injury.

As I left the upper parking lot, a man from Virginia was returning from downriver. I asked him the question that fishermen learn at age one: "Are they biting?"

"I had a little action," he replied, "but then they stopped rising."

This, I thought, is where I usually come in.

I walked down the weedy track and took the seedy railroad car picture. The relic of logging and mining days looked even more forlorn than it had the previous year, but I had no right to criticize it, although I did wonder, as I had before, if it harbored snakes.

I've made no scientific study, but abandoned railroad tracks on warm summer days have always struck me as something that snakes consider Wild and Wonderful, Mountain Mama, and Almost Heaven rolled into one. If they were on or about the tracks, they might also have discovered the railroad car, I thought in an analytical way.

But I saw no snakes, and limped on down the tracks through an old switchyard, where there is not just one set of overgrown tracks to worry about, but four or five. A telegraph shack, or I suppose that was its use, looked as forlorn as the railroad car upstream, and just as snaky.

Farther on, the track returns to one set and enters a long straight stretch that Slaty fishermen call The Culverts section for twin culverts that run under the track. Walking the track, I thought of Nick Adams in Ernest Hemingway's *Big Two-Hearted River*.

I stopped to fish a series of pocket water with a large cliff rising above the river on the south side, and I got a couple of rises and lost a fish, although in general I didn't do as well as Nick Adams. In summer, the Slaty section becomes low and clear, and is a different river from May and early June.

Limping back up the track, and watching for snakes, I jumped the next to last grouse in West Virginia. I say "next to last" to allow for the unlikely possibility that there is another one out there somewhere, like the one I'd seen on the Red Spruce Knob trail. I met a fisherman who was heading downstream. He said he planned to stay until dusk, and I wished him well and was secretly glad that I was heading upstream.

Near the parking lot, I saw a rustling in the weeds between the crosstie I was on and the one I was stepping to. Closer examination revealed a snake of the size that raises the hackles. It had slithered under the end of a crosstie, preventing a good look at it. I think it was a water snake, which, in adulthood, becomes sullen and mean-spirited. But I was too near the car to make new enemies, and I left it at that, and left the Slaty section as well.

Four

Disappearing Act

Elk Goes Underground

In 1896, so the story goes, a fifteen-foot hole opened in the streambed in the vicinity of Blackhole Run and swallowed the river, thus creating the natural phenomenon known as the Dry Bed of Elk. This hole, which Hu Maxwell wrote about in his History of Randolph County, is believed to have largely filled in over the years, but the porous nature of upper Elk is such that the river still finds a way to escape underground.

Underground Elk is not unique in West Virginia. At least two more streams go underground, including the romantically named Lost River in Hardy County, which is "lost" for a mile and a half before reemerging at Wardensville as the Cacapon River.

There is also the Sinks of Gandy in Randolph County, which sinks for a half-mile or slightly more as it flows near Spruce Knob, the state's highest point. The Friars Hole Cave System that originates on Droop Mountain in Pocahontas County and flows to the Greenbrier River is the longest purely underground drainage in the state and one of the longest in the nation, with forty-five miles of subterranean passageways.

But Elk's disappearing act of over five miles occurs on the longest river wholly contained within the state, and which flows to the capital city of Charleston. So it is unique in those respects.

Mike Cumashot calls the area "Swiss cheese" because of its proliferation of sink holes, the largest of which is located on national forest land just off the Mine Road a hundred yards from Old Field Fork. This immense hole is about twenty-five feet deep, and in periods of heavy rain collects water from a small stream that runs into it. The water will fill to a depth of perhaps ten feet, and then eventually goes underground in a whirlpool that resembles a bathtub being drained.

In size and bathtub effect, it is unique within the million acre Monongahela National Forest. I visited the "bathtub" one day with Tim Henry, recreation officer on the Marlinton District, and we were greeted by a wild turkey hen that climbed out of the hole and trotted down a forest road. I'm not sure if trot properly describes a turkey's gait, but so be it. This one was trotting.

When I first came to Blackhole Run, which is usually regarded as the place where Elk goes underground, I thought of the tale of Brandy, a coon dog, and his son, Ben. They belonged to Boonie Sommerville, retired judge, legislator, and raconteur (see Webster Springs). It is a sad story, and, thinking about it, I sat down and wept bitterly, which is something I've always wanted to do anyway..

Boonie, Chuck Cochran, Chuck's son, Clinton, and the Blueticks, Brandy and Ben, went upriver on the railroad side to coon hunt. At the mouth of Blackhole Run the two dogs got into a fight with a bear.

"They fought the bear out of hearing," said Boonie, his eyes misting over. "That was around seven thirty, and sometime after midnight we got the pup back. He was cut and bleeding all to hell. Two hours later we heard the old dog barking treed, or so we thought. It turned out he was still after the bear, and he was baying instead of barking treed."

The dictionary defines baying as "to pursue with barking," or, my favorite, "to utter in deep prolonged tones," and anybody who has ever heard a coonhound baying knows that their tones have no equal in the mystical realm of deep and prolonged.

The bear made a wide circle and came back to the vicinity of Blackhole Run, where Boonie, Chuck, and Clinton managed to corral the baying, cut, clawed, and bleeding Brandy, and carry both dogs back down the railroad track to the vehicle.

On the way home, another fight broke out, this time between the dogs, who, one would think, had done enough fighting for the night. Trying to break it up, Boonie received a severe bite on his thumb.

"Why were they fighting?" I asked.

"You tell me," Boonie replied.

I thought about it at length, and a revelation came to me as one to whom, like the Apostle Paul, was revealed a hidden mystery. "Each one was blaming the other for starting a fight with a bear," I explained to the coon hunting judge in hopes that he would temper his judgment of the dogs with mercy. "Besides that, the father saw his son as a deserter."

This time it was Boonie's turn to think about it. He paused to light his ever present pipe. The birds in the stately trees in his yard in upper Hotel Bottom sang in unison. "I bind them over to the spring term," he finally said, unwilling to completely forgive the cantankerous dogs, but secretly hoping there would be a reconciliation.

And now for the sad part. There was no reconciliation.

"Those two dogs, father and son, hated each other ever after that," said Boonie, his eyes misting over for the second time. "From that moment I never could hunt them together anymore, because all they wanted to do was fight."

It had all started there at Blackhole Run, and I wept bitterly again.

- - -

There is another possibility to explain the aberrant behavior of the dogs, which I call the Darius Cummings theorem. Boonie told me over lunch one day at his home about Cummings, a gentle giant of a man who stood six eight and weighed three hundred pounds.

One day Darius announced excitedly at the mine where he worked that he had either seen seven bears, or one bear seven times. The coon dogs may have had the same thought, which would account for their animosity toward each other since there was the matter of blame hanging between them.

Darius was employed at the Pardee and Curtin No. 2 mine at Curtin, and his strength was legendary. A Pardee and Curtin foreman once asked him to carry a blacksmith's anvil to the top of the mountain to the mine. He was told that if he could do this his day's work would be done and he would receive a full day's pay. The foreman apparently thought it would take him all day to get the heavy anvil up the mountain.

But he picked it up and carried it to the mine without stopping. The foreman wanted to renege on his promise, so the story goes, but the other men said no, he was promised a day's wages and the remainder of the day off, and we will strike if the bargain isn't kept. And so it was.

- - -

Frank Hill of Hurricane, an upper Elk fisherman, had a ringside seat to a bear and dog encounter during bear season 2002. He had started fishing at the railroad bridge above Blackhole Run when he heard a loud and rising chorus of barking.

"I heard something running in the leaves behind me," he said, "and as I turned to look there was a bear paralleling the railroad and cantering upstream like a horse. It crossed the stream at the head of the riffle I was fishing, and soon here came five dogs: two adults and three pups.

"The bear and dogs went up the mountainside, and, I thought, good for them, now I can fish. A short time later I rounded a slight curve in the river and there were the three pups on the river's edge, refusing to jump into the cold water. The bear had again crossed the stream with the two adult dogs in pursuit. I made up with the pups, who were harnessed in their radio gear. They seemed glad to meet a stranger as long as they didn't have to jump into the water.

"I decided to leave that part of the river to the bear and its pursuers, so I hiked farther upstream on the railroad. As I approached the rip-rap area (see The Slaty Section), I again heard a rustling of leaves very close behind me. I turned, and there was the bear in extremely close proximity, skirting the top of the slope behind me.

"It soon came down the slope onto the railroad, and I would have bet my favorite fly rod that it would turn upstream, but it didn't. It came lumbering toward me. I'm convinced it had not seen or scented me. I took off my ball cap, waving it violently, and drew my trusty nine-foot fly rod to defend myself. I guess I thought I would whack it a lick or two.

"The bear came within approximately thirty feet of me and turned down the rip rap slope into the river. The flow of the river knocked it sideways into a boulder, which caused it to grunt loudly. One of the adult dogs was at the top of the slope looking for the bear, which was out of its sight. I yelled at the dog to 'get down here and chase this bear.' The dog saw the bear when it hit the boulder, and nearly ran over me to get to it. The last I saw of them, they were heading up the mountainside.

"After things settled down, I continued upstream toward Big Run and had a good day of fishing."

- - -

Strange things have happened at Blackhole Run, and most of them involve coon hunting, although the river going underground is strange too. Jerome Dean, retired football coach at Webster Springs, Richwood, and Webster County High Schools, was coon hunting there at around age ten with his father, Cal Dean, the renowned poker player (see Company Town), when their dog disappeared. This led to a scene that could have come straight out of an Indiana Jones movie.

"It was in the fall and the water was low," said Jerome," and my dad thought our dog may have chased a coon into a hole in the riverbed. He asked me to take a flashlight and climb down and call for the dog. I crawled through the small opening and came into a fairly large room. The dog was nowhere to be seen, and my calls brought only echoes. But the place was full of large fat crayfish. Each little hole of water contained ten or fifteen. When the light hit them, I could hear their pincers clicking. I got out of there very quickly. I envisioned falling and being eaten alive."

I've never heard crayfish clicking their pincers, but on the other hand I've never been surrounded by them in a dome-like room under a river at age ten. This incident occurred in 1947, and although Jerome doesn't remember exactly where they were, he remembers the dark chamber and the crayfish very vividly.

The story has a happy ending, unlike the fight between Boonie Sommerville's dogs, because the Deans' dog soon showed up. He hadn't been in the black hole at all, but was simply sashaying through the woods as coon dogs are born to do.

- - -

Elk doesn't disappear all at once in a great swoosh. There is a gradual disappearance above and below Blackhole Run as the river flows over the Greenbrier limestone floor seeking its inevitable exit into a dark underground world.

The dry bed is a natural wonder in its entirety, but the most striking single feature is Flat Rock, also called Picnic Rock, which is located seven-tenths of a mile above where the dry bed ends at Cowger's Mill, which is more familiarly known today as Elk Springs or Elk Springs Campground.

As the name implies, it is almost tabletop flat, and fills the entire riverbed for quite a distance. It has the same large parallel fissures, or cracks, as the Split Rock on Big Spring Fork, except on a much larger scale. Square dances were once held on the ample surface of Flat Rock. Ison Folks, the last miller at Cowger's Mill (see Cowger's Mill) , was among those who called the figures.

In July 2004, I visited Flat Rock with Calvin Sizemore, a resident of Campbell's Creek in Kanawha County who was staying at his daughter's camp in the dry bed section. I knew Calvin's wife, Helen, when she worked at the Bible Book Store on Hale Street in Charleston.

Calvin and I drove to the home of Bill and Nina Moles, the property owners on the north side of Flat Rock, and meandered down through their river bottomland to the unique rock, where, with a little imagination,

Flat Rock in the Dry Bed

we could hear the fiddlers performing, and the dancers stomping their feet on the hard surface.

There is a large, shallow pool of water above Flat Rock and a smaller one below that defy the otherwise almost total disappearance of Elk underground during the summer. Ron Hight, a survey technician for the Monongahela National Forest, was born upstream at the mouth of Chimney Rock Run, and recalls swimming as a kid in the lower pool at Flat Rock.

It seemed odd to be sitting in the middle of the river in a vehicle, which in this case was a Kawasaki Mule. The river was dry, of course, but it isn't always so. Calvin and Helen told me that the sound of water rushing over and filling the dry bed after a heavy rain, carrying debris with it, is unforgettable.

In my sheltered world, I have little, if any, familiarity with all-terrain vehicles. One day when I visited Theron Hamrick on Bergoo Creek, he and Donnie Shaffer were working on a tractor and discussing the whereabouts of a neighbor. I overheard Theron say that the person in question had ridden up on his mule the day before. Good grief, I thought, these people are living in a time warp. They rode mules on Bergoo Creek a hundred years ago. Later, when I met Calvin, I realized it was the Kawasaki Mule they were talking about.

Calvin and I left Flat Rock and drove to Chimney Rock Run, which enters Elk from the south another seven-tenths of a mile upstream and is named for a rock formation on a high promontory. On the way, Calvin told me about seeing a mountain lion on the north hillside two years ago during deer season.

- - -

There is a legend of ice being found in Chimney Rock Run into July and even August where the winter snows, driven and packed in among the rocks, and shaded through the spring and summer months by dense foliage, are preserved.

For confirmation, Ron Hight suggested that I contact Eugene Pescosolido, who was born about a hundred yards below the mouth of Chimney Rock Run, as were his brother, Arthur, and sister, Pauline Vigilante. Eugene and Arthur now live in Ohio, and Pauline lives in Michigan.

Eugene remembered that, yes, they collected ice or hard packed snow for Fourth of July picnics, and he recalled the "ice house" as being about a hundred yards upriver from the mouth of the run, where limestone boulders have broken away from a cliff and rest precariously above the dry bed.

His sister recalled the ice house as being farther up the hillside near the rock that gives Chimney Rock Run its name. "There was always a cold wind blowing out of a hole in the side of a cliff there," she said. "We found ice there until mid-July."

Their father, Domenic Pescosolido, was a native of Arce, Italy, near Rome. He came to the United States in 1912 at age fourteen, and worked, as many Italian immigrants did, on the railroad, a career that lasted over forty years. He married Millie Salisbury, a local girl. They rented company land for one dollar a month and built their Chimney Rock home. Domenic became section foreman on the railroad from Slatyfork to below Cowger's Mill. Later he had a little store and service station on Dry Branch Road.

"Father was in the medical corps in the Army following World War One," Pauline said, "and after he returned home it wasn't uncommon for someone to knock on our door in the middle of the night wanting him to come to their house and treat a sick person. He always went."

She remembers fishing trips on Chimney Rock Run with her mother and two brothers. "Mother loved to be outdoors," she said, "and we would take a picnic lunch and spend the day. In the evening, when dad came home from work and saw a big platter of native brook trout on the table, he would say, Oh, I see someone has been up Chimney Rock."

The meal was usually accompanied by sassafras tea and a salad made of a plant that grew along the run. Special treats were pies made from strawberries, blackberries, or raspberries picked along Chimney Rock Run. Occasionally the berries would be served simply as a bowl of fruit with cream and sugar.

Pauline and her brothers attended Rough Gap School, which was located about a mile downriver. "It was aptly named," she said, "because there were boulders everywhere. But it was a good place to play hide and seek."

They learned to swim at nearby Flat Rock. "Father would come in from work tired, sweaty, and dirty," Pauline said, "and we'd want to go swimming. He would always say, Yes, let's go swim."

"The name Flat Rock seemed to follow me," said Pauline, "When my husband, Benny, and I were first married, we lived at Flat Rock, Michigan, about thirty miles south of Detroit. The last two of our four children were born there."

Bill Morgan, who lives on Dry Branch Road, recalls what Domenic Pescosolido once said about the two poisonous snakes of the area. "I don't mind rattlesnakes," he said, "but I don't like copperheads. They no ringa the bell."

Bill and his wife, Dora, live across the river from the mouth of Chimney Rock Run. When they drilled a well, they discovered they were actually closer to the river than they thought. They hit swiftly flowing water at forty-three feet. "The current was so strong," said Bill, "that when I lowered a bucket on a rope, I had to hold on to keep the bucket from being swept away. You could hear the water roaring." They had struck underground Elk in their backyard.

Dora Morgan was born below Cowger's Mill at Hickory Lick, former site of a coal mine tipple. The Samp Hole nearby was named for her grandfather, Samp Conrad. Bill Byrne wrote about catching a brook trout of sixteen and one-half inches there, the largest brook trout he ever caught.

- - -

On a typical summer day in July 2004, when thunderclouds were hovering over upper Elk, I walked to the mouth of Chimney Rock Run, but found no ice. Then I went up the run about a quarter of a mile, climbing over boulders looking for ice, but found none there either.

I returned to the dry bed and visited the "ice house" that Eugene Pescosolido remembered. It is located on the edge of the river, or dry bed as was the case on the day of my visit, and is a collection of limestone boulders. I moved carefully around the boulders so as not to invite further breaking away from the mother cliff.

The air around the rocks had a distinct coolness despite the warm day, and the rocks were cold to the touch, but there was no ice. If this phenomenon still exists, I thought, it would undoubtedly vary in occurrence from year to year, depending on the weather. The "ice house" may actually be located, as Pauline Vigilante recalled, near the rock that gives the run its name. But the day had grown late, so I reserved a visit to Chimney Rock for another time.

Later that month I called Sean Weir, manager of the Elk Springs Fly Shop, and inquired about the status of the dry bed following local thunderstorms. "How's the dry bed?" I asked. I had fed him the perfect straight line, and he was equal to the occasion. "It's dry," he replied.

I drove to Cowger's Mill, following Elk upriver from Webster Springs. Above Whittaker Falls, the road becomes a front end alignment shop's best friend because of potholes that seem strategically placed so it is impossible to avoid them. Sometimes, to escape the potholes, I would take the Point Mountain Road, drop off at Monterville, and follow the Valley Fork Road to Elk Springs. If my destination was the very head of Elk, I would drive over the Highland Scenic Highway via Richwood, a circuitous route but a smoother one.

The scenic highway has a special appeal because of its "high country" look and feel, and because it leads to the headwaters of Elk. Over time, I saw two bobcats there, and a coyote that was feeding on road kill. Unlike the popular image of coyotes as lean and scrawny, this one was large and sleek. Ranchers out west have shot, trapped, poisoned, and otherwise waged genocide on coyotes for a hundred years, but coyotes are still with us, and are in fact expanding their range.

I never saw a bear on the scenic highway, as I had hoped, but one day I did see a very large bear on West Virginia 15 in Braxton County between Gerald Freeman Campground and Diana. It was the second largest bear I've ever seen in the wild, exceeded only by one that I encountered on Otter Creek in Randolph County years earlier.

My sister-in-law, Margaret Johnson, has always wanted to see a bear in the wild. She accompanied her son Rob (my nephew) and I to Bergoo on a trip that coincided with bear hunting season, and along the highway above Curtin we saw a bear that had been killed by hunters and was sprawled in the back of a flat-bed truck. "I really would have preferred to see a live bear," she said.

On the occasion of my call to Sean Weir, I went upriver from Webster Springs to the "catch and release" parking lot above Elk Springs, walked across the river on dry rocks where Mike Cumashot and I had waded a couple of months earlier, and followed the railroad track to Blackhole Run. Just below the run I had caught a brown trout on the day of my visit with Mike. Now, slightly over two months later, that hole and everything else around it was dry.

"Where do the fish go?" I asked myself and got no answer. On a personal level, I wondered what had happened to the trout I had caught, and which I wrote about as probably only renting that hole for the spring.

Only a shrunken pool remained in the Blue Hole immediately above Blackhole Run, where I had photographed Mike. The run itself had a decent enough flow until it came to within twenty yards of the dry bed, where it too disappeared underground.

My intention was to determine to my satisfaction where the dry bed begins. At least on that particular day it wasn't at Blackhole Run, which is usually referred to as the start of underground Elk. As far as I could see upstream the riverbed was nothing but dry rock. Without running water, the quietness was overwhelming, and I sat down and enjoyed it, and was thankful there are still such places in West Virginia where quiet and solitude exist.

I climbed the steep and weedy bank that led back to the railroad track, and continued walking upstream. Soon I could say that I had walked in two counties in one day on one hike: Randolph County below Blackhole Run, and Pocahontas County above it.

The vicinity of Blackhole Run is bear country, as Boonie Sommerville's coon dogs discovered, and I was mindful of this as I walked up the track. A loud noise in the direction of the dry bed, which sounded like a bear ripping at a dead log, got my attention. I took a few steps and something large bolted from the brush near the track. I backpedaled for a better look, and saw that it was a deer. My heartbeat slowly returned to normal. But that still didn't explain the ripping sound, which came from farther away and will remain a mystery.

I did, however, pinpoint the beginning of the dry bed on the day I was there. It occurred where the railroad crosses Elk above Blackhole Run. Immediately upstream from the bridge there was flowing water, but it disappeared at that point. Below the trestle, the riverbed was dry. I walked downriver a considerable distance to confirm this before returning to the railroad track over spongy ground where skunk cabbage flourished. I welcomed the firmness and dryness of the railroad bed, and headed to my car at the lower parking lot, passing with great unease the place where I'd heard the ripping sounds.

- - -

The porous world of upper Elk includes fifty-six known caves, most of them small but a few large ones like the Simmons-Mingo and My Cave system, which totals about seven miles of passageways. Simmons-Mingo tilts precariously on the Elk and Tygart drainages, although most, if not all, of its drainage goes to Elk. My Cave lies entirely within the Elk drainage.

I have been fascinated by the story of My Cave ever since Harry

Mahoney, its discoverer, told me about the day in 1963 when he found cold air blowing out from a softball sized opening on a hillside above Elk. He had gone there looking for caves after reading Hu Maxwell's account of the dry bed.

He enlarged the opening so that he could squeeze through. It led to a large room that was roughly 200 feet long, 50 to 60 feet wide, and 50 to 60 feet high. "I didn't go far," he said. "I'm not a serious caver."

Later he returned, accompanied by Bill Wylie, an ornithologist at West Virginia University who is also not a caver in the technical sense, but who shares Harry's adventuresome spirit. They found a smaller passage beyond the large room that opened to mud slopes and water.

The name My Cave was adopted by a spelunking club from Baltimore after Harry told them about his discovery. He referred so often to "my cave," that they began calling it that. A chilling reminder of the danger involved in caving is that two people have been killed in My Cave, one in a fall and one by drowning.

The caves of upper Elk are considered dangerous because of their technical nature, primarily the existence of many vertical drops. There also lurks the danger of sudden flooding from rainstorms or snowmelt in the headwaters region. In other words, they should be avoided by all but the most experienced and well-equipped cavers, and even then it is "buyer beware."

Caves have different personalities, of course, but "wet and muddy" is a catch-all phrase that seems to cover most non-commercial caves. George Dasher, who works for the Division of Environmental Protection in Charleston and is a spelunker, described the start of a cave on Big Spring Fork as "a tiny entrance, and then immediately a six to seven foot drop to a mud slope."

- - -

I found the fabled "black hole" of upper Elk to be an elusive species. I saw no black hole at Blackhole Run or anywhere else, but I accept the explanations of geologists that "holes" could change with every flood event.

"The black hole [of Hu Maxwell's account] may have filled in, but the river would still go underground," said Linda Tracy, geologist on the Monongahela National Forest. "Sinkholes open or close with catastrophic events."

There have been stories of a "boiling hole" somewhere in the dry bed where the water seems to boil as it disappears underground. Dana

Campbell (see Clendenin and Elkview) remembers seeing a hole that more or less fitted that description downstream from the railroad trestle.

Jack Wallace and Craig Stihler work in the DNR's Wildlife Diversity Program, and one of their assignments is monitoring bat colonies, primarily the Indiana bat and the Virginia Big-Eared bat, two species that are found in West Virginia caves. They have found no colonies on upper Elk, but they did come across a "black hole" possibility.

"We saw a hole on the left ascending side of the river near Black-hole Run," said Wallace, "and we suspected that it may be the black hole of legend, although of course that is only speculation."

Boonie Sommerville probably saw the same black hole at another time. "It was on the left ascending side," he told me, "and the flow of the river was entering what was very distinctly a hole."

George Dasher and a friend, Bob Thrun, were in that vicinity on Labor Day 1998 and were walking in the dry bed. "We could see a hole, although there wasn't a lot to see because it was mostly filled with river rock," said George. "But I remember that we said, that's the black hole."

George took a picture that, when developed, startled them. Bob was wearing clothing that was the same color of the rocks, and blended in with them. Only his head stood out, and it seemed to be floating independently among the rocks and above the possible black hole of legend.

Dry Bed with water near Chimney Rock Run

Five

Cowger's Mill

And the Disembodied Crayfish

The two worlds of upper Elk, hydrologically speaking, meet at the Mill Pool, a picturesque hole of water in the Randolph County portion of the river that is named for the oldtime Cowger's Mill which stood nearby.

Immediately above the pool is a peninsula that separates the two worlds. On the left descending side is the end of the dry bed of Elk, the partly misnamed natural wonder where Elk simply disappears for five miles, but only in dry weather. On the other side is the flow from what is commonly called Elk Springs, which isn't a spring in the true sense but is simply where all the gathered forces of underground flow resurface and carry Elk on downstream in good times, and in bad.

I fished the Mill Pool on an overcast day in early May 2003 with Dave Breitmeier, who had a fly fishing shop on Valley Fork Road. The water temperature was forty-nine degrees but the ambient air temperature was quite warm and in fact was spawning thunderstorms in the region. I watched one thundercloud forming over Point Mountain to the north and I wondered if it would reach us with a fierceness that I knew Point Mountain storms are capable of.

Elk in its upper reaches is host to mayflies, stoneflies, caddisflies, midges, biting nefarious black flies, shrimp, and probably a dozen other things that I don't want to think about. The shrimp are tiny imitations of their better known cousins that are served in restaurants. Shrimp are more prevalent in the Elk Springs section than in the Slaty section upstream, but inhabit both.

The black flies are the same kind that plague fishermen in Northern Canada, but they are not to be confused with black fly midges, which are entirely blameless of any bloodthirsty tendencies. Among upper Elk fishermen, the biters are called "28 that does bite," and the non-biting midges are called "28 that doesn't bite," the 28 referring to the hook size.

Dave and I cast mayfly imitations to the trout of Mill Pool, primarily the Little Blue Wing Olive, and larva of mayflies known as nymphs. The Little Blue Wing is the earliest of the West Virginia mayfly hatches. We were a little early in the season for Gray Fox mayflies, one of the major hatches, but there were a few of them on the water. In one moment of puzzlement we saw a Gray Fox float through a stretch of water where trout were feeding, their swirls and flashes exciting the senses, but the mayfly floated on, its moment of fulfillment as a meal for a trout not yet come.

The river was slightly murky and running with a good flow as it came down from the headwater regions. Elk Springs was contributing most of the water, but the dry bed had a good flow too. They converged at the Mill Pool and raced through the right descending side, their milky hues of green and white very appealing, as was the thought of trout lurking where the water ebbed away from the swift currents of Upper River.

The many springs of upper Elk which are consummated at Elk Springs provide a cool water refuge for trout even in the summer months, and the spring water discourages the river in that section from freezing over, therefore it can be fished in winter, too. Underground springs have a year-round water temperature of about fifty-two degrees, just as coal mines register about sixty degrees on the hottest or coldest days. The trout of upper Elk feed on midges (tiny two-winged flies) even in January, or so I am told.

In a way, I put "or so I am told" to the test on a cold, snowy January 19, 2005, when winter had descended upon us with a fury following an unusually mild period. I called Sean Weir at the Elk Springs

The last Cowger's Mill

Fly Shop. "Yes," he confirmed, "the water is basically open, and even today, should the water temperature warm up two or three degrees, it would be good fishing with midges." The water temperature was thirty-six degrees, the ambient air temperature was eighteen degrees, and the snow depth was five to six inches.

But back to May 2003. Our first fish at the Mill Pool was a brown trout. Its golden brown color and the dark spots on its sides glistened as it was brought dripping into the net and quickly released. The two-mile section of Elk from Elk Springs to Rose Run Bridge is catch and release. Rose Run is named for John and Malinda Rose, who lived at the mouth of the run in the early 1900s.

We caught six browns and one rainbow in our time on the river, and lost one or two of each. Only one of the browns was a wild, or naturally reproduced, trout. The rainbow was a wild trout, and was a thing of beauty with its shining pinkish red lateral stripe and its darkly spotted body.

Any trout, whatever its pedigree, can become "wild" over time in a stream environment, and it is possible that more than one of the browns qualified as such. Regardless of where they come from, the trout of the Elk Springs section eventually develop into more suspicious trout than their neighbors upriver in the Slaty section, or so I'm told. I think the Slaty trout are equally suspicious.

But the conventional wisdom is that the lower section is more accessible and therefore more heavily fished, and the trout become more skeptical of whatever floats by. I had a very nice brown come up at the Mill Pool, take a millisecond look at the fly, and decide he or she wasn't buying. But I've had the same rejection many times from smallmouth bass, so I didn't take it personally.

Browns are stocked in the Elk Springs section as fingerlings, and there is some natural reproduction. The same is true of rainbows. Brook trout are rare in this stretch. Trout Unlimited believes the reproduction of rainbows in the Elk Springs section is sufficient to maintain the population, and therefore has suspended its participation with the Division of Natural Resources in rainbow fingerling stocking there. The DNR isn't as convinced, and continues to stock fingerlings.

The Slaty section, where Elk begins, is best known for its excellent population of wild rainbows, although it also has some wild browns and brook trout. This section benefits from trout that spawn in its tributaries, where there is considerably less water fluctuation than in the river. But native brook trout, once *the* trout of mainstream upper Elk, have become a minority.

The most comprehensive list of wild trout streams (those containing reproducing populations) in the Elk watershed, and probably in the
state, is stored in Ed Hayne's computer. Ed lives in Charleston and is a
member of Trout Unlimited.

The list has been compiled over a period of years, and is ongoing.
He has personally spent hundreds of hours on it, but with considerable
help from fishing friends and DNR personnel. It includes water tempera-
tures, stream chemistry, stream flow, geology of the area, and the particular fishery.

Most of the fisheries data resulted from "rod surveys," which is
Ed's term for fishing a stream. "Those kinds of surveys are "very accurate
and very much fun," he says.

The list also includes streams with resident smallmouth populations. My fishing experiences with Ed were on New River fishing for
smallmouth. We caught some fish, but I can't remember the details. I do
recall that on another trip, minus me, Ed caught an 18-inch smallmouth on
a fly rod and popper.

The Elk watershed contains hundreds of tributaries. Most of the
trout streams are located above Webster Springs, beginning with Crooked
Fork in Pocahontas County, but the remaining five counties of Elk con-
tain trout streams too, including Clay and Kanawha Counties. Fingerling
browns are stocked in the Buffalo Creek drainage in Clay County, and
in Blue Creek in Kanawha County. From Crooked Fork to Blue Creek is
approximately one hundred and seventy eight miles, and to have trout at
both ends of the spectrum illustrates the remarkable versatility of Elk.

Ed was once crawling through a rhododendron thicket on Rock-
camp Run of Buffalo Creek with a backpack containing two hundred
fingerling browns when he saw a large dark object that was sharing the
thicket with him. When he moved, it moved. Maneuvering for a better
look, the water in the backpack shifted, and he fell forward. It was then
that he saw four very thick black-haired legs moving back and forth not
twenty-five feet away. "I do not recall how I ended up standing back in
the middle of the Jeep trail," he said. "I was amazed at the dexterity that
carried me through the rhododendron. I suddenly realized that I had on
my back two hundred tiny fish that all but made me a walking sushi bar
for a bear. I immediately set off for a better site."

There are approximately twenty native brook trout streams on
upper Elk in Pocahontas, Randolph, and Webster Counties. Some of them
already are, or will in subsequent pages, become familiar names to readers of this book: Crooked Fork, Big Spring Fork, Cup Run, Chimney Rock
Run, Slatyfork Run, Big and Little Sugar Creeks, and Desert Fork of the
Right Fork of Holly.

Others have reproducing populations of brown or rainbow trout, including the renowned Slaty section of main Elk, which Ed has fished since 1976. "Its wild rainbow population," he says, "is a remnant from the 1930s that has survived by moving into the small tributary streams."

- - -

An argument could be made that God in His infinite wisdom created Cowger's Mill and added Elk River as an afterthought. The first mill was established around 1800, and the last one was torn down in the 1960s. But the area continues to serve as a handy reference point for fishermen. A typical exchange might go like this:

"Where did you catch that big brown?"

"Above Cowger's Mill."

"Where did you lose that big rainbow?"

"Below Cowger's Mill."

"Where did you fall in the river and drown?"

"At Cowger's Mill."

"Where do you want your ashes scattered?"

"Under Cowger's Mill."

Fulfilling the above request will require some thought and imagination, but in this computer age of virtual reality anything is possible, and I truly believe the drowned fisherman would accept a simulated burial under a nonexistent mill.

Lou Hevener Sage and her sister, Pearl Hevener, were born near the site of the last mill, which was located a stone's throw from the river on slightly raised ground near the present Elk Springs Fly Shop. Their grandfather, Ison Folks, who died in 1960 at age ninety-four, was the last miller. He operated the mill until around 1957. The sagging structure was torn down a few years later.

Prior to her death in June 2004, Pearl recalled helping her grandfather repair the sloping wooden chute that carried water to the mill from one of the nearby springs where underground Elk emerges. The mills there have always been spring fed, with the possible exception of one that Lou Sage believes was located on Elk downstream at Hickory Lick in the dim past.

The last Cowger to operate a mill was Conrad 'Coonie' Cowger, great grandfather of Lou and Pearl. Ison Folks took over the mill in the 1930s, and later built a second one a short distance away that became the last mill.

A story in *the Clarksburg Sunday Exponent-Telegram* on August 28, 1932, described Coonie Cowger as "the oldest active miller in the United States." He was born near the mouth of Valley Fork, an Elk tributary. At the time of the interview he was ninety-four years old. He said in the newspaper article that he was "never more than a rifle shot from home" in his life.

His mill was a log structure with clapboard shingles, and was about ten feet square and eight feet high. It was one story, although there was a raised portion over the wheel and hopper. It stood about one hundred feet below the spring that was its water source.

The mill was described as "overshot water power," meaning that falling water was required to turn its vertical

Coonie Cowger, Emma Folks, and Jerl Hevener, circa 1930

wheel. The wheel turned the millstones, or buhrs, which ground the corn. Coonie Cowger's fee was one gallon of corn out of each bushel ground.

Coonie Cowger was a strong Democrat, and his son-in-law, Ison Folks, was an equally strong Republican. After a disagreement over politics, Coonie moved into a small shanty near the mill. He did eventually return to his son-in-law's home, although it is unlikely that either changed their minds, politically speaking.

- - -

There is a subliminal message for fishermen in the story of Glen Sage, one of the legendary anglers of upper Elk who got religion and gave up fishing.

Glen, a Virginia native, came to Slatyfork with his parents and later moved to Cowger's Mill to work at the Hickory Lick coal mine, which was located on the Back Fork side of Point Mountain. A tunnel connected the mine to the tipple on the Elk side.

Glen's passions were fishing and baseball, and he was good at both. He once received an offer from a major league team to attend a tryout camp, and although he didn't go, the invitation said a lot about his ability.

"He was an adequate defensive player," said his son, Ronnie Sage, "but hitting was what he was all about. He could hit a baseball purely and instinctively." Ronnie now lives at Leesburg, Virginia, and his brother, Earl, lives at Mechanicsville, Maryland. They started fly fishing with their father before they were teenagers.

Glen was both a live bait and fly fisherman. "He fished a lot with softshell crawfish," said Ronnie. "He would cast the crawfish to the head of a riffle, and let it bounce along naturally with the current." In other words, the same technique used in fishing a nymph.

Glen was not a catch and release fisherman, and he would have opposed the present catch and release water on upper Elk, according to his wife, Lou Sage. But he did have a code of ethics about keeping fish. In the 1950s he hooked a brown trout at Whittaker Falls that was found later to be thirty-one inches long. He brought the exhausted fish to the bank, where the hook fell out of its mouth. He gently nudged the fish back into the water with his foot. "My hook was not in its mouth," he explained. "It wasn't my fish."

About a week later another fisherman caught and kept the same fish. Glen recognized it from a distinctive lump on its throat.

The largest fish that Glen caught and kept was a twenty-five and one-quarter inch brown trout below the Priss Hole in 1974. It wouldn't hit a crayfish, nor a night crawler, but it did hit a streamer fly after he put a small sinker on the line to get the fly deeper. The Priss Hole is located

Glen Sage the ballplayer

between the Mill Pool and the Rose Run Bridge. It is named for Priscilla Hamrick, who lived nearby.

Ken Yufer caught a twenty-five inch rainbow near the Priss Hole in 2003. He told me he caught it on a 24 Baetis, which I assumed was a code name for a secret government project he was involved in, and which will eventually be made into a blockbuster book and movie. I hesitated to ask more, for security reasons.

Glen Sage occasionally orchestrated his fishing trips with his sons. "One day," said Ronnie, "he told us to try a certain spot, and we did, but without success. Dad came over and promptly caught a nice trout. He turned around, grinning, and said, I thought there might be a fish there."

In 1982, Glen was converted, and, later, at a prayer service at Friendship Baptist Church near Valley Head he found himself thinking not about prayer but about how he might catch a certain large trout he'd seen. "He realized that his thoughts were still on fishing and not on religion," said Ronnie, "and he never fished again."

He died seven years later, in 1989, and is buried at the Randolph County community of Mingo. Upper Elk fishermen named one of the pools on the river "Sage's Pocket" in his memory.

- - -

My return to the Elk Springs section was delayed in spring 2004 by a throat ailment and a series of thunderstorms that muddied the water. Reduced to watching television during the ailment, I became enamored of a new program called "Searching for Satellite Signal. Please Stand By." I enjoy search stories, and standing by is something I do well, although I felt the plot was a little thin.

But I did return, like MacArthur in World War II. The day was warm, almost oppressively so, and thunderclouds were building up, although they never came to fruition as I had come to expect them to on upper Elk. It was disappointing, but for that matter so was the fishing.

I'm sure there were extenuating circumstances at work. John McCoy, my outdoor writing friend in Charleston, summed it up nicely when he wrote about the catch and release regulations on upper Elk: "The stream quickly developed a reputation for producing large, finicky trout that have become increasingly difficult to catch."

Still, at some point between the Engine Hole and the Priss Hole, I said to myself while changing fly patterns, "You're impersonating a trout fisherman, and you should be ashamed of yourself." The more I thought about it, the more ashamed I got, and for once in my life I did the right thing. I laid my fly rod aside, wedging it between ubiquitous rounded rocks, and enjoyed the moment.

The first thing I took notice of was the head of what had been a large crayfish. Its long and sinister looking antennae lay limply on the rock in front of me. Its grotesque protruding eyes were lifeless, as might be expected of something whose body was missing.

I wondered what fate had befallen it, but with crayfish you can pick almost any scenario. I've seen enough crayfish remains strewn along streams to know that something likes to eat them. We have long accepted as dogma that raccoons love them, as do various kinds of birds, turtles, snakes, fish, and perhaps even the two mink I was soon watching.

The mink were not fully grown. One was exploring the opposite side of the river, and its fellow explorer was on our side, "our" being me and the crayfish. They were hunting to eat, which is the most honest and defensible kind of hunting. But it must be hard, I thought, without having the luxury of stopping by the grill at the Elk Springs Fly Shop, as I had in mind for later in the day.

Three ducks that I could not identify flew upriver, and soon came floating down. I looked for their identification later in my three excellent bird books, but as usual there was nothing pictured in the books that remotely resembled what I had seen.

They floated down in a neat row, as well organized ducks should do. The current of Upper River gave them a good ride through Sage's Pocket, or wherever I was. I called it the Disembodied Crayfish Hole. I had planned to begin fishing at the Horseshoe just above Rose Run Bridge, but a vehicle was parked there, and I chose a stretch farther upstream.

One of the classic split rock formations of upper Elk lies in this stretch. It appears that someone with a chisel and a fine sense of symmetry had created the pattern, prying the rock apart with giant hands. The best known split rock is located at the pool of that name on Big Spring Fork, the largest is located in the dry bed and is called Flat Rock, and there is another split rock formation below Whittaker Falls.

A few nights later, I had split rocks on my mind and couldn't sleep. The next day I called Steve McClelland of the West Virginia Geological Survey, who explained that such fissures, or joints, usually occur as a regional pattern, and not over the entire state. He said they are created by huge titanic forces underneath the surface associated with the movement of the earth. Over time, the cracks are widened by the forces of nature.

- - -

I followed a buffalo trail upriver to where I could climb the steep road bank and return to the car. My feet were sweating in waders, but at that I was better off than the crayfish that was missing its body. Actually, the trail wasn't made by buffalo, but by fishermen. But it resembled what I've always imagined a buffalo trail would look like, and there were deer tracks imprinted here and there to give it a look of hoofed foot authenticity.

At the Elk Springs Fly Shop, I joined a convention of outdoor writers and photographers, or so it seemed. Rick Steelhammer and Kenny Kemp of *the Charleston Gazette* were there doing an article for the *Sunday Gazette-Mail's* Wild and Wonderful page, and Mike Fisher, a freelance writer and photographer from Centreville, Virginia, was there also on a story.

Rick and Sean Weir were fishing the Mill Pool. I could not see Rick, but Sean was across the river on the railroad side, waist deep in the water, casting a fly with practiced precision. At the upper end, he caught a nice brown trout.

Even though it was only early June, the dry bed of Elk was already drying up, although there were still pockets of water. When I had fished the Mill Pool in early May of the previous year, the dry bed still had a strong flow. Without that contribution, the pool loses the swift current that otherwise flows down the right descending side, and it more closely resembles a placid mill pool.

I enjoyed seeing Rick and Kenny again, outside the pages of the newspaper, meeting Mike, and seeing Sean catch a trout, but my heart belonged first of all to the grill inside the fly shop, where I had a hot dog, a.k.a. The Usual.

I admired again the collection of insects in the vase that is labeled Elk River Cocktail (see The Slaty Section). Bill Harkness, the assistant manager, provided further details. He said they were sulfur spinners, or the molting stage of the mature dun mayfly. They were so thick that he had scooped them up on the front step of the shop. I had been an eyewitness to the hatch when I arrived there in late evening from a fishing trip upriver with Mike Cumashot. Upper Elk is famous for its hatches, but we all agreed this was one for the history books, which leads me to the following sermonette:

The abundance of insect life, and the limestone water, are the corner-stones of Elk's reputation as a fine trout stream. But a stream environment is fragile. The fragility begins at the lowest level with plankton, the tiny animal and plant life that is the lifeblood of a river. Plankton provides food for insects, and insects provide food for fish. Any significant disturbance of a streambed in any way automatically diminishes the quality of the stream, and the stream it flows into. This is true of any stream, not just a trout stream.

Bill was watching something through the window. It was the former trout hatchery raceway, which has been resupplied with trout for the simple pleasure of seeing them. "It's our Outdoor Channel," he explained. The "programming" also includes a river at their doorstep called Elk.

- - -

I saw Ken Yufer one day at the Mill Pool after the May and early June hatches had run their course. He was fishing a tiny fly called a Black

28 something or other, the scientific name of which defied both our powers of inventive spelling and pronunciation. But, regardless, he caught a brown trout on it. Ken holds brown trout in high regard, including their color scheme, which he likens to "a Brooks Brothers' paisley tie."

Later he looked up the tiny fly, and it is a Number 28 Black Chronomid. Ken and Dave Breitmeier once compiled an Elk River Small Fly Hatch Chart, which the Black Chronomid leads off. The chart contains twenty-five tiny insects, all so small you can barely see them, but sometimes on upper Elk, less is more.

Ken learned to fish by accompanying his father on Elk Creek in central Pennsylvania. He was instrumental in founding the organization Friends of the Elk (the West Virginia Elk River), and is passionate about upper Elk. His enjoyment of the river led him to build a cabin nearby on Point Mountain, from where he can be on Elk in a short time.

I sat on the large rock at the upper end of the Mill Pool and talked with Ken and his friend, Jim Thomson. The conversation turned to places we'd heard of but hadn't seen, and when we finally see them they're not as we imagined them. The only place that might be as we imagined it, I said, was Buffalo, New York, which we imagine as a great mound of snow.

"By the way, Jim," I asked, "where are you from?"

"I'm from Buffalo, New York," he replied.

~ Six ~

Whittaker Falls

A Place of Puzzlement

Elk leaves Randolph County and enters Webster County at Whittaker Falls, thirteen miles below Slatyfork. There are actually three falls, beginning with a small one on the left descending side of the river. The second one extends all the way across, as does the final and real Whittaker Falls, which drops five to six feet at normal flow and is nicely curved in a moderate horseshoe shape.

Geologists say the main ledge is being inexorably worn down by the water's flow and in another ten million years there won't be a Whittaker Falls. But I have resolved not to lose any sleep over that possibility, just as I have decided there's nothing I can do about warnings that the Cranberry Glades, West Virginia's version of northern muskeg country, are drying up and will disappear at about the same time as Whittaker Falls.

Whittaker Falls lies four hundred yards below the second catch and release trout fishing section on upper Elk. Those who prefer to fish with a fly rod and a tiny imitation insect can do so above the falls. Those who prefer a spinning rod and cheese eggs have the falls and below.

On a pleasant Sunday in July 2003, Gibbs Kinderman of Slatyfork, his wife Cheryl, and Cheryl's daughter, Kama Weatherholt, visited Whittaker Falls and saw a bizarre sight. Dozens of large fat crayfish were climbing up the ledge all the way across the river, except in the middle where the heaviest volume of water was going over.

I've never heard that West Virginia crayfish have migratory tendencies, although in at least one genus the mating and egg laying occurs in late spring and summer. I don't know if this would have anything to do with them climbing the ledge at Whittaker Falls in such numbers, and people with more knowledge of crayfish than I have, if such a thing is possible, didn't know either.

Another unsolved mystery is the origin of the name Whittaker Falls. It may have had the same namesake as Whittaker Run on the Cass Scenic Railroad, and if so was probably named for a railroad person. There is also a Whittaker Falls in Canada's Northwest Territory. A connection to our Whittaker Falls is unlikely, but I wouldn't completely rule it out.

As Elk proceeds toward Webster Springs, its biota gradually change from trout to smallmouth bass, although in this day of trout stocking the complete switch doesn't take place until below Webster Springs. Even there, large brown trout are caught occasionally in the deep holes.

Retired football coach Jerome Dean has fished Elk often between Whittaker Falls and Parcoal, and he told me that he begins to catch smallmouth on trout flies in the Bergoo area, which is nine and one-half miles below Whittaker Falls. But smallmouth are also caught at the Calvin Hamrick Canoe Hole, or Boat Hole as it is commonly called, not far below the falls where the long ago community of Samp was located.

I was surprised to learn that smallmouth are found above Whittaker Falls as well, proving that there are few absolutes in nature. Ray Menendez, the retired fisheries biologist, saw smallmouth in the Rose Run area near Cowger's Mill in 2002.

The best way to determine the biota of a stream, as far as fish species are concerned, is to fish it, so on a pleasant day in late June 2004 we fished Elk from the Twin Bridges below Bergoo to the Curtin Bridge. The verdict went to smallmouth on a technical knockout, although we did catch two rainbow trout. One of the rainbows was seventeen inches long, and was the largest fish of the day. It was caught at the Vincent Hamrick Canoe Hole at the lower end of the Don Gilkeson farm.

A mystery fish that assaulted the brown grub I was using and broke my line at the same hole was probably a large brown trout. It is a likely place to find a large brown, although we caught smallmouth there too. Lee Wolfe, a forester for Pardee and Curtin, told me about walking along the railroad on the south side of the river above Curtin one year during a drought

Elk below Whittaker Falls

and seeing a huge brown trout in one of the pools.

Despite the mystery fish and the rainbows, the numbers on our trip weighed heavily toward bass. Four of us caught and released a total of thirty-two fish, of which thirty were smallmouth or rock bass. The largest smallmouth was sixteen inches. Fishermen are very good at keeping count of their catches, especially when they are approached by a writer with paper and pen in hand at the end of the day. The tally as I wrote it down began to resemble a baseball box score in the newspaper.

Our fishing group included my nephew, Rob Johnson, and Larry Massile (both of whom work for Appalachian Power Company in Charleston), Mike Surbaugh, a science teacher at Webster County High School and a partner with Jim Casey in Horizon Line Adventures (see The Voyageurs), and myself.

Jim may have made two or three casts that day, but if so I missed them. When I asked him what he caught, he replied, "A cold." My fondest recollection of Jim on a river was when he and a number of others, including my nephew, were running the middle section of Birch River. Barney Lilly, who leads this annual West Virginia Wildwater Association Good Friday outing, made a safety talk prior to departure and asked if there were any questions. "Yes," said Jim. "Do you expect the price of gasoline to go down anytime soon?"

Mike described the river when we left the Twin Bridges as "bony," meaning there were many rocks showing. But upper Elk is excellent whitewater at higher flows, and in my opinion the canyons of Elk in the Curtin area and below Webster Springs are every bit as impressive as the New and Gauley River Canyons, both of which are federally protected river corridors.

I am a little envious, but only a little, of Dwayne McCourt, a Bolair Webster County resident who paraglides over Elk in the Webster Springs area. He told me that at several thousand feet he can see sunlight reflecting off Snowshoe Mountain Resort at the head of Elk, and the upper end of Sutton Lake in the other direction. The idea of soaring above the rugged Elk canyon wearing a pair of wings is something I would have to give long and careful consideration to; just as I would to ending a sentence with a preposition, as I am going to.

Dwayne and Lee Wolfe made newspaper headlines in 2001 when they discovered the wreckage of a plane that had been missing for six years. The pilot of the twin-engine Cessna had taken off from Sutton, and was last seen near Webster Springs. The ceiling was low and the rising mountainous terrain was partially obscured by clouds. Dwayne and Lee, a private pilot, searched often, and eventually found the plane on the head of Big Beechy of the Middle Fork of Williams River.

Elk from Bergoo to Curtin is a series of pools, rapids, and underwater rocks, and is therefore appealing as a bass stream. It drops four hundred feet from Bergoo to Webster Springs, an average drop of forty feet per mile. One of the fine views of the river canyon in this area is from an overlook on the Point Mountain Road.

The surrounding hills are high and rugged. Potato Knob, a prominent feature near Curtin, is 2,203 feet, but there are higher elevations nearby, including 2,932 feet near the head of Mill Run. On the north, or Point Mountain side, elevations exceed 3,500 feet.

Geologists say that Elk once flowed behind Potato Knob, but gradually carved out a new route in front. There is another Potato Knob nearby on Point Mountain, and probably a dozen other Potato Knobs, runs, forks, branches, hills, and rows scattered around the state.

The one on Point Mountain supposedly got its name when a horseman's sack of potatoes fell off his horse and he went to a nearby house and asked for help in hoisting it back on. "Where did it happen?" the farmer asked. "On Potato Knob, I reckon," the horseman replied.

I've tried over the years, but have failed, to see any resemblance between Potato Knob above Curtin and a potato. Maybe there was never intended to be one. Maybe there is another explanation, such as the above, and if so I hope it's a funnier story.

On our fishing trip, we came to the Bill Triplett farm, which borders Elk for a considerable distance on the highway side, and crosses to the south side at Mill Run. At the lower end of the farm is a pool where long ago residents of Mill Run boated across to attend services at Pleasant Grove Church. The spot where they came ashore is still known today as "The Boat Landing."

Mill Run is steeped in the history of the area. Isaac Gregory, an early settler on upper Elk and the man who killed the last buffalo in Webster County (see End of the Line), lived on Mill Run, as did, in a later time, Rattlesnake Bill Dodrill, author of *Moccasin Tracks and Other Imprints*. Rattlesnake Bill was teaching school in Webster Springs at the time he lived on Mill Run.

By the time we left the Mill Run area, we had been on the river for over five hours and my interest in fishing, history, and geography had waned. I thought only of the Curtin Bridge, where our trip mercifully ended an hour later. But others, perhaps primarily my nephew, were casting lures to the very last drop of water.

Elk at Curtin is about a thousand feet lower than Gauley, which lies across the mountain to the south, not that I cared at that moment. Elk is the older river, and therefore has had more time to cut a deeper path through the mountains. It may have also met less resistance in the soft red shale of upper Elk. During high water, the river takes on the color of light chocolate.

Curtin was first called Ralph for a nearby post office. Then it became Barton for Barton Pardee, the co-founder of Pardee and Curtin Lumber Company. But Barton was being confused too often with Bartow in Pocahontas County, so the name was changed to Curtin.

My favorite post office name in the area, although long gone, is Mopo, which was located on the Bergoo Road in the early 1900s. Doris Gilkeson, who lives between Curtin and Bergoo, has a postcard with the Mopo postmark dated April 20, 1909.

- - -

I returned another time to the historic Bill Triplett farm. From Bill and Barbara Triplett's home there is a superb view of Elk bending around the broad river bottom where cattle graze. The pilot of a small plane once used the bottom to great advantage when he either ran out of gas, or was about to run out, and landed there. The wings were removed, and the plucked bird of the sky was hauled away in a truck.

The Triplett farm is where the Hamricks and Gregorys of Webster County got their start. Isaac Gregory came into the area around 1800 from Bath County, Virginia. He settled on Gauley River, and later moved across the mountain to Elk. He may have lived the final years of his life with a daughter and son-in-law. A chimney still stands where they are believed to have lived.

Isaac Gregory died in 1852 and is buried on Keener Hill on the south side of Elk above Curtin. Bill Triplett and I visited his grave in June 2003. His weathered tombstone notes that he served in the War of 1812 with "Cooke's Virginia Militia." Whether his unit saw action is uncertain.

Visiting cemeteries is an avocation with me, except for the final visit, which will be an imperative. But I was delighted, avocation-wise, when Bill suggested that we also visit the Meadowland Cemetery at Bergoo, from which there is a pleasant view of the

Bill Triplett

Upper Elk Valley. Bill commented on various graves, and then he pointed to a sunken place in the ground where nobody is buried. He related the story:

Neighbors were informed that a former resident of the area would be buried at Meadowland. They gathered to dig the grave, which was once a communal custom. They waited, and waited, but the body never arrived. Someone called the funeral home and was told that there had been a change of plans and that the burial had taken place elsewhere. They refilled the empty grave and went home.

In another part of the cemetery I saw a fresh grave with the flowers still in place. I went over to read the funeral home marker, and was stunned. It was the grave of a woman I had talked with recently on the phone. She was to give me information on Sugar Creek of the Back Fork of Elk. Bill told me she had died rather quickly of pneumonia.

- - -

The story of the Hamricks of upper Elk is a remarkable one, and we are indebted to Les Hamrick, author of *Roots & Wings*, the family genealogy, for its telling in considerable detail. Les is a Charleston native whose avocation is freelance writing. That, and considerable patience and perseverance, saw him through a voluminous book that was several years in the making.

I first met Les in August 2002 in Webster Springs, and later interviewed him in Charleston, where we met "halfway," he from his home near Ravenswood, and I from Braxton County. The primary purpose of the interview was to obtain information on Rimfire Hamrick, the mountaineer whose renown (see Rimfire) reached beyond the hills of Webster County. But the conversation also included discussion of the Hamricks generally.

The centerpiece of the story is Benjamin Hamrick, a Revolutionary War soldier who served from 1775 to 1781. For his service, he received a land grant in what is now Braxton County, but which was then Kanawha County, and later Nicholas County. When Benjamin Hamrick moved to Frame's Run of Strange Creek in 1796, or perhaps a few years later, it was part of Kanawha County.

Benjamin and his wife, Nancy McMillion Hamrick, had eleven children, and three of them migrated to upper Elk to begin the Hamrick presence there. The *Roots & Wings* account says that sons Benjamin and William left Frame's Run in 1811, presumably in search of adventure and to make their own mark in the world. They probably followed Elk to present day Webster Springs. A few miles farther upriver, in the Curtin-

Bergoo area, they settled down. Benjamin built his home on what is now the Bill Triplett farm, and William built a short distance upriver.

A third brother, David, joined them in 1820, settling about twelve miles upriver at Whittaker Falls, thus becoming an early pioneer in that well known locale. It is believed that at some point Benjamin and William returned to Frame's Run and brought their father back up Elk with them. Their mother had died on Frame's Run in 1832. The three brothers' marriages produced large families, and most of their children lived to adulthood.

The elder Benjamin Hamrick died in 1842 and is buried on the lower end of the Triplett farm. Son Benjamin, with whom he lived, died in 1863 and is also buried on the farm, although at a different place. William died in 1850 while on a business trip to Summersville, and is buried in an unmarked grave on "the old Robinson farm" near Summersville. It is said that he was a great hunter, and would regale family and friends with hunting stories. David died in 1875 at Whittaker Falls and is buried in an unmarked grave.

About two hundred yards below Bill Triplett's house is "the church barn," where Methodist services were held starting in 1833. Webster County historian Ron Hardway wrote that religious services were a rarity on isolated upper Elk because ministers were rare. Funerals were often held six months to a year after a death, and marriages were sometimes held with the couple's two or three children in attendance.

I walked down to the church barn with Bill on a day when the calendar said June but the cold wind said March. The gusts ruffled Bill's luxurious beard and my jacket collar. The barn was built by brothers Ben-

The Church Barn

jamin and William Hamrick, and their sons, in 1830. When Addison Hite, a Methodist evangelist, came into the area to hold a series of meetings, they volunteered the use of the barn, and services were held in the loft. This continued intermittently until 1845 when the Pleasant Grove Methodist Church was built nearby on what is now the Bergoo Road.

That the barn has survived all these years is a miracle of Old Testament proportions. In the 1980s a renovation drive began, reminiscent of the Israelites returning to Jerusalem to rebuild the temple. Portia Hamrick, who owned the farm then, deeded the old structure to the Methodist Historical Society in 1983.

Portia and Viola Hamrick were sisters of Mayme Hamrick, who became the first woman to obtain a law degree from Duquesne University, and who worked as an attorney for the U.S. Treasury Department in Philadelphia and the U.S. Department of Justice in Washington.

In the 1980s, I interviewed Portia and Viola for *the Charleston Gazette.* They were retired teachers with masters degrees, were in their eighties, and tended cattle and sheep, most of which they had names for. Once a man who helped them on the farm began to curse a cow that had ventured out to an island in Elk and wouldn't return. Viola waded into the water and yelled at him, "We don't curse our animals." "Well," he replied, "then you get the SOB across."

The sisters had an ancient Jeep that Viola drove to the river bottom to feed the cattle. I rode with her on the day of the interview. We bounced along with the cows plodding patiently behind, waiting for the bales of hay that were tossed out of the Jeep like manna from heaven.

Portia had a philosophical view of life. "It takes half of your life to have anything," she once told Bill Triplett, "and the other half to keep it, and you're damned if you do and damned if you don't, but such is life."

She would have been a soulmate of Granny McPhail, a Cabin Creek resident whose words of wisdom were inscribed by *Charleston Gazette* artist Bill Pitzer and put on the wall of the Dungeon, a small offshoot of the main newsroom. Her grandson, Bill Christian, who worked with my brother Bob at Columbia Gas, said that Granny McPhail's philosophy was "Life's a bitch and then you die." Granny McPhail died in November 2004, two weeks shy of her ninetieth birthday.

Some local residents still call the Bill Triplett farm "the Miller farm" for brothers Robert and Lee Miller, who lived there all their lives. Robert kept a diary, and was honest about it. If he didn't do anything on a particular day, he wrote "Done nothing." One day he wrote that "Lee done nothing. I washed."

Seven

Pardee and Curtin

Her Eminence

From Whittaker Falls to Parcoal is Pardee and Curtin country. George W. Curtin and Barton Pardee, the co-founders of the venerable company, bought the huge tract there in 1888 that is still the core of the company's presence on upper Elk. Somebody in the company must have read Margaret Mitchell's *Gone With the Wind*, especially the part where Scarlet O'Hara's father says to her: "Land is the only thing in the world that amounts to anything, for 'tis the only thing in this world that lasts, and don't you be forgetting it."

The tract is known as "the Pratt lands," named for C.M. Pratt of Standard Oil Company, who purchased it around 1883. It contains 32,867 acres on Elk and Gauley Rivers, and was the last large stand of virgin timber left in the state. William Seymour Edwards, who commissioned the mountaineer statue at the State Capitol in Charleston (see Rimfire), handled the purchase for Pratt.

Curtin and Pardee were said to have paid $800,000 for the Pratt lands, or approximately twenty five dollars per acre. They owned the tract as individuals until March 7, 1904, when they deeded it to Pardee and Curtin, the company. Since that time, the company has bought other properties and now owns 182,000 acres of timberland or minerals in West Virginia, Virginia, and Kentucky, most of it in West Virginia.

George W. Curtin was the son of Andrew G. Curtin, the governor of Pennsylvania during the Civil War. The son was captured by Confederate forces in the Battle of the Wilderness in Virginia on May 6, 1864, and sent to the Confederate prisoner of war camp at Andersonville, Georgia,

Logs at the mouth of Granny's Creek
Photo courtesy of Craig Smith

one of several infamous camps on both sides. He survived, but many did not.

Soon after the war, he became superintendent of a log boom at Lock Haven, Pennsylvania. He later came to Grafton, West Virginia, to manage a boom on the Tygart River. Grafton was said to have been the largest sawmill town in the Eastern United States during the Civil War and for a short time afterwards. It was at nearby Fetterman in 1873 that George Curtin and Barton Pardee of Hazelton, Pennsylvania, formed the Pardee and Curtin Lumber Company. Barton Pardee was the son of Ariovistus Pardee, the family patriarch who decided he was too old for the venture and recommended his son instead.

The Pardee and Curtin mill, and others in the area, were destroyed by a huge flood in 1888, and Pardee and Curtin moved to Sutton, Braxton County, in 1890, where the company was incorporated. They operated a log boom and mill at Sutton until 1904. In that fourteen-year period, logs from Webster and Braxton Counties were floated down Elk to the mill. The boom was a separate corporation called the Elk Island Boom Company. It consisted of logs chained together end to end and anchored to stone-filled piers and abutments.

The mill stood in the river bottom below the mouth of Granny's Creek. George W. Curtin lived on a knoll above the mill, and his house, built of the finest hardwoods, is still a Sutton landmark. My aunt and uncle, Virginia and Oldham Berry, once lived there. The present owners are John and Merleen Campbell. Their son, J.L. Campbell, grew up in the house from age ten, and fished Elk often. He recalls seeing timbers in the river from the boom operation.

Pardee and Curtin also had a mill at Holly Junction above Sutton from 1901 to 1907, and in 1900 began a twenty-five year presence in Nicholas County with a large mill at Old Curtin at the mouth of Cherry River. Other mills followed at Coal Siding in 1905, Hominy Falls in 1909, and Deer Creek in 1921. The company had its own railroad in Nicholas County, the Cherry and Hominy, with eighty-five miles of track. The logging was done by horses, and the logs were brought to the mills on the narrow gauge railroad.

The move to the Pratt lands of upper Elk began in 1925 with construction beginning on a mill at Bergoo. The Old Curtin mill, shop, and rolling stock, including the Shay engines used in the Nicholas logging, were moved there, first on Baltimore and Ohio flatcars to Holly Junction, and then on the West Virginia Midland to Bergoo. By that time, Pardee and Curtin had purchased the West Virginia Midland, and used its own Shays to transport the mill over the narrow gauge track.

The Bergoo mill opened in 1928 and operated until January 1945, when it burned for a second time and wasn't rebuilt. Today its ghostly walls still stand in bottomland across Elk from the mouth of Leatherwood Creek.

The Pardee and Curtin mills in Nicholas County cut 720 million board feet of lumber in twenty-five years, and the Bergoo mill cut 220 million board feet in seventeen years. Production records don't exist for the Grafton, Sutton, and Holly Junction mills, or at least haven't been found.

Included in the cut at Bergoo was thirty-five million board feet of American chestnut. The blight that eventually destroyed the native chestnut forests was already well under way by the time the mill opened. The majority of trees fed to the mill were poplar, followed by hard maple, and then chestnut.

Pardee and Curtin's announcement in 1945 that it would permanently close its Bergoo mill sent economic shock waves through Webster County. At its peak, employment was 350 men at the mill and in the woods, although this number was down to 160 by the time of the closing. At one point, the company employed 2,000 men in its various operations, including coal mines, tipples, company stores, Bergoo mill and shop, logging

Bergoo Mill in its heyday

crews, train crews, etc.

In 1955, Pardee and Curtin built the first all-electric single band mill in West Virginia at Barton (now Curtin), and operated it until 1981, when the hardwood timber market declined in a recession. Three years later, the mill was leased to the Jim C. Hamer Company, which still operates it. Pardee and Curtin reorganized, and its present function is as manager of its timber, coal, and oil and gas properties.

The current president is George D. 'Dee' Curtin III, who lives at Parcoal. He is the son of George D. Curtin Jr., who lived in Newark, Ohio, and was an engineer for Owens-Corning Fiberglass. Dee joined Pardee and Curtin in 1970 and became president in 1990.

George W. Curtin, the company's co-founder, is buried in Town Hill Cemetery in Sutton, as is his wife.

- - -

Although the Pardee and Curtin company name says only "Lumber," and indeed that is appropriate, the company also mined coal on upper Elk in a major way.

Camp Four, the first community on Elk below Whittaker Falls, was the site of the tipple for Pardee and Curtin's No. 4 mine, which was located on Point Mountain. Camp Four was also known by its railroad name of Byers. Clarence Bennett, who died in 1975, was tipple foreman from the time the mine opened in 1935 until it closed in 1959. He ran the first lump of coal through the tipple in December 1935.

Camp Four was one of nine coal mines operated on Elk and Gauley Rivers from 1928 until 1959 by Pardee and Curtin. The company dug 23 million tons of coal during this period.

Bill Gillespie, former State Forester and Assistant State Agriculture Commissioner, and present head of Gillespie Forestry Services, was born in Webster Springs, but grew up at Camp Four where Lower Big Run comes into Elk from Point Mountain.

Bill's brother, George Gillespie, remembers the miners playing poker with scrip, the "coin of the realm" of coal towns. The poker games took place at Snake Rocks on the river at Camp Four. "We would look for and usually find scrip that had fallen into cracks in the rocks," he said.

The names of the mines still resonate today: Bergoo No. 1 at Parcoal, Bergoo No. 2 at Curtin, Bergoo No. 3 on Leatherwood Creek, Bergoo No. 4 at Camp Four, Bergoo No. 5 across the river from No. 4, Bergoo No. 6 on Gauley River, Bolair No. 1 and Bolair No. 2 on Gauley River, and Britton No. 1 on the Back Fork of Elk.

Symbolic of Pardee and Curtin's coal mining presence is a large lump of coal on display in front of the Webster County Courthouse. It came from the Sewell seam at the Bergoo No. 2 mine at Barton (now Curtin), and was placed at the courthouse in the mid-1930s by employees.

Esther Mansfield Bennett, a native of Hominy Falls and wife of Clarence Bennett, has lived at Camp Four since 1936. She was a Pied Piper to the kids there. "When I went to the river," she said, "the kids followed. I think I taught every kid in Camp Four to swim." Their "swimming pool" was the Boarding House Hole on Elk, named for the Pardee and Curtin boarding house that stood across the river.

One of the highlights of summertime at Camp Four was a monthly fish fry, featuring roast corn, potato salad, and of course, fish. In one of life's small ironies, the fish came from the company store, not from Elk.

When Esther Bennett and her husband arrived at Camp Four, the road wove back and forth on both sides of the river, and wasn't paved. She and her husband got stuck more than once at the Chestnut Ford Bottom crossing below Camp Four, and each time Charley Hamrick, a local farmer, came to their rescue with his team of horses.

The coal mining era on upper Elk ended in the late 1980s. Esther has a picture of a Bergoo and Western locomotive taking the last trainload of coal out of Bergoo. The final mining was done by Elk River Sewell Coal Company, Westmoreland Coal Company, and Phoenix Resources, all on Leatherwood Creek.

- - -

I've always envied Webster County its rattlesnakes, so when someone suggested that I visit the front porch of Kathy and Robert Woods at Camp Four and see their splendid collection, it became a royal imperative.

Braxton, my home county, has a few rattlers, but they are mostly Webster, Nicholas, or Clay County snakes that have slithered across the poorly patrolled borders at night. Many times I have lain awake wondering why God favored those counties and not Braxton.

I walked tentatively up on the Woods' porch, and there in a glass aquarium were thirteen timber rattlers. The aquarium is large, but its inhabitants were all mingled in a haphazard if cozy pile at one end. "They do that," said Kathy. "When we add a new snake, there's no animosity. The newcomer simply slithers over and joins the pile."

The rattlers, black or sulfur yellow in color, were caught on Leatherwood Creek and Gauley River, mostly on former strip mines or logging roads. I sat down near the aquarium, yellow legal pad and pen in hand, and interviewed the inhabitants. They watched me with their beady little vertical eyes, and I tried not to offend.

"Why are you in a pile?"

"Why not? Would you like to join us?"

"I'm the one asking the questions."

A faint rattling.

"Are you sinister?"

"Don't push it, newsman."

"Are you truly cold blooded, as they say?"

"Who's they?" Their tongues flicked out, and I withdrew the question.

"Why do you shed your skin?"

"Frankly, that's none of your business."

"Why do you rattle?"

"Look, fella, don't get personal."

"Did you beguile Eve?"

"Yes, and she asked for it."

"Do you go blind in dog days?"

"Of course not, you idiot."

"Would you bite me?"

"Not if you don't bite us."

We shook hands, figuratively speaking, on that offer.

The snakes' captivity is temporary. Kathy and Robert turn them loose around Labor Day weekend near where they were captured, giving them time to become readjusted to the wild and to locate a den before cold weather.

"How can you tell which snake was caught where?" I asked.

"We just know them," replied Kathy, and I accepted that as one would ask for the time of day and accept the answer given.

~ Eight ~

The Creeks

Bergoo and Leatherwood

The best known tributaries of Elk above Webster Springs, with the possible exception of Blackhole Run, are Bergoo and Leatherwood Creeks, particularly the latter, being the largest tributary above the Back Fork.

Bergoo Creek comes into Elk a mile and a half above Bergoo, while Leatherwood Creek enters at Bergoo. This raises the obvious question: Why then isn't the village of Bergoo called Leatherwood? Rimfire Hamrick had as good an answer as anybody. He said the Leatherwood Post Office, established in 1876, was discontinued for a time and then reestablished. By then, another post office somewhere else had been named Leatherwood, so the reestablished one was called Bergoo.

Bergoo Creek begins on Gauley Mountain in the Monongahela National Forest in Randolph County at an elevation of 3,750 feet. The head of the creek is rough and boulder strewn, and is bear country. In the early 1940s, a two-seat open cockpit military trainer crashed near the head in bad weather. So inaccessible was the site that the engine and other salvageable parts were hauled out by horse. The two crewmen were not injured, and walked out.

National forest land begins about five miles up Bergoo Creek. From the vicinity of Carol Hamrick's store at the mouth of the creek, looking south toward the higher elevations, red spruce can be seen. Generally speaking, this marks the westernmost range in West Virginia of this legendary tree of the big logging era.

The headwater origins of the creek join in the vicinity of what was known in the coal mining days as Baldwin Mine, a deep mine that operated into the early 1940s. It was named for Jim Baldwin, who lived at the mouth of the creek. In the 1930s, he "faced up" the mine opening with pick and shovel. The mine refuse dump is still there, as are pieces of cable from an overhead skidder that brought logs to the railroad.

There was some talk about salvaging the coal that remained in the refuse, which led to the "hauling the gob to Bergoo" conversation that Tim Henry overheard (see Lofty Beginning) when he came to the Monon-

gahela from Wisconsin and had never heard of either gob or Bergoo. Later he visited the mine site, and discovered that at least the view toward Elk is nice from the gob pile.

On a sultry day in July 2004, I visited Bergoo Creek with Theron Hamrick, a retired heavy equipment operator who grew up on the creek and still lives near the mouth. His grandfather, Curley Dave Hamrick, a farmer, miller, and blacksmith, was born on Bergoo Creek in 1875. Curley Dave was the son of Curley James and Rebecca Baughman Hamrick.

"Watch where you step," Theron cautioned me as we tramped through weeds to the Curley Dave mill site, which I had asked to visit. "A man wouldn't want to step on a rattlesnake."

No, a man wouldn't, I thought.

Curley Dave built the mill in the early 1900s, and around that time also built a blacksmith shop and a barn. The blacksmith shop is long gone, but the remains of a footbridge that crossed the creek to the shop are still there. The weathered barn still stands in relatively good condition for its years.

Curley Dave Hamrick

Theron's father, Russell Hamrick, grew up helping at the mill. Later he was an engineer on a Shay engine for Pardee and Curtin Lumber Company. A 1939 picture shows him with Pardee and Curtin's No. 12 Shay, along with fireman Gordon Dorsey. Two other men are standing on a car behind the engine with three logs that had been cut from a single giant poplar.

Like much of upper Elk, Bergoo Creek is Hamrick country. The Hamricks tended to grow tall, and probably the tallest of them all was Elza Hamrick, who was born in 1880 near Whittaker Falls and later lived on the Bergoo Creek headwaters. He was said to have been a seven-footer, or thereabouts.

Milton Hamrick, a woodsman and farmer on Bergoo Creek, wasn't as tall as some of the others, being "only" six foot three. But he was one of the strongest. The story is told that he was hired by a neighbor to build fences, and he cut and carried eleven-foot fence rails all day for several days until the job was done.

Milton's grandson, Richard Hamrick, lives near the mouth of Bergoo Creek on his grandfather's homeplace. "Yes," he was very strong," Richard said. "He also had a reputation for catching rattlesnakes with his hands, and for working with honey bees without wearing a face net." Exactly how he accomplished the rattlesnake feat isn't clear, but he got away with it, because he lived to be ninety-two.

Seven-footer Elza Hamrick

- - -

Leatherwood Creek begins on Gauley Mountain at an elevation of 3,850 feet. The Left Fork, which originates in Randolph County near the head of Blackhole Run, is considered the main fork, but the Right Fork, which starts on the Randolph-Pocahontas County line near Sharp's Knob, is more scenic, and contains brook trout that are "almost" native. The two forks become one stream 3.35 miles above the village of Bergoo.

In his book, *Logging South Cheat*, George Deike wrote about a wreck on the Left Fork when a West Virginia Pulp and Paper Company train loaded with logs came down the steep grade in the vicinity of Rock Run and got away from the crew. Wreckage was scattered everywhere, but the crew jumped to safety.

Artie Barkley, shop foreman at the Cass Scenic Railroad, told me the rest of the story. The Shay engine, No. 6 by name, was brought to the shop at Cass and repaired, and was housed at Slatyfork, where it continued to be used on upper Elk. When the Elk logging ended, the engine was sold to an individual, who eventually sold it to the State of West Virginia. Thus it came back to Cass and is still there, although its only function is to provide parts from its cylinders and trucks for the Shays that are used on the Cass runs.

Each year, retired fisheries biologist Don Gasper and members of the Mountaineer Chapter of Trout Unlimited carry in fingerling brookies and stock them in the one and one-half miles of the Right Fork of Leatherwood up to a large waterfall. Just above the falls is "Little Canada," so named because it contains plants that are usually found in more northern life zones. Larger and better known examples of such areas in West Virginia are Canaan Valley and Cranberry Glades.

Gasper described the stocking and the Right Fork generally:

"The Right Fork up to the waterfall is a beautiful, steep, boulder strewn streambed. This is where we annually place 2,000 fingerling trout, which is about thirty-two pounds of three and one-half inch fish, and it takes eight bags of water and oxygen to do it.

"Just a quarter mile above the falls is national forest land, and

Falls on the Right Fork of Leatherwood

in the thirty plus years I've been doing this, I've never seen the stream muddy. For the first time in one hundred years, something good has happened to a West Virginia trout stream. Streamside shade has grown up, and brookies are able to occupy downstream reaches in summer. The cooler water makes them more robust and more competitive with creek chubs.

"The fish we stock in the Right Fork are hatchery brook trout. In the early 1960s there were native trout above the falls, and three other fish species also. We never wanted to mix the wild trout with hatchery brook trout genes, so we never stocked above the falls. The DNR does not stock hatchery brookies within three miles of native trout streams, except that we can stock safely below barriers such as falls.

"The Right Fork above the falls extends for five to eight miles on national forest land, and is undisturbed, except for acid rain. In the 1970s, this reach became too acid and lost all its fish, including the relatively acid tolerant native brook trout. It is barren today, but it could be restored by liming. Though the watershed continues to acidify, we plan to do this with helicopters and, hopefully, congressional help.

"Our fingerlings grow an inch a month, and become seven to eight inch trout by June of the following year, when we restock. Though attempts are made to spawn at ten inches in October, the eggs do not hatch, just as the native trout above the falls failed to do in the 1970s. Therefore, we must bring in a new batch each year.

"Most of our fish would live longer and grow to around twelve inches, but the majority of them are caught out before this can happen. Most of them are caught before October, as soon as they become at all a desirable size, but there is good fishing and some catch and release fishing.

"The land below the national forest is owned by Pardee and Curtin Lumber Company, which about twenty years ago cut the steep hillsides very expertly, with little damage. They used the old railroad grade that had been improved to get a crashed helicopter out. [The crash occurred in 1972 when the helicopter struck the Webster Springs to Marlinton power line and crashed on the Right Fork, claiming the lives of the pilot and a passenger].

"The national forest planned to sell timber about that time, to be taken out along the stream and this road, but changed its mind following a request from the West Virginia Highlands Conservancy. Today, the road is used by four wheelers up to national forest land, where they are supposed to stop.

"One day, with continuing acid deposition, our fingerlings will die soon after we put them in, because the watershed and stream continue to acidify. It will become barren, like above the falls. We do plan to lime it, and restock native brook trout from Bergoo Creek, and perhaps from the Left Fork of Leatherwood as well.

"The Left Fork is considered the head of Leatherwood Creek. It and Bergoo Creek are a little richer in the body-building calcium that brook trout require, and have perhaps twenty years before they turn acid and barren, but the Left Fork is often muddy and disturbed, as is main Leatherwood below the forks.

"A short distance above the mouth of Leatherwood in Bergoo, a little stream enters. It probably adds a few native trout, and a few may come from the Right Fork. Some of our fingerlings wash out, I'm sure, and are caught below."

(Don Gasper, a Missouri native, retired from the West Virginia DNR in 2000 after forty years with the agency. He is known for his work on mountain trout streams, and particularly on the threat posed to these streams by acid rain).

- - -

I visited Hartsell Evans on Leatherwood Creek on a very warm day in late August 2003. From his porch, we could see Point Mountain to the north. It is difficult to escape a view of Point Mountain from anywhere on upper Elk.

Hartsell lives in the former Windy Rose house, which is shown in Mark Romano's 2002 *Pictorial History of Webster County*. I'd seen the picture, but had forgotten that it includes a view of the Rimfire School, and the Red Oak and Pardee and Curtin coal tipples, both gone now. "The school stood there," Hartsell said, pointing to the creek bottom across the road from his house. The school, which was closed in the early 1940s, was named for Bergoo native Rimfire Hamrick.

"Are there still trout in main Leatherwood Creek?" I asked.

As if on cue, his neighbor, Max Farley, came riding in on a four-wheeler. Behind him, holding up a brook trout, was his smiling six-year-old son, Logan, who had just caught the fish. It was a brilliantly colored trout of probably ten inches.

Logan was starting his first day in the first grade the following morning at Webster Springs Elementary School. I hope he grows up to catch at least one of every trout that swims on the North American continent, although none will mean as much to him as this first one on Leatherwood Creek.

I was drawn inexorably to the waterfall on the Right Fork. It had begun well down the list of things I wanted to do before Halley's Comet returns in 2062, but had gradually worked its way up to second place. Number One was still a desire to swim at the Big Falls of the Back Fork. Nobody knew why I wanted to do this, especially since I would be passing up several nice swimming holes that are easier to reach. I couldn't explain why, because I didn't know either.

In the course of writing this book, there was a handful of people I turned to for projects that required walking, which as we know is a lost art. One of the handful was Don Gilkeson, a friend from my newspaper days who came to Elk above Curtin in 1958.

There is another thing about Don, or more specifically his dogs. They never barked at me. When I approached his pleasant farm house, they came out to greet me, tails wagging and tongues drooling, their dark soulful eyes transformed into looks of blissful contentment when I rubbed their ears and whispered terms of endearment.

Usually it wasn't that way. I was barked at or growled at by every known breed of dog in the six counties through which Elk flows. Once a small dog that was up in years and losing its hair growled at me nonstop for forty-five minutes while I conversed with its owners, a canine accomplishment that I considered submitting to the Guinness people for entry in their Book of Records. Another time I was preparing to get out of my car when a dog came bounding up. It looked friendly, but you can never be sure. "Will your dog bite?" I asked a man who came into view. "Only if I tell it to," he replied.

I asked Don to accompany me to the waterfall on the Right Fork, a walk of a mile and a half, including two creek crossings. We got a late start on a humid day in June 2004, and as we left I envied his dogs their reclining positions on the porch. We drove to where the two forks of Leatherwood meet, and walked up the Right Fork, following an old logging railroad grade that is now used by four-wheelers, to whom walking is definitely a lost art.

I was overjoyed to reach the falls, and I suspect Don was too, because it meant I could take a few pictures and we could start back to the car. There were two streams of water coming over the ledge into a nice pool, and it is indeed a very scenic spot, except for the beer cans that had been thoughtfully left there by previous visitors.

As we admired the falls, Don told me about turkey hunting on a flat above us where he and his son, David, each killed a turkey. The flat is adjacent to the former Paris Green farm on Fork Ridge, which lies between the two forks of Leatherwood. It is said of Green, a lanky six-footer, that he would walk to the store at Bergoo, buy two feed sacks full of groceries and other items, and, balancing one on each shoulder, walk all the way back up the mountain.

I took pictures of the falls, being careful to complain about light conditions, a hedge that I learned from accompanying newspaper photographers for many years. But I admired their ability to take good pictures under adverse conditions. One trip that I especially remember was when *Gazette* photographer Chris Dorst and I walked through the rain and fog searching for Mount Porte Crayon near Dolly Sods. We never found it because of the fog. Nevertheless, Chris got a graphic picture of our guide, Joe Tekel of the U.S. Forest Service, with his arms wrapped around a trail sign. His flapping raincoat and the fog-obscured background told the story of our futile search. I thought that one picture was worth a six-hour walk through a soggy Roaring Plains, although Chris may disagree.

When Don Gilkeson and I walked to the falls on the Right Fork of Leatherwood, the only complaint, recorded above, was late afternoon light conditions in the deep gorge. Well, there may have been others, but they were minor, and included mist from the falls, slippery rocks, gloom and doom, hunger, thirst, and an absence of righteousness.

On the return walk, Don and I talked about bears, mountain lions, rattlesnakes, and the pictures I had taken. We were in favor of bears and mountain lions, but somewhat ambivalent toward rattlesnakes, although we conceded them their place in the grand scheme of things. We didn't know exactly what to think about the pictures.

"If they aren't good, I'll come back and try again," I said.

"Don't return alone," Don cautioned.

"Why?"

"You might be attacked by a mountain lion." He knew of my obsession with the animal.

"In that case," I replied, "I'll die happy. I will have seen one."

~ Nine ~

Bergoo

Finding Bearskin

Seven miles below Camp Four, Elk arrives at Bergoo. Mankind has marveled at the name Bergoo since Genesis One, and Rimfire Hamrick once offered an explanation. "The story goes," he wrote, "that meny years ago, when moonshiners had to begin to hide their stills, some of them went on this creek and put up their stills. So they run out of grain and gathered a lot of ramps and run off the steam as they did the Corn Licker. When one man tasted it and another man asked how it was, he said, nothing but a Boogaboo, and that name got changed around till it was called Bergoo."

George D. Curtin Sr. of Pardee and Curtin Lumber Company told Harry Sturm, co-author of *Rimfire: West Virginia's Typical Mountaineer*, that Bergoo was named for burgoo stew, which he said was a highly seasoned soup that was served three times a day in the lumber camp boarding houses.

Bill Byrne had a different version. He said that a party of hunters camped at the mouth of present Bergoo Creek when the region abounded in game and fish, and for weeks they feasted on bear, deer, grouse, squirrels, turkeys, and trout. One day, for variety's sake, the cook made a stew of all of the above, and flavored it with applejack. The meal was a smashing success, and they named the place Camp Bergoo after burgoo stew. At least he agreed with Curtin on the stew part.

When I visited Bergoo in November 2002 with Bill Triplett (see Rimfire), I wasn't sure if we were visiting the same place. I, an outsider, pronounced Bergoo with the emphasis on goo. Bill, a native, pronounced it with the emphasis on Ber. I silently thought about this, not wanting to correct a man on the pronunciation of his birthplace when we were standing there, and remembering also that I have devoted a lifetime trying unsuccessfully to instruct outsiders, of which there are six billion, on the pronunciation of my birthplace, Herold, as in Hare-old, which the emphasis on Hare.

Gordon Hamrick, a Bergoo native, believes the name Bergoo predates any of the above versions. He said that Danish sailors of the 1700s ate an oatmeal dish they called burgoo. As to proper pronunciation, Gordon contends there is none because the root or source of the word is unknown.

The dictionary defines burgoo as "a stew or thick soup of meat and vegetables," and places the accent on bur, as Bergoo natives do. But I suspect the concoction brewed at the long-ago hunting camp was a gooey mess, with the accent on goo.

There was an Associated Press writer in Charleston named Tom Stimmel, who was from out of state. He was fascinated with West Virginia place names, and Bergoo led the list. We had an imaginary contest in the newsroom in which the first prize was a week in Bergoo, the second prize was two weeks in Bergoo, and the third prize was three weeks in Bergoo. The imaginary winners came back with wonderful stories about a place where Upper River flowed past, someone named Rimfire was born,

The village of Bergoo. Renowned mountaineer Rimfire Hamrick is believed to have been born on the mountainside in background.

and Bearskin Bill caught bears.

Bergoo was a lumber mill and coal mining town whose heyday was from 1928, when the large Pardee and Curtin Lumber Company mill opened, to the 1950s, when Pardee and Curtin's Bergoo mine closed. Other companies continued to mine in the area into the 1980s. There is presently no mining being done at or near Bergoo, and virtually all the people who live there are either retired or work elsewhere.

"We have a lot of four-wheelers and trout fishermen," said Sam Nichols, who works at Pardee and Curtin's office at Curtin and has lived in Bergoo since 1968. In his younger days, when he was living on Miller Mountain at Webster Springs, he remembers playing softball on the former site of the mill pond.

In addition to the Pardee and Curtin mill, which stood across the river from Bergoo, there was a two-story boarding house with porches at both levels, machine shop, railroad, Pardee and Curtin office, company store, mine entrances and tipples, and a school. In 1939, the enrollment at the eight-room Bergoo School was 450 students.

Prior to the mill and mining, Bergoo was a farming community, as was virtually all of rural West Virginia. Out of this setting came the Benjamin 'Kelly Ben' Hamrick family, one of the most prominent families of upper Elk.

Kelly Ben was born near Curtin in 1834, the son of William Hamrick, one of the three brothers who came to upper Elk from present day Braxton County (see Whittaker Falls). Kelly Ben married Naomi Mollohan, a Braxton County native, in 1856. They lived in Braxton County for a time before moving to Bergoo at the start of the Civil War. The reason for their move was believed to have been to escape the "copperhead," or southern sympathies, that existed in Braxton County during the war.

Kelly Ben and Naomi had fourteen children, among them Bearskin Bill and Rimfire (see Rimfire chapter for a more complete record of the Kelly Ben family). It is believed that Rimfire was born on Dodrill Flats on the south hillside above Bergoo. The likelihood is that some of his brothers and sisters, including Bearskin, were born there as well.

Gordon Hamrick, great nephew of Rimfire, remembers his father, Benson Hamrick, taking him there and remarking, "That was where Rimfire Hamrick was born." His father told him that Kelly Ben

Kelly Ben and Naomi Hamrick

hewed poplar logs and built the house. Part of the walls were still standing at the time of Gordon's visit. Dodrill Flats is named for Henry Dodrill, a later resident.

- - -

Bearskin Bill Hamrick was born in 1865, the sixth of Kelly Ben and Naomi's children. In the family genealogy, *Roots & Wings*, Les Hamrick said of Bearskin: "He is noted in most published work as Bearskin Bill or Billy G. Bearskin Bill applied to his public persona, but family and close friends knew him simply as Billy."

Across the road from the Bergoo Community Building, on a small flat, is where Bearskin Bill kept his bears. "The story I heard," said Berlin Cummings, his grandson, "is that grandfather trapped bears in the woods, fattened them in pens, and then shipped them live by rail to restaurants in Baltimore. I remember

Bearskin Bill Hamrick

my mother saying that she had fed the bears on occasion."

Berlin Cummings is a Slatyfork native, but grew up on Bill's Knob near Bergoo. He is retired from the Maryland Department of Health and lives at Perryville, forty miles north of Baltimore. His mother, Angie Hamrick Cummings, was a daughter of Bearskin Bill.

By all accounts, Bearskin Bill was at least the hunting and fishing equal of his brother Rimfire, although the latter got more "press" in his lifetime and beyond. But Bearskin was one of the luminaries of *Tale of the Elk*, while Rimfire is nowhere to be heard of in the book.

When Bill Byrne first came to the head of Elk in 1908, he was with Bearskin. He told about fishing Split Rock Pool of Big Spring Fork with "my old friend and fishing partner, Bearskin Bill Hamrick," adding that "he and I had previously made numerous trips to the Upper River, as it is called."

Strangely, Byrne didn't write about Bearskin's obsession with bears, and never mentioned Rimfire. The closest he may have come was when he wrote that "one of Kelly Ben's boys" helped Bob Herndon, Byrne's companion on an 1886 trip to Bergoo, dig fishing worms.

The question "Which one of the boys?" has been left hanging for one hundred and eighteen years. It wouldn't have been Arnold, Isaac, or

Adam. They were in their twenties, and young men in their twenties don't dig worms. Rimfire was eighteen, and therefore a very marginal possibility. Boys in their late teens have learned to say no and are sullen about it. It wouldn't have been Bearskin Bill, or Byrne would have said so. Ellis is unlikely at seven, and George is ruled out at four. That leaves Simpson, who was twelve, and Felix, who was eleven, both of the worm-digging age. But Simpson became a minister and a fisher of men, not trout. That leaves Felix, who became a dairy farmer. Tilling the ground would have come naturally to him at an early age. It was obviously Felix.

Rimfire certainly knew of Byrne, whom he called "Birns." Writing about Elk River during a hospital stay in 1931, he said: "Thus it runs on for a distance of thirty miles through which it gathers nine other streams at which place we will stop and leave the other part to Mr. William Birns to chase it on out as it passes Elk Lick [Webster Springs] and flows on to the watters of Kanawah River at the Capital City at Charlston."

In a circa 1920 newspaper interview, Rimfire made a brief reference to his brother's interest in bears. "Will [Bearskin] took a fancy to chasing bears," he told the interviewer.

Indeed he did. Homer Riggleman wrote in *A West Virginia Mountaineer Remembers* that Bearskin "would always set traps and bear pens back on Gauley. Sometimes he had eight or ten bears in a big log house. I have peeped through the cracks many times and saw them in there. We named him Bearskin Bill."

Bearskin's traps were cages mounted on sled runners. When the trap door slammed down, the cage would be pulled back to Bergoo by a pair of mules, and the bears would be transferred to pens. Bearskin kept the mules tied near the pens so they would become accustomed to the scent of bear. Normally a whiff of bear will send mules and horses into a towering frenzy.

Gordon Hamrick believes the "back on Gauley" of Riggleman's account was on the head of Gauley under Sharp's Knob. "I know that was one place he trapped bears," said Gordon. "Billy G. lived for hunting and fishing, mostly hunting, and he had three hunting camps scattered across the Gauley River watershed, one on each of the North Fork, Middle Fork, and South Fork."

Billy G. is said to have been likeable but contrary. Gordon tells a story that came down through the family that, in an apocryphal way, may illustrate the latter characteristic. "Billy G. and his nephew, Levi Gregory, were having a dispute about something and Levi threatened court action," related Gordon.

To which Billy G. replied, "I'll be thar."

Levi continued, "If you beat me there, Uncle Billy, I'll take you to the circuit court."

"I'll be thar."

"And if you beat me there, I'll take it to the State Supreme Court."

"I'll be thar."

"And if you beat me there, I'll take it to the U.S. Supreme Court."

"I'll be thar."

"And if you beat me there, I'll take it to Hell."

"I'll send Wysong (Billy G.s lawyer)."

Homer Riggleman's version of the origin of the name Bearskin Bill is no doubt true, but of course other versions exist, and they are quite colorful. The story is told in *Rimfire: West Virginia's Typical Mountaineer* that a feral hog was raiding Bearskin's corn patch, and he "dressed himself up in a freshly killed bearskin, lay in wait in the cornfield for the razorback and made a surprise leap at the pilfering porker." This so scared the hog, the story goes, that it didn't stop running until it reached the mouth of Leatherwood Creek.

Another version appears in *The Blue Hills of West Virginia* by Ray Hamrick, who accompanied Bearskin into the hills near Bergoo in the fall of 1908 to repair or build pens. Later, Bearskin took one of his mules to check the pens, and found an old she-bear that was too poor for the carcass to be worth anything, so he killed her, skinned her out, and started home with the hide. On the way, he detoured to check on some hogs he had on the divide between Leatherwood and Bergoo Creeks. 'They all came running at the sound of his voice," Ray Hamrick wrote, "but when they caught scent of the bear hide they disappeared over the hill, snorting and squealing."

When Bearskin arrived home he found all of the hogs there, led by an old sow who had gone into his corn field, the others following. He got them all out except Old Sow, who delighted in being surrounded by corn. At that point, he began dragging the bearskin across the field, and Old Sow bolted through the fence and kept on running. She ran all the way to Sam Dodrill's, who lived several miles down Elk. Bearskin recognized her about two weeks later when he was visiting Dodrill. It was therefore Sam Dodrill, according to this version, who gave Bearskin the name.

Mary Jane Hamrick, wife of Brasil Hamrick, a great nephew of Bearskin, said that when her husband worked at Union Carbide in South Charleston his fellow workers called him "Bearhide." Brasil hunted with Bearskin when the latter had a lean-to camp on the head of Gauley.

Bearskin had a store, post office, and sawmill on Leatherwood Creek at Bergoo. Berlin Cummings recalls stories of his grandfather cutting ice, either from Elk River or Leatherwood Creek, and storing it in sawdust for the summer. Bearskin left Bergoo in 1912 and moved to Webster Springs, opening a store there. He lived in Dorrtown where the present road crosses the route of the old West Virginia Midland Railroad.

Around that time he bought property in Colorado, and spent some time there in the summer. One of the views was of Pikes Peak, the 14,110-foot prominence in the Rockies. Probably the primary attraction to Bearskin, though, was the trout fishing and hunting of the American West. Les Hamrick wrote in *Roots & Wings* that Bearskin "spent much time in later years at his large [600-acre] ranch in Colorado."

In the summer of 1914, he took his daughters west in a Model T Ford touring car. Berlin Cummings remembers his mother describing the trip. "There were no road signs, and we would stop from town to town and ask directions. At stream crossings, logs were chained to the car and it was floated across."

Bearskin has been described as an exuberant extrovert, but Cummings recalls his grandfather as a man of few words. "My brother Billy and I would ride the caboose from Bergoo to Webster Springs and stay overnight with grandfather," said Cummings. "He liked wild grapes, and we'd pick as many as we could up on the mountain above the old Vincent Hamrick place, and take them to him."

"In the evening, he'd say, Okay, you boys get ready for supper. After supper he'd say, Okay, you can go in and listen to the radio (while he read his newspaper). Later he'd say, Okay, it's time to go to bed. When we got up the next morning, he had already left for the store."

"He drove a Model A Ford coupe at that time," Cummings recalled, "and fishing rods would be sticking out of the rumble seat in the back. More often than not, he would be heading up toward Whittaker Falls."

Like many fishermen, Bearskin was tight-lipped about his catches. The story is told that if someone asked him for details, particularly as to where he caught them, he would say, "Yeah, I got some," and keep on walking.

Bearskin Bill died in January 1945 and is buried in the Hamrick Cemetery at Webster Springs, as are his parents, Kelly Ben and Naomi Hamrick, and others of his family, including Rimfire.

- - -

Illustration by Jordan Hudkins

One warm day in July 2003 I stopped at Bergoo for a sandwich and cold drink, and was engaged in conversation by a former Bergoo resident who lived in Ohio and had returned for Bergoo Days, an annual Fourth of July event.

I was listening, but not closely enough, a terrible habit that I fall into about midway through the second year of writing a book. I was aware, however, that I was being told coon hunting stories. My problem was that the conversation had shifted smoothly and without noticeable pause from coon hunting to bear hunting, and I hadn't realized it.

"We were hunting way up on the head of Leatherwood Creek," the Bergoo native said, "and the dog treed one and we shot it out."

That happens in coon hunting, I thought.

"It wasn't a big one," he continued. "It weighed no more than two hundred and twenty-five pounds, but still it was a long drag to the nearest road."

I was left speechless. Usually I can think of something to say other than the mundane "Is that right?" or "That's remarkable." But nothing seemed appropriate to cover a two hundred and twenty-five pound coon, especially since there are larger ones out there.

I paid for my sandwich and drink, wished the man from Ohio happy Bergoo Days, and headed down the road to see Emmett Hamrick at the Twin Bridges. It was there that a bizarre and tragic incident occurred in 1884.

Trigger Ben Hamrick and a companion, George Cowger, approached a flood swollen Elk on horseback, and Cowger was reluctant to attempt the crossing. To persuade him, Trigger Ben proposed swapping horses. Trigger Ben's horse, a large animal accustomed to bearing its rider in deep water, made it across safely with Cowger, but the smaller horse fell and Trigger Ben was swept away. His body was found far downstream thirteen days later.

Across the river from Emmett Hamrick's was the former settlement of Bernardstown, named for Sampson Bernard Hamrick. He was president of the Webster County Commission when the Twin Bridges were built in 1923 by the Luten Bridge Company of York, Pennsylvania. Emmett carried water to the workers for one dollar a day.

The upper bridge crosses Elk. The lower one crosses what in 1923 was a mill race that carried water to a grist mill. Both bridges are narrow, and their concrete sides are scarred from being scraped by vehicles.

Emmett and I walked out onto the upper bridge, which is not a good thing to do because of its narrowness. A sign warns that fishing from the bridge is prohibited. We were there to read the plaque that tells about the building of the bridge, not that we were any safer for that reason. But we did watch and listen.

Emmett was born on Point Mountain. As we talked in his living room, the mountain loomed large across the river. Also visible is the dip in the hills where Baltimore Run comes into Elk. Just upstream is Metcalf's Bank, a popular fishing hole named for William T. Metcalf, a Methodist preacher circa 1837.

In the book *Moccasin Tracks and Other Imprints*, Rattlesnake Bill Dodrill said that Baltimore Run got its name from a man who lived farther up Elk and didn't like it there, so he decided to move to Baltimore. He got as far downstream as the mouth of the aforementioned run, where he built a cabin and stayed. Naturally, local people began calling it Baltimore Run.

Ten

Company Town

Parcoal Remembered

Three miles above Webster Springs, sprawled in a long river bottom, is the former Pardee and Curtin coal mining town of Parcoal. The name may be a blending of Pardee and coal, although another version is that Parcoal derives its name from the French word "parcoal," meaning "by coal."

One person who knew Parcoal in its heyday was Brack Davis, a native of Strange Creek, Braxton County. He came to Parcoal with his family in 1930 at age one, and grew up there. His father, Brack Sr., managed the company store, and his uncle, Ed Davis, was general manager of Pardee and Curtin's Bergoo office from 1928 until the 1960s.

Brack Jr. retired in 1991 from Silver Burdette Publishing Company and he and his wife, Virginia Lou Strader Davis, a Gilmer County native, live in Winter Haven. Florida.

He wrote the following remembrance:

"All the buildings in town belonged to Pardee and Curtin. At one time this company owned and operated three towns and four coal mines along Elk River. Each town had a store, an office, a post office, a school, a church, a community building, and a barber shop. A room located in each company office served as a doctor's office.

"In Parcoal, the families who lived downriver from the office occupied the "lower" part of town, sometimes called Golden Ridge, which was the name of the company that opened the first coal mine in Parcoal. The families who lived upriver from the office occupied the "upper" part of town.

"It was thought that upper town families enjoyed a better status than those in the lower part. This wasn't because of the houses in which we lived, because all company houses were built alike. Rather, it was because of the manner in which people lived. Even in a coal mining town, a social state of mind was present.

"Believe it or not, we had our own "Fats Arbuckle." He drove a gasoline and kerosene truck for Gulf, and came to town about once a week. The two hand-pumped gas pumps were located just off the porch in front of the store. Six gallons of 'low test' or five gallons of 'high test' could be bought for a dollar.

"Kerosene was kept inside the wareroom in a hand pushed tank cart, and sold for two cents a gallon. Most people used kerosene for starting fires in their stoves, but some did have oil lamps for emergencies. In 1936, the company built a filling station in Cherry Falls and gasoline was no longer sold in Parcoal.

"The store wareroom was located in the back and was usually well stocked. If the store was out of anything, people just had to wait until 'the truck came in.'

"In the early days, ice cream was delivered in heavy padded containers that were packed with dry ice. Several flavors of Imperial were enjoyed, including cherry, cherry nut, strawberry, peach, chocolate, chocolate ripple, vanilla, and raspberry. Other treats included Imps, Popsicles, and Creamsicles. We always looked forward to finding a wooden stick from an Imp, Popsicle, or Creamsicle stamped 'free,' which meant we could take it to the store and get a free treat.

"Some years later the dry ice cooler gave way to the electric ice cream freezer. Power outages occurred occasionally, and when this happened the store would treat us with ice cream because there was no way to keep it. We loved those power failures!

"During the cold winter months, the company store served as a gathering place for men off work and boys who had nothing to do. My reason for going was to listen to the men talk as they stood around the pot-bellied Burnside stove. Without exception, the talk always got around to a Tom Mix, Gene Autry, Tarzan, or Roy Rogers picture show. All who had seen a particular show added their part to the dialogue. By the time the discussion was finished, it was time to close the store. When dad called out, 'All ashore that's going ashore,' that was the signal for closing and everyone would leave.

"Just about every brand of chewing tobacco, plug, sack, or twist was sold at the store, as well as snuff. A tobacco cutter was kept on top of the counter for cutting the plug tobacco into the size wanted. Most miners who chewed plug bought five or ten cents worth at a time.

"Most brands of cigarettes were sold. Wings and Avalons were cheaper than Camels, Lucky Strikes, or Chesterfields. Also, several kinds of cigarette tobacco were available, including Butler, R.J.R., Five Brothers, Prince Albert, and Sir Walter Raleigh. Each came with a small package of cigarette papers, but a good package of O.C.B. papers, with glue, could be bought for a nickel. A 'roll your own' cigarette machine could be bought for about $1.98.

"Two kinds of matches were available, the big five cent box, called 'farmer's' matches, and the penny box, Copperheads or Diamonds.

"Employees of the company could go to the office and draw scrip against wages earned. Payday was every two weeks, but during those Depression years most miners didn't have much money. Coins were issued in denominations of penny, nickel, dime, quarter, and half dollar. These were cast in metal alloy by the Ingle-Schierlok Company of Dayton, Ohio.

"Paper denominations were issued in one, two, three, four, five, ten, and twenty dollars. These were about the size of today's business calling cards.

"Scrip could be taken to Webster Springs and exchanged at stores or other places of business at the rate of seventy five cents in silver for one dollar of scrip. Businesses in the position to make this exchange liked this arrangement because they returned the scrip to the company for face value in silver." (Scrip is defined by the dictionary as *paper currency or a token issued for temporary use.*)

- - -

At the upper end of Parcoal, in the Union Cemetery, there is a tombstone that says in classic simplicity: Cal Dean. 1913-1979. Cal lived in Hotel Bottom in Webster Springs, and it is said that he was such a good poker player that he couldn't get a game in Webster County, or at least not one that involved serious money.

Cal's son, retired football coach Jerome Dean, said his father, a coal miner, acquired his skills with cards during the times the mines were idle for one reason or another. "He said you've got to eat," his son recalled, "so he learned to play poker."

His favorite game was five card stud in which four cards are dealt face up and the fifth face down. "He had a phenomenal memory for cards," said his son. "If he was holding two sevens, for example, he would remember if someone else had been dealt a seven, or if someone had a seven when they folded and tossed their cards on the table. He would say the odds against getting another seven were too great, and he would get out of the game."

He was also good at card tricks. Retired judge Boonie Sommerville, who coon hunted with Cal, once asked for a demonstration of the art of sleight of hand. "He picked up a deck and dealt me four Jacks," said Boonie. "Then he dealt himself four Queens."

When Cal learned that he was dying of cancer, he wrote the inscription he wanted on his tombstone. It says: *"The saddest words I ever spoke: Deal around me boys, I'm broke."*

Eleven

End of the Line

The Demise of Last Buffalo and Friends

There are always pockets of wilderness that survive longer than others because of their inaccessibility. One was the Gauley Mountain region on the head of Elk River which was referred to in old writings as "the wilds of Pocahontas County." Another was the Pratt lands centered around Bergoo (see Pardee and Curtin).

This large reserve of wilderness was a refuge for bear, deer, and wild turkeys, and they never completely disappeared from the Pratt lands, as they had in most other places in West Virginia by the early 1900s. Among the remnant deer herds remaining in the state in 1910 was one on the headwaters of Leatherwood and Bergoo Creeks.

But it does not pay to be the last of your line in Webster County. The last buffalo was shot in 1806, the last elk in 1815, the last mountain lion in 1877, the last wolf in 1897, the last wild hog in 1933, and the last Republican in 1936. I cautioned my nephew, Rob Johnson, who was the photographer for this book, to search his life and those of his ancestors five generations back to determine before entering Webster County whether he was the last of something or other.

If Uncas, the *Last of the Mohicans* in James Fenimore Cooper's classic novel, were to start down Elk from Slatyfork today, he would get no farther than Whittaker Falls, the county line.

Isaac Gregory, an early settler, shot the last buffalo on Point Mountain about five miles from Webster Springs. The date is given as "before the War of 1812," and it may have been as early as 1806. Point Mountain parallels Elk on its south side and Back Fork on its north side. Last Buffalo was shot on the Back Fork side on present West Virginia 15.

There are different versions of the event. One is that the buffalo, a lone bull, was shot on what is known today as Buffalo Bull Knob, but ran across Point Mountain to Valley Head before expiring. Another is that Last Buffalo died where he was shot on the fateful knob. They say that if you go there on a dark night, you can hear the shot and the sigh of the buffalo, but of course "they say" cannot necessarily be trusted to tell the truth

A third version is that the bull was shot and killed a short distance from the knob at what is known as the Old Dodrill Place, and that a cow with it ran across Point Mountain and was killed at Valley Head.

"It really makes no difference," said Dudley Dodrill, a Pickens native who grew up on Point Mountain, "but the story I always heard is that Isaac Gregory hid among some large rocks and waited for the buffalo to come up the hollow. He shot the bull, and the cow ran to Valley Head, where it was killed."

Years ago, I saw a roadside marker at Valley Head that told about the buffalo, although perhaps I only dreamed it. One day when Dudley and I visited Valley Head, I asked two people about the marker, and they both stared at me with bemused looks.

Earlier that day, Dudley showed me the site on his homeplace where, according to family tradition, Isaac Gregory crouched behind a rock and shot the bull as it came up the hillside from the Back Fork. The family tradition began with Charles Dodrill, Dudley's great grandfather, who was born about thirty years after the shooting, and continued with his grandfather, James Dodrill.

Point Mountain was roadless wilderness at the time. The Summersville and Slavin Cabin Turnpike, which was the forerunner of West Virginia 15, wasn't built until 1856, and it was no more than a muddy path that hardy souls traveled only because there was nothing else. It was still a muddy path in the early 1940s when an aroused citizenry demanded and received a paved road. Perhaps the Department of Highways had heard the "last of" stories.

In 1806, what later became a road over Point Mountain was probably only a "buffalo trace," which was the name the early settlers gave to buffalo trails. This "trace" led to the salt sulfur lick where the Elk and Back Fork meet and which attracted buffalo, deer, and elk in large numbers.

The last elk was shot and wounded on Elk River between Bergoo and Whittaker Falls, and supposedly ran across the mountain to Gauley River near Straight Creek, where it was killed. There is a rounded rock on the south bank of Elk diagonally across from Chestnut Ford Bottom, where, according to legend, the elk was standing on a fateful day in 1815 when it was wounded and pursued to its doom.

The man who wounded the elk and later killed it was C.W. Cottle, according to Rattlesnake Bill Dodrill in his long-lived 1915 book, *Moccasin Tracks and Other Imprints.* Dodrill said that Cottle lived at the community of that name in present day Nicholas County and was returning from a trip to Greenbrier County. He was a justice of the peace and was elected the first member of the Virginia General Assembly from Nicholas County.

There is a sadness attached to the end of an animal species in a region, but if there is such a thing as "saving grace," in this instance it is that Last Elk was standing in Elk River in its final hours. If elk are ever reintroduced into West Virginia, as Pennsylvania and Kentucky have done, the proper symbolic place to start would be at Chestnut Ford Bottom, where we could say a prayer and wish them god speed.

Native chestnut sprouts still cling to life on the riverbank at Chestnut Ford Bottom. This is not uncommon in West Virginia, because the fungal blight that wiped out the vast chestnut forests in the early 1900s did not affect the root system. But it is especially appropriate at Chestnut Ford Bottom.

Whether the buffalo shot on Point Mountain and the elk shot at Chestnut Ford Bottom were the last in the state would be a dubious claim to make. Probably every county or region has its "last of" stories. For instance, the book *Trans-Allegheny Pioneers* says the last buffalo in the Kanawha Valley was killed on Little Sandy Creek of Elk about 1815 by Archibald Price, and the last elk was killed on Elk Two-Mile near Charleston in 1820 by Billy Young.

The last mountain lion in Webster County was killed by Kelly Ben Hamrick on Leatherwood Creek, his son, Rimfire, wrote during a 1931 hospital stay. He gave no details, but said the demise of Last Cat took place "near fifty years ago." That would coincide with the time of the disappearance of mountain lions generally in West Virginia in the late 1800s.

Corroboration of Rimfire's story appeared in *the Weston Democrat* in 1982 in Bill Adler's *Yesteryears* column. Adler printed an account of an 1877 trip up Elk by Louis Bennett, a Weston attorney, whose party stopped for dinner at Kelly Ben's home at Bergoo. Bennett wrote: "Kelly Ben had shortly before killed a large panther, whose skin I obtained and will bring home with me."

The last wolf in Webster County and maybe in West Virginia

Last Elk Rock (smaller rock in background)

was killed on the head of the Back Fork of Elk in 1897 by Stoffer Hamrick, who was seventeen years old and a member of the party that had hunted the wolf relentlessly for eight days. Stoffer's family lived on Elk just below Whittaker Falls. He wrote an account of the hunt in 1941. Lone Wolf, a male, roamed Point Mountain in the 1890s, killing sheep, and all efforts to hunt him down had been unsuccessful.

Stoffer said the final chase began on New Year's morning in 1897 with two feet of snow on the ground. About fifteen men and boys took part. "We followed that wolf track for eight days in subzero weather over four counties," he wrote, "but most of the time in Webster and Randolph."

The chase ended on January 8, 1897, on Turkeybone Mountain, where the Back Fork heads near Pickens. "I was standing on a log that was lying against a large maple tree," Stoffer said, "when I sighted the wolf and fired the shot that brought his depredations to an end."

Later examination revealed that Lone Wolf had eaten only a grouse in eight days, yet he had led fifteen hunters on a monumental chase through deep snow over four counties. We are reminded of the ragged, starving band of Nez Perce Indians, who in 1877 were chased across two thousand miles of the western landscape by the U.S. Army before surrendering at Bear Paw Mountain in Montana within sight of refuge in Canada. But there was no such refuge for Lone Wolf.

At first the Webster County Commission refused to pay the fifty dollar bounty on the wolf because it had been killed in Randolph County, but the youthful Hamrick obtained a court guardian, hired Webster Springs lawyer E.H. Morton, and won judgment in magistrate court.

Stoffer Hamrick was born in 1880 at Samp, a community on Elk near Whittaker Falls, and died in 1975 in Detroit, where a daughter lived. He is buried at Thomas, Tucker County, where he worked in the coal mines for many years and was a policeman.

Dan Hamrick, grandson of Stoffer Hamrick, has a picture of

the hunters and the frozen carcass of the wolf. "My grandfather was a handsome young man and a physically fit adult who believed in a good diet and a lot of exercise," Dan recalled. "I remember he took me for a walk one time, more than four miles to Mingo [Randolph County], across Mingo Flats for about a mile or two, and then he said we would turn toward home at the head of Ralston Run. That was another four miles or so over rough terrain. Only in recent years have I realized that he was about eighty-five at the time."

Homer Riggleman claimed to have killed the last wild hog in Webster and Randolph Counties in 1933. Wild Hog was a Randolph County resident, but he roamed into Webster County at night to feed. This is an "iffy" situation as to which county can claim credit for its shooting, but for my purposes it has Webster County written all over it.

"No hogs had been tracked in that area for some time," Riggleman wrote in his 1980 book, *A West Virginia Mountaineer Remembers*, "and to my knowing there has never been another wild hog killed in Randolph or Webster County or even in the state."

A "wild hog" in West Virginia at that time was a domestic hog gone wild. There were never any native wild hogs in the state, although European wild boars were stocked in Southern West Virginia in 1979 and are still there.

Riggleman was a farmer, logger, and coal miner, and the brother of Leonard Riggleman, who was president of Morris Harvey College, the forerunner of the University of Charleston, from 1931 to 1964.

The brothers grew up on Elk near Cowger's Mill, and attended Cowger School, a one-room log school on the Valley Fork Road that is long gone. Its successor school closed in 1960, but the building still stands as mute testimony to the thousands of small schools that once dotted West Virginia's rural landscape. An oldtime post office known as Blue Spring was located nearby. It was named for a spring whose water took on a bluish color in the summer.

When the Riggleman brothers were growing up, they preferred fishing for brook trout on the rugged and isolated Back Fork, and they would walk two or three miles over Point Mountain to that stream, when Elk was at their doorstep. Homer Riggleman died in 1976. Leonard Riggleman died in 1983.

- - -

Republicans, who disappeared from Webster County in the Roosevelt landslide of 1936, have been reintroduced through restocking. Returning a viable population is being hailed by wildlife biologists as one of their major successes. But there is still work to be done. The last Republican presidential candidate to carry Webster County was Nixon over McGovern in 1972, and that by only forty-five votes. Since then the Democrat has won: Carter over Ford in 1976, Carter over Reagan in 1980, Mondale over Reagan in 1984, Dukakis over Bush One in 1988, Clinton over Bush One in 1992, Clinton over Dole in 1996, Gore over Bush Two in 2000, and Kerry over Bush Two in 2004.

When Boyd Dotson Sr., editor of *the Webster Republican* for many years, was elected to the West Virginia Legislature in 1943 he attributed his victory to the popularity of his coon dog, Old Mutt. But Boyd was popular too. West Virginia Route 15 east of Webster Springs, commonly called the Point Mountain Road, is named the Boyd Dotson Sr. Memorial Highway in his honor.

His son, Boyd Jr., was a fine athlete at Webster Springs High School and West Virginia Wesleyan College. Boyd Jr. edited the newspaper after his father, and now works for the Department of Highways in Charleston.

- - -

Not all birds and animals go quietly into the dark night. Take the case of the attack hawk at Cherry Falls. Mike Collins, who works at John's Exxon, was helping a customer fill his propane tank when suddenly a red-tailed hawk swooped down from a nearby tree. "'It flew right in my face" said Mike. "I ran and the customer ran."

But the hawk wasn't finished with them. "We returned to the propane tank, watching our back trail all the while," said Mike, "when here it came again. I swatted at it, and it ran under the propane tank, and took me on a third time. I ducked and it flew off and didn't return."

Apparently it had made its point, whatever its point was.

Around this same time in early 2005, a hawk made a "strafing run" at legislator Joe Talbott's cat in Webster Springs. The cat flared up and made hissing sounds, its hair on end, and the hawk flew away to fight another day. Joe suspects it was the same bird that took on Mike Collins and his customer at the propane tank.

One night Joe and Boonie Sommerville were coon hunting, and an owl swooped down and knocked Joe's hat off. But they did soon discover a reason for that gallant bit of daredevilry. They found a freshly killed opossum lying on a stump nearby. The owl was obviously guarding its dinner.

~ Twelve ~

Rimfire

Enshrined in Bronze - Or Is He?

On a gray and drizzly November day in 2002 I went to Leatherwood Creek and Bergoo in search of Rimfire Hamrick, the renowned Webster County mountaineer, although I didn't expect to find, in a physical sense, a man who died fifty-seven years ago.

But I did find a very good pencil sketch of him on the wall of the Bergoo Community Building, which was once the office of the Pardee and Curtin Lumber Company. He shares the wall with many others, including J.M. Cofer, the legendary company doctor who rode log trains to remote areas to deliver babies.

Although Rimfire is best known for his days at Webster Springs, in a spiritual sense he belongs to Bergoo and Leatherwood Creek, where he was born on March 28, 1868. The most likely site is Dodrill Flats (see Bergoo). The flats can be seen by looking south from in front of the Bergoo Baptist Church.

Bill Triplett, great great nephew of Rimfire, accompanied me on that late November day that was an early warning sign of the cold and snowy winter to come. It was the kind of day that makes West Virginians wonder what the weather is like in the Cayman Islands.

We proceeded to find Rimfire in another way in a picture of the Pardee and Curtin mill that stood across the river. Its walls are still partially standing, although now surrounded by trees, and they presented a ghostly tableau on the day of our visit. To the left of the mill in the picture are two pieces of cultivated ground that were Rimfire's garden and tobacco patches when he worked for Pardee and Curtin. He made "twist" tobacco for chewing. Bill has a piece of the "Rimfire twist" at his home that is almost petrified with age.

Other reminders of Rimfire are a large mantel clock and matching salt and pepper shakers. Inscribed on the clock is "Eli Hamrick, jeweler." Rimfire had a watch repair shop in Webster Springs in the early 1900s. He made the clock cabinet and ordered the mechanism. The salt and pepper shakers are inscribed "Eli to mother. Norfolk, Va. 1906."

Although Rimfire's public persona was as a man of the mountains, he made several trips outside the state, including to Norfolk, where he was custodian of the West Virginia Building for the Jamestown Exposition in 1906-1907. The exposition observed the 300th anniversary of the founding of Jamestown, the first permanent English settlement in America.

The years of his proprietorship of the jewelry store were 1902-1917, although intermittently. An item appeared in the "Local Notes" column of *the Webster Echo* on October 31, 1902, that said: "If your watch needs repairing bring it to Eli Hamrick when you come to Court."

He also worked at the grand Webster Springs Hotel, was a game protector and fire warden, and worked for Pardee and Curtin Lumber Company. When he applied for a job with the latter in 1928, he was asked, "What can you do?" He is said to have replied famously, "Most anything anybody else could."

The final fifteen years of his working life were spent with Pardee and Curtin, where he belonged to a union called the Elk River L. and L. Association. A letter written by Ed Davis, general manager at the Bergoo office, says that in the last two or three years Rimfire "had no duties except the things he chose to do, which was mainly cultivating and caring for the beautiful flowers he grew in the office lawn and his little garden and tobacco patch."

He was employed at the Webster Springs Hotel in the fall of 1907 after he returned from Norfolk, and was appointed game and fire warden about 1912. Sampson Miller wrote in his book, *Annals of Webster County*, that the fire tower was located on Turkey Mountain on the Gauley drainage near Jerryville.

Miller devoted a short chapter in his book to Rimfire. He knew him, hunted with him, and said that "in dress and appearance he was a typical pioneer backwoodsman, a true mountaineer hillbilly." This image served him well when he was employed at the Webster Springs Hotel.

- - -

Bill Triplett and I walked past the Bergoo Post Office in the drizzle to the back of the community building. Bill pointed to where Rimfire had planted flowers, and nearby on the bank of Leatherwood Creek where he planted a patch of ginseng.

The 1967 booklet *Rimfire: West Virginia's Typical Mountaineer* by Harry P. Sturm and H.G. Rhawn, tells that during a winter Rimfire spent in Florida, "there were no flowers at the place he lived, so he planted a garden which delighted the Floridians."

He was said to have been a masterful painter of buildings. Bill Gillespie's family book, *A Brief Genealogy of Elijah Hedding Gillespie, His Ancestors, Descendents and Their Families*, tells that when Bill's grandfather built a new store building, *the Webster Republican* of April 3, 1913, carried this item: "Eli Hamrick, with brush and paint, is giving the finishing touches to the Gillespie building. It is a splendid job, a testimony to Eli's mastery of the painter's art."

In 1910, Rimfire and Cherry Woodzell built a bigger Lover's Lane boardwalk on Bell Street, which ran from the courthouse up the Back Fork for several hundred yards. The original was built around 1875 so circuit clerk Ben Conrad could walk to the Courthouse without wading through red clay mud.

One of the earliest records of Rimfire as an entrepreneur was this item in the March 13, 1896, *Webster Echo*: "Eli Hamrick passed through here going to the Yew Pines [mountains on the head of Gauley River] to get a load of canes to take to Addison." The American yew is a shrub whose heavy, fine grained wood made good canes. An oldtime fiddle tune celebrates the Yew Pine Mountains.

Rimfire was a pig farmer of sorts. In the spring, he would take shoats into the woods near the Turkey Mountain fire tower and turn them loose. He would kill the pigs in the fall and bring them into Webster Springs to be sold. After running loose in the woods all summer and fall, the meat was lean and tough. Whenever someone got hold of a tough piece of meat, they would say "Must be one of Rimfire's razorbacks."

Rimfire's only marriage was to Zella Cogar, daughter of William and Margaret Payne Cogar. They were married in 1920 and divorced in 1925. Part of that time they lived on Turkey Mountain at the fire tower. Wade Pepper, longtime sports editor of *the Clarksburg Exponent,* wrote in the November 1923 *West Virginia Wildlife* that Rimfire "built a neat little log cabin near the fire station."

Helen Lee Lyke, Zella's daughter from a later marriage to Bennett Lee, said her mother, and not Rimfire, was the fire warden during the time of their marriage. "My mother was the first woman in West Virginia to be a fire warden," said Helen, who lives in North Ridgeville, Ohio. "Rimfire was the game warden." In a way, the original fire tower was the forerunner of present day tree stands that hunters use. It was a platform built high up in two black cherry trees at the head of Gum Bee Tree Hollow.

Once Rimfire was offered a twenty-dollar reward to trap a sheep-killing bear on Gauley Mountain, and Zella partially cooked a ham as bait. They carried the ham and a heavy double-spring trap on a horse or mule, and headed into the area where the offending bear roamed. "But before they arrived where they were going to set the trap," said Helen, "it got dark and they had to camp for the night. Mother told me that she looked back and Rimfire was slicing off pieces of the ham and eating it." But she believes they did ultimately catch the bear.

Zella filed for divorce in 1925. "There was no bitterness on mother's part toward Rimfire," said Helen. "But she had lost a baby [a son that was stillborn in 1922], and her sister Ella had died of pneumonia, and I think those things were weighing on her mind." Zella died in 1978 and is buried in the Odd Fellows Cemetery at Cowen.

- - -

Rimfire was six three or six four and weighed perhaps 155 in his heyday, although he became "stoop shouldered and painfully skinny" in his final years, according to Les Hamrick, a fourth cousin who wrote the Hamrick genealogy, *Roots & Wings*. Employment records at Pardee and Curtin in 1935, when Rimfire was sixty-seven years old, list him as weighing only 135 pounds.

Rimfire, his eight brothers, and his father were all over six feet tall, the tallest being brother Ellis, who stood six foot six and weighed 280 pounds. Ellis has been described, perhaps fortunately for anyone who may have riled him, as "the gentlest of men."

Rimfire was a fisherman. If van Gogh liked to paint pictures, Rimfire liked to fish. He fished Elk, the Back Fork, Gauley, and Williams, and he went fishing whenever the whim struck him, regardless of what he might have been doing otherwise. Bill Gillespie, a Webster Springs native, said Rimfire "was as independent as a hog on ice."

Bill, his associate Jim Brown, and I were having lunch at Vickie's Food Palace in Webster Springs when Bill made that imperious announcement. I glanced at Jim, and his dark brown eyes were riveted on the menu. I retreated to my thoughts and thought about a hog on ice. I envisioned it sliding this way and that way, totally out of control. Knowing that hogs are independent anyway, I silently conceded that a hog on ice could be very independent. As I ordered the fish special and a Coke, I had a vision of a half dozen men the size of Bill Gillespie advancing on my hog. Jim asked for a cheeseburger with a slice of onion, so I knew he must have seen something that alarmed him too, because only frightened people would ruin a cheeseburger by putting onion on it. But by the time our food was served, the hog had slid away and escaped, its icy independence preserved.

Rimfire spent a lengthy period in a Clarksburg hospital in 1931 recuperating from a broken leg and lacerated head he received at the Pardee and Curtin machine shop when a steel door blew shut on him. During the hospital stay he wrote what amounted to his "autobiography," committing to paper his thoughts on wildlife, nature, and Elk River.

He was not a man of letters, but he *was* a man of rivers, as the following excerpt from his writing clearly shows. It is part of a longer passage in which he describes in his mind's eye an outing on upper Elk. Whether it was a specific occurrence, or a composite of his experiences, isn't known.

"*Next we heare the sound of the clear, sparkling river as it ripples over the rocks, and soon we are at the side of it. We set down on a rock and watch, and soon we see a nice brook trout jump out after some kind of a fly. It is getting late and we must get a fiew fish for our supper an breakfast. We cut a small pole an hunt us a crawfish and use the tail only for baite. We throw in the baited hook and - swish - we have a ten inch trout. We repeat this till we have ten an quit. Next we gather some wood and finde a pine tree that answers for a shelter if it rains, an then we start a fire and get our supper. We have bread, coffee, jelly, butter an five nice trout.*

"*Next we gather small pine limbs an make us a nice little bed an lay down and soon are at peace with both men an animals.*"

When Bill Gillespie was a boy, he went camping on the Back Fork and met Rimfire, who was then in his seventies. "His hat was lying on the ground beside him," Bill recalls, "and he was with another man I knew only as Old Man Rutherford. Rimfire had a fire going and was frying a skillet full of trout. He invited me to share the trout with them, but I declined."

Rimfire could relate to that. Lanky Henderson of Cowen told me about meeting Rimfire on Gauley River near the mouth of Straight Creek in 1924. Straight Creek flows off Turkey Mountain from the southeast and is the first major tributary of Gauley below the Three Forks. Lanky had caught two nice trout, and Rimfire had caught none. When Lanky offered Rimfire one of his trout, the independent Rimfire replied, "Thank you, but I'll catch my own fish."

Lanky described him as "a tall man with gray hair wearing bib overalls and the back of his shirt was torn. He was fishing with a pole he'd cut in the woods, and he carried a little basket on a shoulder strap." (Lanky Henderson died in April 2003 at age ninety-nine).

- - -

Little is known about Rimfire's early life. He is said to have attended school for six years, presumably on Leatherwood Creek and probably around 1875 to 1881. There was no high school in Webster County until 1910, and six years of schooling was average for the time.

Later he worked on his father's farm and helped in the store at Bergoo. He told an interviewer that he was twenty-two years old when his father, Kelly Ben, gave him a choice. "Now, Eli, you're your own man and have to make your own living. But you're a good hand and if you want to remain at home, I'll pay you seventy-five cents a day." "That was top wages in that day," Rimfire said, "and none but a good man could earn it. I said, Well, Dad, I'll stay and it won't cost you a cent."

Sampson Miller told an engaging story about Rimfire and a relative, Neal Hamrick, both in their early twenties, making some money cutting timber, and then setting out to see the sights of Charleston, walking most of the way.

A young Rimfire Hamrick

During a night of revelry at an old-fashioned square dance, they indulged freely in cocktails and wine, and spent all their money. On the way home, they decided to pass themselves off as evangelists and make a little money, so they offered to hold a revival meeting at a schoolhouse. They felt it would be hypocritical to do this in a church. "I will do the preaching," Neal said to their farmhouse hosts, "and Eli can do the singing." The revival went well, collections exceeded expectations, and they headed home with some money in their pockets. When they got back, friends joked about them being hypocrites to claim the evangelical call, and Neal replied: "Eli did a good job of singing, and really I felt good while I was trying to preach."

Rimfire is said to have "called the figures" for Saturday night square dances in the Webster Springs Hotel ballroom. Portia Hamrick told me in a 1980s interview that she had heard that "one night Rimfire was pretty full [he'd had a few drinks], and took his mule right onto the dance floor."

Kelly Ben Hamrick and his nine sons.
Standing, from left: Felix, George, Ellis, Rimfire, and Simpson.
Seated: Bearskin Bill, Adam , Isaac, Arnold, and Kelly Ben.

A defining moment for the Kelly Ben and Naomi Hamrick family occurred on a summer day in 1900 when two family heirloom pictures were taken. Rimfire was thirty-two years old then. One picture is of the entire family, and the other is of Kelly Ben and his nine sons.

The pictures were taken at the Arnold Hamrick farm on Point Mountain seven miles east of Webster Springs. Arnold was one of Kelly Ben's sons. Patsy Hamrick Weikart, a granddaughter of Arnold, said her father told her that was where the pictures were taken.

In the larger group, a hound dog stands beside Kelly Ben and Rimfire. In the picture of Kelly Ben and his sons, the dog is lying down nearby. Whether the dog belonged to Rimfire isn't known. But it appears to be a redbone hound, a favorite of coonhunters.

Gordon Hamrick told me an amusing (except to him) story about Rimfire the coonhunter. In the late 1930s at Bergoo, Gordon's father went out to feed the livestock and encountered Rimfire and his hound returning from an all-night hunt. "In the country tradition," relates Gordon, "Rimfire was invited in for breakfast with the dog being given its share. After breakfast, Rimfire was guided to my room, where he placed his coat on the floor for his hound and crawled into my bed, fully clothed. My room smelled like wet hound for a week."

The best known Rimfire picture, taken in 1923, shows him with a Walker hound, identified in the photo caption as Jack, who was said to have been "death on rattlesnakes." Jack belonged to Rimfire's wife, Zella.

In the picture, Rimfire is holding a mountain rifle and wearing a badge that identified him as a game warden. John W. Davis, a West Virginia native and Democratic nominee for president in 1924, displayed it in his Wall Street law office. He said that Rimfire's countenance "was as sad as that of Lincoln." After the election, Davis may have joined Rimfire in looking sad. He lost to Repub-

Rimfire Hamrick and Jack
Photo courtesy of Mark Romano

lican incumbent Calvin Coolidge in a landslide. The country had bought the slogan "Keep Cool With Coolidge."

The mountain rifle in the picture was used only at shooting matches, according to an interview with Rimfire by Wilbur Swiger. In the interview, Rimfire listed his weaponry as a Smith & Wesson .38 revolver, the mountain rifle, a 32-40 Marlin rifle, and a double-barreled shotgun, which raises the question: where was the rifle that fired rimfire cartridges and led to the name Rimfire? Les Hamrick believes that at some point Rimfire owned a .25 caliber J. Stevens rimfire rifle for squirrel hunting.

The stories of the origin of the name are analogous to Rimfire's life in general. There were as many different views of him in his time as there are logos on a race car driver's jacket today. Gordon Hamrick tells one facet of Rimfire:

"Although he is portrayed as a simple mountain man, he was really a complex person, a consummate actor and, in later years, something of a misanthrope. Around the turn of the twentieth century when the railroad first reached Webster Springs and hotels were being built to house the influx of tourists, the 'sports' wanted a typical mountain man, and Rimfire, with his tall stature, gangling walk, sad face, and the ever-present rimfire rifle fit the part.

"For the twenty-five years or so that Webster Springs was a tourist mecca, he cultivated this image, both in appearance and in speech. Weekends, during the tourist season, he would catch the West Virginia Midland train to Holly Junction, catch the B & O train to Clarksburg, and wind up at the Waldo Hotel, where he would give a little speech or talk that always ended with his exit line, 'I'm going back to my little old mountain home.' His 'little old mountain home' was, however, a two-story mansion in Webster Springs."

It is generally believed that the name Rimfire originated when he worked at the Webster Springs Hotel. The most familiar version involved J.W. Wooddell, the manager. He supposedly asked Rimfire one day how he killed the chickens that were served at the hotel, and supposedly Rimfire replied with the now familiar line, "With a rimfire rifle, by God."

The adverb *supposedly* is a popular one with those who write about Rimfire. Supposedly, circuit judge Jake Fisher gave Rimfire the rifle. Around the end of World War I, Fisher and others built a clubhouse on Elk above Bergoo. The fishing was spectacular in that roadless time, and Rimfire was a frequent and welcome guest. Members of the club got together, so the story goes, and presented him with the .25 caliber rimfire rifle.

An article in the *Richwood News Leader*, date and author unknown, said that John T. McGraw, who owned the hotel, gave Rimfire the name because on hunting trips Rimfire carried a .25 caliber rimfire rifle. The article said Rimfire himself told this version.

- - -

In 1915, Rimfire was one of the organizers of the Rimfire Scouts of America, and held the title chief scout. Ward Huffman, a Webster Springs businessman, wrote that it was the duty of Rimfire to count the ballots taken for scouts who were up for induction. "It was usually a long, drawn out affair," said Huffman, as old Rim could hardly count." One time the ballot box was being "stuffed" by prankish boys, and Rimfire looked out over the top of his glasses with his gray eyes and said: "I 'saze' brethren, there is something wrong here. There has been more ballots cast than there are brethren present."

Rimfire had a fling at courting votes instead of counting them. In 1932, he was persuaded by the Republican party to run for the State Senate in the district that included Braxton, Calhoun, Gilmer, Pocahontas, and Webster Counties. Obviously the thinking was that his renown would translate to victory at the polls. Wade Pepper wrote one of the more memorable campaign slogans in the history of West Virginia politics: "You put him at the Capitol in bronze, now put him there in person." Pepper was referring to the mountaineer statue that stands on the Capitol grounds in Charleston. There is a popular perception that Rimfire modeled for the statue, which may not be true.

Pepper's slogan for Rimfire had its counterpart in modern times when my former colleague at *the Gazette*, Danny Wells, was elected to the House of Delegates from Kanawha County in 2004. His slogan was a quote attributed to his wife Sandy: "Get him out of my house and into yours."

The Rimfire slogan might have worked in another time. But Rimfire had the misfortune of being a Republican in what turned out to be an overwhelmingly Democratic year as Franklin D. Roosevelt swept to the presidency and carried most Democrats around the country into office with him. He was defeated by Albert Mathews of Calhoun County, 19,442 to 11,086.

- - -

Rimfire was an anomaly in a family of high achievers. Kelly Ben, the patriarch, was a farmer and merchant, and when he moved to Webster Springs he built a two-story home that he lived in, and a large store building that he rented. He appreciated the value of a dollar, and it is said that when he died in 1906 he had over $45,000 in the bank, a tidy sum for that day.

Of his sons, Simpson and Isaac became ministers, Bearskin Bill became a merchant, George became a merchant and funeral director, and Arnold, Adam, Felix, and Ellis became farmers. Adam was the only one who remained on Leatherwood Creek all his life. In Mark Romano's *Pictorial History of Webster County* there is a picture of him attending a singing school taught by Singing Sam Simmons.

Of Kelly Ben's daughters, Mariah, Diana, Elizabeth Jane, and Rebecca became housewives, and Mary became a teacher. There is a story told about Rimfire receiving the news of Mary's death in a car wreck in Clay County. A young girl was sent to tell him. He had grown hard of hearing, and she was having difficulty getting him to understand. Finally, Dr. J.M. Cofer said "Rim, she's trying to tell you that your sister was killed in a car wreck." Rimfire supposedly (that adverb again) looked up and rather truculently replied, "What do you expect me to do about it?"

Les Hamrick is ambivalent about Rimfire. "He had a huge following. He worked in a public place [the hotel], and he had a way with words. He perhaps had the misfortune of coming from a high-powered family. The rest of the male members of the family were serious business people. Rimfire was cut of a totally different cloth. He was a free spirit who took life as it came.

"He was more of a fisherman than a hunter. He came of age in a time when he saw too many people using too little land. They killed off the deer and bear almost to extinction. If there is any legacy for Rimfire, that's it. He spoke out against the trend, and anybody who likes the outdoors owes him at least a nod."

In the 1931 hospital interview, Rimfire virtually repented of shooting deer. "I was thinking today as I viewed my broken leg," he said, "if I would ever have the heart to shoot another deer. As innocent and crafty an animal really deserves a better fate than to be crippled by the gun and suffer like I know they must."

- - -

The centerpiece of the Rimfire story, and that of his brother Ellis, stands seven feet tall in bronze on the northeast corner of the State Capitol grounds in Charleston. The statue is called the Mountaineer Soldier, or Union Soldiers Monument. Another title is The Mountaineer, and that is the way most West Virginians over the years have perceived it: the typical mountaineer. And they have perceived the typical mountaineer as being Rimfire.

The statue was unveiled on a sunny December 10, 1912, at the old capitol downtown. Governor William Glasscock and governor-elect H.D. Hatfield were in attendance. Collier's and Harper's Magazines covered the event, a band played, and the state militia fired a salute.

The next day *the Charleston Gazette* devoted extensive coverage to the story, including pictures of William Seymour Edwards, who commissioned it, and Henry K. Bush-Brown, who sculpted it. Bush-Brown was a giant among American sculptors. Three of his works stand on the Civil War battlefield at Gettysburg, and a fourth stands at the national cemetery where Lincoln delivered his Gettysburg Address.

Edwards gave a speech that apparently didn't mention either Rimfire or Ellis. He was quoted as saying that the figure was that of no single man, but instead a composite. The newspaper story said that the first series of serious sketches and models were prepared by Bush-Brown, and later he spent time in the mountains of West Virginia "gaining familiarity with the West Virginia mountaineer that he has now so successfully portrayed."

The question becomes whether Rimfire and Ellis were among those sketched by Bush-Brown, and did one or both of them model for the sculptor? Rimfire said in a 1920 interview that Bush-Brown did sketch him at the jewelry shop in Webster Springs.

Sampson Miller, writing in *Annals of Webster County*, said that Ellis was the one who posed, and he cites Rimfire as his source. "He told me," Miller wrote, "that he did not pose or model for the mountaineer statue, but that he attended the unveiling. He said that after the unveiling the governor said to him, What do you think of your brother's statue? He replied, it should have been mine."

The Ellis Hamrick family holds an annual reunion in Circleville, Ohio, where George Hamrick, the only surviving son of Ellis and Georgianna Ambler Hamrick, lives. In 2002, the family divided into teams and, in good fun, debated the "Who Posed?" question.

There is no doubt in the mind of Bettie Hamrick Clark, Ellis Hamrick's only surviving daughter. "My father went to Washington to pose," she told me when I interviewed her and George in May 2003 in the rolling southern Ohio farm country where their father lived the final seventeen years of his life.

Over lunch at the original Bob Evans Restaurant, Bettie said that Ellis' family grew up believing that he modeled for the statue. "Father never mentioned modeling or being sketched that I know of," she said, "but our family belief is that the sculptor selected him because of his physique."

At six feet six and 280 pounds, Ellis Hamrick was indeed of imposing size. At one time he weighed 315 pounds. Among today's gargantuan football players, he would have stood out in a crowd of them. One of Ellis' sons, Charles, played three years of varsity football at Ohio State, and in 1936 was named to the All-America team as a 230-pound tackle.

Bettie said there once existed photographic evidence that Ellis was in Washington around the time the statue was being created. A postcard size picture that has become lost over the years showed him with William Howard Taft, who was president from 1909 to 1913. She showed me another picture which may close the case. It is a picture of the completed statue, with the following inscription in faded ink: "*To Ellis Hamrick with compliments of H.K. Bush-Brown.*"

Bettie accepts that many West Virginians prefer to believe that Rimfire was the one who posed. "Uncle Eli was a West Virginia legend," she said, "while my father left the state and never returned to live."

In July 1932, Ellis returned to Webster County for what proved to be a final visit. He had become sick, and thought that the Webster Springs salt sulfur water might help him. While there he became gravely ill, and died of liver cancer on July 26, 1932, in a Charleston hospital at age fifty-three. He and his wife, who died in 1949, are buried in the Mound Hill Cemetery that overlooks the Ohio River at Gallipolis.

- - -

Rimfire's residence of record from 1906 until his death in 1945 was his parents' home in Webster Springs known as "the Kelly Ben mansion house," a two-story structure on the hill near the courthouse. After Kelly Ben died in 1906, Rimfire lived there with his mother until her death in 1917. She had previously deeded the house to him.

In his final years, Rimfire was cared for by Raleigh and Eula Hamrick Gregory. Raleigh Gregory owned a gas station and tire dealership in Webster Springs, and was town recorder, and a fishing companion of Rimfire. He once said that Rimfire would wrap bread dough in oil cloth, put it in a scooped-out hole in the ground, place hot coals over it, and they would have fresh baked bread around their campfire.

At some point, Rimfire asked the Gregorys to move in with him, and they did. In a handwritten will dated November 7, 1942, Rimfire gave the house and his personal possessions to Raleigh. The house burned in 1980, and Raleigh and Eula rebuilt on the same site. The present owners of the Raleigh and Eula Gregory house are Greg and Carol Stout.

Rimfire liked rye whiskey. One evening after a few sips of the nectar he said, "Raleigh, you know what makes a good drink? Pour all the 'Coley' out of a bottle except a small amount, and then refill it with rye whiskey." When soda pop came along, Rimfire called it 'Coley,' as in cola, no matter what kind it was.

He had a fondness for ginger snaps, and he liked the combination of ginger snaps and rye whiskey. He would sip the whiskey and chase it with ginger snaps. Sometimes in mellow moments he would sing a little song which went like this: "Zella went to Bill Cogar's and never came back, never came back." Zella was his former wife; Bill Cogar was her father.

When Joe and Bill Talbott were small boys, they lived beside the Gregorys and Rimfire. They recall that Rimfire kept raccoons in a pen in the yard, including three white ones. "I have this faint recollection of Rimfire peeling apples for his coons," said Joe.

Rimfire died on the morning of Sunday, April 1, 1945, in an upstairs bedroom of the Kelly Ben house following a ten-day illness. He was seventy-seven years and three days old. He once said that he felt so good that he believed he would live to be a hundred, but he didn't come close.

He is buried in the Hamrick Cemetery near where he lived. I went there on a warm early spring day in March 2003 when ramps were beginning to come up. The inscription on his tombstone says: "Eli (Rimfire) Hamrick. West Virginia's Typical Mountaineer."

(above) Rimfire Tombstone
(below) The Statehouse statue, Charleston, WV

~ Thirteen ~

Point Mountain

The Fatherland

West Virginia was born and grew up on Point Mountain, the summit that divides the drainages of Elk and the Back Fork. The road and the mountain perfectly present the West Virginia hills. When John Denver stepped onto the stage at the Cultural Center in Charleston with Larry Groce in that memorable midnight moment in 1985 and sang *Country Roads*, they could have been singing about the drive over Point Mountain.

The mountain runs for twenty-five miles in an east-west orientation from Valley Head in Randolph County to Webster Springs. Mountains tend to run in a north-south orientation, Point Mountain being an exception. The highest elevation on the highway is 3,872 feet at the Randolph-Webster line near Monterville. The highest elevation *on the mountain* is 3,979 feet two miles west of Monterville.

Point Mountain is locally famous for its severe winter weather, as is the Randolph County village of Pickens, which is located twelve miles from Monterville. Any family album of longtime Point Mountain residents will show pictures of snow piled everywhere. District forester Jim Hays with the State Forestry Division said he has seen remnants of snow in the ditch lines in late June after an especially bad winter.

Carol Warren, who lives about a half-mile off Route 15 near the Point Mountain Fire Tower, told me that she and her husband, Todd Garland, have used snowshoes to reach their home every winter in the ten years that they've lived there. The winter of 1995-96 was particularly severe, with a total of three hundred inches of snow and a single storm depth of forty-two inches. The deepest snowfall of the winter of 2004-05 was "only" two feet, but it came on top of fourteen inches already on the ground. "We've had snow on May 19, my birthday," she said.

I made several trips to Point Mountain and the upper Back Fork in the process of writing this book, and I carefully scheduled them to escape any possibility of snow, or so I thought. But on April 27, 2004, when I was certain it was safe to return to The Fatherland, as I named Point Mountain, I encountered a whiteout snowstorm.

My host on that trip was Wayne Eads, who lives at Curtin but grew up at Waneta, a former coal mining community on Point Mountain. He was less surprised by the snow than I was, and seemed to think it wouldn't be necessary, as I had suggested, to drop off the mountain to Elk to escape a repeat of the blizzard of 1888 or some such cataclysmic event.

Instead, he changed the subject. "There were once two hundred and fifty people who got their mail at the Waneta Post Office at the Loy McAtee Store," he said. "There were probably thirty-two company houses in the area, but they are all are gone now." At the moment, I believed I understood why.

The mine was Pardee and Curtin's No. 4. The coal was transported down to the tipple at Camp Four in monitors, or covered coal cars. The cable system enabled the loaded cars to pull the empties back up the mountain. A cluster of nineteen houses at the No. 4 mine was called Dogpatch for the mythical town in the comic strip Li'l Abner.

An apocryphal story is told about Boots Hall, who worked at No. 4 and liked to rabbit hunt. Earlier he had lived in Kentucky, and during a snow he tracked a rabbit all the way from Kentucky to Webster County, so the story goes. When the snow disappeared, he couldn't find his way back to Kentucky, so he stayed in Webster County the rest of his life.

I am haunted by fire towers. I like to climb them for the view, but I find it scary when they tremble and sway in the wind. Sadly, most of them are gone, but the one on Point Mountain remains, one of the few to survive after foresters began using airplanes. It owes its afterlife to a decision by the State Forestry Division, the Webster County EMS, and the Division of Natural Resources to use it as a communications tower.

It stands proudly ten miles east of Webster Springs at an elevation of 3,538 feet, the highest point on the western end of the mountain. The view is toward Hodam Mountain to the north and across Elk to Red Oak Knob to the south.

The wind picked up in intensity and the sky was darkening to the east, a precursor of the approaching snow squall, as Wayne and I walked up to the one hundred foot tower and saw the sign, "Climb at your own risk." Wayne told me he had once carried his oldest daughter, Rhonda, 3, to the top of the tower when his father-in-law, Orden 'Pipe' Hamrick, was warden there in the 1970s.

The least I could do was climb it on the day of our visit, although I hedged by saying that I'd probably only go halfway. As it turned out, that's exactly what I did. At the halfway point I could feel the tower trembling in the wind, and my resolve flickered and then went out completely like a candle hid under a bushel.

Trembling Tower is the successor to the original, a wooden tower that was located on Noah Bonner Ridge, a steep and rocky thrust of land on the Elk side of Point Mountain above Bergoo. It was also located near Hoot Owl Ridge, which should pinpoint it to everybody's satisfaction.

- - -

There were five schools on Point Mountain. In order, starting at the Webster Springs end, were Sunrise, Lower Point Mountain, Big Swamps, Waneta, and No. 4. Sunrise was named when the school was being built on the Ray Hamrick farm, and the workmen were inspired by the sight of the sun coming over the horizon and slicing through the fog. Big Swamps School was named for a swampy area about halfway out the mountain. When the Summersville and Slaven Cabin Turnpike was built in 1856, chestnut logs were cut and placed in the bog as a corduroy road.

Locally famous, like the weather, is Buffalo Bull Knob, or just Buffalo Knob, which is where tradition says Isaac Gregory shot the last buffalo in Webster County (see End of the Line). The Webster County Watershed Association put up a sign in memory of Last Buffalo, and is also restoring a spring and concrete water box near the site of the buffalo's demise. The water box was built by the Civilian Conservation Corps in the 1930s for a very useful purpose: cars chugging up Point Mountain invariably overheated, and motorists could stop and take on water, like the Shay engines at Cass.

The oldest structure still standing is Point Mountain Community Church, which was built in 1892 by the Methodists, and renovated in 1987 as a community church. It is well worth a visit in the spring when its large cemetery is carpeted with a showy red phlox. Among the graves are those of woodchopping legend Paul Criss (see The Choppers), horseback mail carrier Lee Hamrick, author Ray Hamrick, and Esta Cowger Dodrill, the first elected woman sheriff in West Virginia.

Homer Riggleman wrote of Lee Hamrick: "He was a great character, one of the great mountaineers. He was known, I suppose, by more people in Webster and Randolph Counties than any other person. He had a little store and a little filling station. Kept a little stock. Owned some coal land and some timber. Carried the mail from Waneta to Bernardstown three days a week on horseback. When the automobile came out, he bought a Model T Ford. He never drove a car himself. His grandsons drove his cars for him all the time, and they kept them pretty well torn up."

Esta Cowger Dodrill was elected sheriff of Webster County in 1960, and served from 1961 to 1964. A reporter from Charleston came up to interview her, and asked for a comment about herself. "Well," she replied, "I put up one hundred quarts of beans today."

She was the mother of Dudley Dodrill, who accompanied me one day to Point Mountain. Dudley showed me his homeplace, where Perry and Norma Mollohan now live. We walked down through the meadow to a large rock in the woods that his family called Indian Rock because Indians supposedly sheltered under it and prayed to the Great Spirit from its expansive top.

On the way back from Indian Rock, Dudley became "overheated" in the sultry weather, like cars climbing Point Mountain long ago. Norma gave him cold water from the same spring he knew as a youngster, and he soon felt better.

- - -

Point Mountain is reunion country. There is the Point Mountain Community Reunion that is held on the Lee Hamrick farm near Waneta, the Upper Point Mountain School Reunion at the Albert McAtee place, and the granddaddy of them all, the Hamrick-Gregory Reunion, now called the Pioneer Family Reunion.

The Hamrick-Gregory gathering started informally in 1926 at the head of Little Run Hollow, where, according to legend, the original "picnic table" was a flat rock. In 1927 it was moved to Moore Hamrick's yard, and the next year to his chestnut orchard. Later it was held at the Henry Beckwith farm, but in 1954 land was acquired for the present reunion park back on the Moore Hamrick farm.

This granddaddy reunion grew out of summer picnic gatherings after church. In its heyday, it attracted huge crowds, and speakers over the years have included the likes of senators and governors. Senator Jennings Randolph rarely missed a Hamrick-Gregory reunion.

"If you wanted the vote in Webster County, you showed up," said Les Hamrick, author of *Roots & Wings*, the Hamrick family genealogy.

Bill Byrne, author of *Tale of the Elk*, spoke at the 1935 reunion, as did Governor H.G. Kump, Senator M.M. Neely, and Senator Rush D. Holt. A 1937 speaker was native son Rimfire Hamrick. Leonard Riggleman, the Cowger's Mill native who became president of Morris Harvey College (now University of Charleston), spoke in 1954 and 1955. Another 1955 speaker was Cal Price, legendary editor of *the Pocahontas Times*.

Little Run Hollow, the original site of the Hamrick-Gregory Reunion, begins a stone's throw from Bill Gillespie's camp, which sits on a knoll at over thirty eight hundred feet elevation with a nice view toward the Back Fork country.

One steamy day in June 2003, Peter and Elizabeth Silitch and I stopped there for a rest. Bill wasn't "home," but the Point Mountain breeze was. We relaxed on his front porch and drank in the view of West Virginia's Fatherland.

Earlier that summer I visited Ivan and Anna Dodrill, who live near Monterville. Anna attended the first Hamrick-Gregory Reunion in 1926 at age three, and hasn't missed one since. She recalls when people came on horseback, wagon, and automobile, an eclectic mix that would intermingle on the reunion campground. Anna is the granddaughter of Moore Hamrick.

She is famous for her Hummingbird cake. I was tempted to ask how many of the tiny birds are required, but perhaps she saw the words forming on my lips and saved me the trouble. "The ingredients," she said, "are crushed pineapple, chopped nuts, chopped bananas, three eggs, flour, sugar, soda, salt, cinnamon, and vegetable oil." Ivan, who helps bake the cake, nodded. "No hummingbirds," he said.

The reunion wasn't held during the World War II years of 1942-45, a time that Ivan remembers well as a rifleman in the 83rd Infantry. On the wall of his home is a Purple Heart and three clusters, representing the four times he was wounded in France and Germany.

- - -

Perhaps it is the soil or climate, but Point Mountain grows good apples. In the old days, Point Mountain apples were put to their best and highest use in making applejack, the colloquial name for apple brandy, or distilled apple cider.

"The apples didn't look like much," said Les Hamrick, "but they made great applejack." Once at the Hamrick-Gregory Reunion, Les mentioned that he'd like to have some good applejack. Nobody said anything, but as he left the reunion grounds, a bottle of this nectar of the gods rolled out from under the seat of his car, wrapped in a beach towel.

From post-Civil War days into the 1940s, Point Mountain apple-jack was something to be cherished as well as clothed in a veil of secrecy. "The credo," said Les, "was still your apples and keep your mouth shut."

Maybe the making of applejack on Point Mountain is a thing of the past. I inquired of several people if it was still being made, and the answers ranged from the all-purpose "Not that I know of" to a silent negative shake of the head.

Some of the apple trees may be descendants of those planted by Henry Moore, a native of Clinton, Maine, who came to Point Mountain around 1850. Nobody ever knew why he left Maine, or why he came to Point Mountain. He acquired four hundred acres on the mountain, and then made a journey back to New York State and returned with apple and other fruit trees.

Later owners of the Moore farm, or at least a large chunk of it, were the Bonners, starting in 1913 when brothers George and Lee Bonner bought the farm from Currence Chapman. The Bonner presence on Point Mountain would continue for the next eighty-two years.

Parker Bonner, George's son, was born there in 1920 and lived on the mountain until he sold the property in 1995 and he and his sister, Viola, moved to Webster Springs. I visited them in early April 2004. From their window, we could see Point Mountain blanketed in a robust coating of snow. The western end of the mountain reaches into Webster Springs in the vicinity of Morton Hill, the courthouse, and the post office.

I returned in June 2004 and Parker and I drove to his old home-place. I admired a large red spruce that stands in the yard, towering over the house. Parker told me the story of the tree. Currence Chapman had a store on Point Mountain, and he drove a horse and wagon to the railroad at Pickens for supplies. On one trip, he dug up the spruce, brought it back, and planted it. "I was always afraid lightning would strike it," said Parker, "but it never did."

The two hundred and seventy six acre Bonner farm is

Parker Bonner at his homeplace

located just west of Waneta. Lou Fletcher, who was staying there on the day I visited the farm with Parker, said he had been competing with local bears for Early Transparent apples that grow on the farm. "I went out to the tree one day," Lou said, "and the apples weren't quite ready. I went back in a few days and the bears had eaten them all."

Thinking about this later, I thought that maybe instead of the bears eating the apples, they had drunk them. I've been asking the wrong people, I concluded, about whether applejack is still being made on Point Mountain.

Elk tributaries Granddaddy Run, Baltimore Run, and Coalbank Run all head on the farm. There is a splendid view looking south toward Elk, a view that includes Red Oak Knob, Gauley Mountain, and, light blue in the distance, Cheat Mountain. Lou said that in winter he can see the lights at Snowshoe Mountain Resort when they are turned on for night skiing.

Parker raised cattle, timbered, and worked at the Pardee and Curtin No. 4 mine. As a youngster, he once turned the grindstone that sharpened the axe of Bearskin Bill Hamrick (see Bergoo). Parker and his father were sharpening a mower bar at the farm when Bearskin came along, heading down to the Back Fork to cut a bee tree. He planned to cut a tree as a "bridge" over the Back Fork, and then cut the bee tree. "He was a powerful woodsman," said Parker.

Parker told me about shoveling paths through the snow to his mailbox, or to uncover his car to go to work at the mine, if getting to work was possible. He said that a neighbor had this pithy comment about Point Mountain winters: "That cold north wind blowing right out of the east would freeze a man to death."

- - -

From Parker's homeplace, we continued to Turkeybone Mountain, where I wanted to photograph Turkeybone School (see The Back Fork). On the way, he told me about the Snoring Ghost of Point Mountain. His grandfather, John Bonner, and uncle, Harmon Bonner, were spending the night in a vacant house while they worked on the house and the property.

"My grandfather was asleep and snoring loudly," said Parker. "My uncle was awake, and he heard footsteps on the porch and then in the first floor of the house. It was two men who, his uncle believed, were moving from one logging camp to another, and had spent the night there on previous occasions. When they heard the 'snoring ghost,' they ran out of the house and kept on running."

Going out the Pickens Road toward the school, we drove through a portion of Kumbrabow State Forest, a green and inviting oasis in an otherwise heavily timbered area. Most of Kumbrabow lies on the Buckhannon River drainage, a secondary portion on the Tygart River drainage, and a small portion on the Back Fork drainage.

Kumbrabow was the focus of a high profile court case in 1995 that went to the State Supreme Court and resulted in a decision favorable to the State Forestry Division. The West Virginia Highlands Conservancy had challenged a proposed timber sale at Kumbrabow, but the high court ruled that the state had the right to harvest and sell timber from its forests. The timbering went forward, although none has been done since.

The 9,165 acre Kumbrabow is one of the oldest state forests, having been purchased from the Midland Corporation in December 1934. The origin of the name Kumbrabow stumped us both, and I made a mental note to check it out. I photographed Turkeybone School, and we headed back to Point Mountain. It was a gloriously warm and sunny day, and I envied those who live on that high mountain in the heartland of West Virginia. I envy them in summertime, that is.

The next day, I called Dave Lilly at the State Forestry office in Charleston, and he explained the origin of the name. It is a combination of the surnames of the three men who were instrumental in its purchase as a state forest: Governor Herman G. Kump, Spates Brady, and Hubert Bowers.

There was to be yet another trip out the Pickens road. The pictures I took of the schoolhouse were not of book quality, I was told in funereal tones by Neal Gentry, my design and layout man who hands out life and death decisions under the corporate name of Wolfpen Digital. Something about a low megapixel count. I first thought I was coming down with a fatal illness, but fortunately for me it was the camera that was sick and dying.

I returned with Parker Bonner and my neighbor Denzil Baughman, and a different camera that had been declared healthy by a panel of doctors. Parker and Denzil stood behind me, hands hovering over their holsters, the sun at their backs. I circled the little school, pointed the lens menacingly, and clicked the shutter with the rapidity of an Old West gunfighter fanning the hammer of a Colt .45. The pictures were okay, I suppose.

~ Fourteen ~

Webster Springs

A Town Well Named

Three mountains loom over Webster Springs: Miller Mountain to the north, McGuire Mountain to the south, and Point Mountain to the east. Elk River flows through a steep canyon to the west, completing the picture of a town held captive by its own terrain and lying in an immeasurable abyss. Visitors approaching Webster Springs for the first time can be forgiven for thinking that the only way to gain entry is to be born there.

One of the "sink or swim" airplane rides of all time must have been the takeoff from the old Skyline Airport on Miller Mountain. Once airborne from the nine hundred foot grass strip, the pilot was immediately out over the precipitous mountainside, with the town far below. Because of a line of trees on one end of the runway, the approach for a landing dictated the same route back over the town.

The road sign upon entering Webster Springs could read, Welcome to Elk Lick, Fork Lick, Webster Court House, Addison, and Webster Springs. Pop. 818. The sign would be right in all instances.

In earlier times, elk, deer, and buffalo came to lick at the salt sulfur spring that seeped out from underground on a rocky bar near where Elk River and the Back Fork of Elk met in splendid isolation. Hence the name Elk Lick, which was the original and unofficial designation of Webster Springs. Elk disappeared from Webster County in 1815, but the name Elk Lick still resonates.

The first official name was Fork Lick, which was bestowed in 1852 by a Virginia General Assembly that obviously didn't appreciate what a great name for a town Elk Lick is, and how perfectly it matched the river that flows by.

Fork Lick was also the first post office name. The post office was opened on May 31, 1852, and the first postmaster was John E. Hall. Retired postmaster Philip Cooper and the late Webster County historian Sampson Miller collected pictures of most of the previous postmasters, including Hall, and they are displayed in the post office lobby on Back Fork Street.

On January 10, 1860, Webster became the last county created before our separation from the mother state of Virginia. There is a partly apocryphal story which claims that Webster County didn't become organized along traditional county lines, with elected officials and such, until near the end of the Civil War. But it didn't matter much because Webster Countians were an isolated and independent sort who had paid no attention to outside authority before, and still didn't.

The wheels of organization edged slowly forward. In 1861, Fork Lick became Webster Court House, and remained that way until the town was incorporated as Addison in 1886 in recognition of Addison McLaughlin, who donated the land for the Courthouse Square.

McLaughlin was a native of Richmond, Virginia, who later came to what is now West Virginia, became a lawyer, was elected to the Virginia General Assembly, owned land in Webster, Nicholas, and Braxton Counties, and engaged in the saltworks business.

There is a clause in the McLaughlin deed which stipulates that Courthouse Square will return to McLaughlin's "heirs, assessors, and assignees" if the town should cease being officially called Addison. The spectre of a great multitude of people descending on the courthouse to assert their ownership in the Webster County seat of government is a chilling one.

The first courthouse was built around 1865. It was burned on June 17, 1888, allegedly by arsonists seeking to destroy legal records. The county court met for six years in the First Baptist Church, which is located behind the present courthouse, until a new courthouse was completed in March 1896.

Webster County Courthouse

The street leading to Courthouse Square, and the streets on two sides of the square, were paved in 1904, and were thought to be the first paved concrete streets in the nation. It turned out that wasn't the case, but they *were* the first in West Virginia. The Portland Cement Association said the city of Belfontaine, Ohio, paved the streets around its courthouse in 1891-93.

On April 7, 1902, the U.S. Post Office Department gave the name Webster Springs to the post office. The agency may have done this in acquiescence to those who wanted to capitalize commercially on the salt sulfur water, but whatever the motive the name accurately reflected the town's status as a mountain resort.

- - -

The years of Webster Springs as a resort town were roughly from 1897, when the original version of the legendary Webster Springs Hotel was built, until 1925 when the enlarged version burned. It stood in majestic splendor in the broad river bottom that today is known as Hotel Bottom. The Mineral Springs Motel is located near where the old hotel stood.

It is difficult to imagine that such a large hotel once existed in such a remote setting. In 1925, the hotel was larger than The Greenbrier at White Sulphur Springs - 265 rooms versus 250. Greenbrier historian Robert Conte explained: "The Greenbrier, which had opened in 1913, was considerably smaller than it is today. It underwent a dramatic expansion in 1931, bringing it close to today's size of 600 rooms. I am speaking solely of the hotel building. There were cottages here in 1925 but I do not believe I could come up with a very accurate estimate of the number of rooms in those cottages at that time."

The original Webster Springs Hotel was built by Johnson N. Camden, a Lewis County native who spent his childhood in Sutton. He became one of the founders of the oil industry in West Virginia and a U.S. Senator. He also brought the railroad into Cowen in 1892, and built the Camden Hotel that he envisioned would turn Camden on Gauley into a resort town. But that never panned out.

In 1903, John T. McGraw bought the Webster Springs Hotel from Camden and began a 115-room addition that was completed in the spring of 1904. McGraw was a Grafton native and a lawyer for the Baltimore and Ohio Railroad.

Of the eighty-nine non-guest rooms in the McGraw enlargement, forty were for "taking the waters." The salt sulfur baths occupied the entire first floor of one wing, and a bath cost the modest sum of one dollar.

The grand Webster Springs Hotel

McGraw wasn't the originator of the baths, but he added more of them. Perhaps more importantly, he was faithful to the hotel's Victorian summer resort style architecture.

For the hotel to flourish, a railroad was needed to bring in passengers from the outside world, and McGraw built one. It was completed in 1902. McGraw's railroad was first known as the Holly River and Addison because it ran from the Baltimore & Ohio line at Holly Junction up the Right Fork of Holly to Diana, and over the mountain to Addison, a distance of about thirty miles. It became the West Virginia Midland in 1906 with new incorporators and more money.

The arrival of the evening train was an event on the order of the "3:10 to Yuma" of Old West legend. There was a definite Old West flavor to a posed picture taken at the Webster Springs train platform that appeared in *Pictorial History of Webster County*. It showed the conductor with celebrated mountaineer Rimfire Hamrick, both holding rifles.

Oscar Marsh, grandfather of Jim Marsh (see The Wildcats), was the first conductor on the West Virginia Midland and later its general superintendent. The Midland's offices and shops were located at Palmer near Holly Junction. Palmer now lies under the waters of Sutton Lake.

The largest of many trestles on the Midland was the Clifton. It crossed a deep chasm near Diana, where the climb up the mountain began. The trestle was eighty-eight feet high on one end, and was named for

The Clifton Ford Trestle

John F. Clifton. The story is told that Clifton declined to move when the railroad was built, and passengers crossing the trestle could look down his chimney.

In addition to opening the remote town to visitors, the railroad provided its own sense of excitement. Passengers disembarked on the south side of Elk near Baker's Island, crossed the river on a swinging bridge that was called "McGraw's Lightning Express," and strolled to the hotel.

An extension of the Lightning Express was a boardwalk that became known as "McGraw's Promenade." The promenade ran from the salt sulfur well to the river, and followed the riverbank upstream to the site of the present Webster Springs Elementary School.

Although the Webster Springs Hotel was obviously the largest, it wasn't the only one during the resort era. It is said there were once thirty-one hotels in Webster Springs, although many were of today's bed and breakfast variety.

The only challenger to the resort hotel in size and Victorian elegance was the Oakland, which was named for a large grove of oaks that grew where the First Methodist Church now stands. It opened in 1904, about the same time the Webster Springs Hotel enlargement was completed. To the joy of preservationists, it still stands as an apartment building.

- - -

The fire that brought down the Webster Springs Hotel was grandiose in its own right. A yellowed Western Union telegram dated July 21, 1925, sent to Alexander & Alexander, an insurance firm in Clarksburg, serves as an epitaph for the resort hotel, which was said to have been the largest wooden structure in the state at the time of its demise. The telegram said simply: *"Webster Springs Hotel completely destroyed by fire Monday night."*

The sender of the telegram was the West Virginia Sales Company, an insurance brokerage firm in Webster Springs. A letter that followed gave further details. It said the fire was discovered about 9 p.m. and apparently originated on the fourth or attic floor in the east end of the building. It also said the origin of the fire was unknown, but was generally supposed to have been from electrical wiring. The few guests staying at the hotel at the time all escaped without injury.

Even Sam McGee from Tennessee in the memorable Robert Service poem, *The Cremation of Sam McGee*, would have gotten warm when the hotel burned. "Sparks were falling thick all over town," said a story in *the Clarksburg Exponent*, "and there were fears that other buildings would be set on fire, but the dampness of the night prevented any danger from that source."

The owners of the hotel at the time of the fire were John M. Hoover, a lawyer at Webster Springs, Dr. William York of Huntington, and Senator A. Blaine York of Washington, D.C. They had purchased the hotel from C.S. Riggs of Fairmont, who had bought it from the McGraw estate.

Present day residents of Hotel Bottom can hardly plant flowers in their yards without dredging up relics. Joe and Sue Talbott have found silverware, pottery, porcelain doorknobs, and a brass coat hanger with the year 1906 inscribed on it. Foundation stones from a portion of the hotel are visible under the grape arbor in their backyard.

When the hotel burned, only James W. Wooddell of the principal figures in its heyday was alive to know about it. Johnson N. Camden died in 1908, five years after he sold the hotel, and John T. McGraw died in 1920, five years before it burned. The West Virginia Midland Railroad lasted until June 1933.

Wooddell was a native of Green Bank, Pocahontas County. His parents, William J. and Martha Jane Gum Wooddell, came to Webster Springs in 1873. The book, *West Virginia In History, Life, Literature and Industry*, said that the elder Wooddell "engaged in the hotel business."

Upon the elder Wooddell's death in 1880, his wife assumed charge of the Wooddell Hotel, and it was there that James W. Wooddell became familiar with the hotel business. When the Webster Springs Hotel was built, "he and his mother assumed active charge of the same," according to the above book. Wooddell was manager of the hotel until 1911, when he left to manage the Willard in Grafton. In the spring of 1914, he became manager of the Waldo in Clarksburg and remained there for thirty-five years.

Wooddell died on March 1, 1953, at age seventy-nine and is buried in the Bridgeport Cemetery near Clarksburg. With his passing, the final chapter had been written to the story of the Webster Springs Hotel in its salad days.

Martha Jane Gum Wooddell, remained in Webster Springs for the rest of her life and reached the century mark. She died on December 20,

1938, at the age of one hundred years and one month. She and her husband are buried in the Wooddell Cemetery on Morton Hill.

- - -

The original salt sulfur spring that led to the resort era no longer exists, or at least cannot be seen. It was buried when a new bridge was built in 1932 over Elk on the left descending side of Baker's Island. A cement enclosure once marked the spot, but it was moved by floodwaters and eventually covered by sand and rock.

The identity of the first white settler to "discover" the original spring is open to debate. One possibility is Abram Meirs, who was credited in surveyors' notes of August 30, 1785, as the discoverer. Another possibility is John Miller Sr. and Henry McQuirter when they were staking claim to land on the Back Fork in 1784.

There is a tantalizing third possibility that surfaced in a "Re-Echo" column in *the Webster Echo* written by Wendell Ware. Citing as his source the Boston Public Records Archives, he wrote that the first white men to see Elk River may have been brothers Andrew and James Cobb, early English settlers of Massachusetts who escaped from an engagement with King Phillip's Indians and made their way down the Ohio River and up the Kanawha.

From there, the account goes, they reached the mouth of Elk and followed it to Webster Springs and beyond. They reported seeing elk, deer, bear, wolves, panthers, wild turkeys, and large numbers of smaller game. They described a salt water spring where they killed a buffalo. Their adventure ended in late summer 1675 when they came to the waters of the Potomac and reached fellow colonists.

The first salt sulfur well was drilled by John E. Hall, the town's first postmaster, and an associate identified in Sampson Miller's *Annals of Webster County* only as "Skidmore." This well was believed to have been thirty-two feet deep.

Between 1850 and 1860, Addison McLaughlin enlarged the well to a depth of 169 feet, where it produced a strong flow of salt sulfur water and spawned a hotel, a tourist era, and a water company. The Webster Water Bottling Company shipped out forty-two thousand quarts of the elixir in one season. A World War II soldier from Webster County reported seeing a bottle of Webster Springs water in Germany.

The Hall-McLaughlin well was located on the edge of Hotel Bottom behind the present apartment building for seniors. In the early 1900s, the well was enclosed by a gazebo which is a familiar image in old pictures of Webster Springs. Later the structure was replaced by a handsome pagoda roofed gazebo with stone pillars. All that is now gone except for a concrete basin.

In 1937, the Webster Springs Lions Club raised money for a new well on the Courthouse lawn which was drilled to a depth of 120 feet. West Virginia native Louis A. Johnson, the assistant secretary of war, came to town in 1938 for the inaugural Rhododendron Festival and dedicated the well house as a Veterans Memorial.

Happily, the salt sulfur water is still flowing. There are two fountains, one offering West Virginia-American Water Company water from the firm's Elk River plant, and the other offering water from the salt sulfur well. The salt taste is always there, but not necessarily the sulfur. "That's because the fountain isn't used a lot," explained Jason Hyre, who tests the water for the Webster County Commission. "But if you run it long enough, I guarantee you'll smell it and taste it."

The salt sulfur water still evokes memories of home for some. Chuck Armentrout, president of the county commission, told me that many people who formerly lived in Webster Springs and return for visits fill gallon jugs of the water to take home with them.

- - -

The year of the well house dedication was a contentious one for Webster Springs. The town council installed parking meters of the kind where a nickel was inserted and a flag pushed down. When an hour had expired, the flag popped up and a parking ticket was probable.

But there was trouble brewing. The meters were opposed by the Webster County Court and the town's businessmen, and they sought an injunction. Circuit Judge Jake Fisher ruled in favor of the plaintiffs, calling the meters "a public and private nuisance."

Battle lines had been drawn.

Mayor Kenneth White and town council appealed to the State Supreme Court, where, in June 1939, the parking meters triumphed by a vote of four to one. But the heady win didn't last. Businessmen continued to protest the loss of revenue from potential customers, and in 1940 town council reversed its course and voted the meters out. But parking meters have lives of their own. At some point, they were reinstalled. As one who has dutifully placed money in the Webster Springs parking meters, I have come to admire their gentleness of spirit and kindness of heart, and I offer this tribute:

On broad avenues of commerce you stand,
Receiving coins from all the land.
Your generosity is widely known,
For one quarter ten hours are sown.

Injunctions come and injunctions go,
The lawyers tell us it's always so.
But injunctions, like snow, do not last,
With the Supreme Court in their path.

A nuisance you well might be,
And God knows you have your fee.
But majority opinions always rule,
And four to one is very cool.

- - -

The best known island of upper Elk is Baker's Island at Webster Springs. It is twenty acres in size, boasts a municipal swimming pool, picnic facilities, baseball field, tennis court, basketball court, miniature amusement park, and the Arden Cogar Pavilion where woodchopping festivals are held.

The swimming pool is located on the upriver end. The banks where Elk sweeps around the pool have been built up, fortress-like, with rock gabions to turn aside floods that periodically fill the pool with debris. The tip of the island now resembles the bow of a large ship slicing through the waves.

Sandra Mitchell Given, who was elected mayor of Webster Springs for a fifth time in 2003, has spent a lot of time with a shovel in her hands. She was mayor in 1985 when the new swimming pool was filled with floodwater debris, and it has happened twice since, most recently in November 2003.

Baker's Island is named for J.C Baker, a Braxton County native who bought the island in 1941. He lived in Webster Springs in the early 1940s, and owned three Texaco stations and a taxi service. Sons George Baker of Gassaway and J.P. 'Preach' Baker of Summersville recall driving two big Packard taxicabs. "Webster Springs was a thriving town at that time," said Preach, "primarily because of the coal mines. We were very busy taking people to places like Parcoal, Curtin, Bergoo, and Diana."

At the time J.C. lived in Webster Springs, Baker's Island was at the mercy of Elk even more than it is now. J.C. bought a steam shovel, dredged the river channels on each side, and used the material to build up

J. C. Baker

the island.

The Army Corps of Engineers, which regulates the dredging and filling of navigable streams, showed up unhappy. Mike Baker of Gassaway, a grandson, remembers his grandfather telling him that the Corps representative spent two days in Webster Springs, saw that the project had merit from the town's standpoint, although not from the river's standpoint, and left with a reprimand. "In essence," said the grandson, "he told grandfather, don't do it again."

In 1971, J.C. leased the island to the town for one dollar a year. In 1996, J.C Baker and Sons, a Gassaway firm, donated the island to the town with the stipulation that it always be used for public recreation.

- - -

A legend of the taxi era in Webster Springs was Elsie Hamrick, who drove for fifty years. Her taxi "stand" was a phone on the side of the Nichols Building, which housed a hardware store and funeral home. She would park beside the building and wait for calls.

She also owned The Custard Stand. The hot dogs were called "Elsie's Dogs." "My brother Kevin and I grew up on Elsie Dogs," said Kenney Hamrick Jr.

Webster County magistrate Gary Payne, Elsie's nephew, recalls that his aunt "drove all over the state." The Department of Welfare hired her to take clients to doctors and hospitals, and during World War II she took servicemen to military bases.

Elsie drove until 1995, when she fell and broke her hip. She passed away in 2000.

Kenney Hamrick Sr., who died in 2004, was also a driving legend in Webster Springs, but of a different kind. He was one of the pioneers on the Grand National Circuit, which was the predecessor of NASCAR. He competed against the likes of Lee Petty, Buck Baker, and Ralph Earnhart.

Sons Kenney Jr. and Kevin are carrying on the tradition. Kevin competes in super late model races, and Kenney is his crew chief. Kenney works for the Department of Highways, and Kevin works for the West

Virginia-American Water Company.

Their father leased and operated J.C. Baker's Texaco stations. "I always tell people," said Kenney, "that Kevin and I slept at our home on the Back Fork, but were raised at the service stations. It seems like I was pumping gas when I was still in diapers."

Kenney Hamrick Sr. drove a red 1934 Ford coupe in races in West Virginia, Pennsylvania, Ohio, and Virginia. "Racing was an obsession with him," said Kenney Jr. "There were no tracks around here, so he went outside the area."

In a 1953 race at Elkins he won the feature in a memorable way. As the race ended, his throttle stuck and he sailed by the flagman and continued around the turn at full speed. He vaulted over a safety fence and crashed through a ten-foot high board fence, then made a "U" turn and came back through the pit gate to claim the checkered flag.

- - -

Perhaps there is something in the mountain air or salt sulfur water that has spawned memorable legislators from Webster County. The first was Eskridge H. Morton, who is credited with writing the original highway law in West Virginia that became the framework of the present highway system.

The amendment authorized the selling of bonds for road construction, and when Morton returned home he went to work campaigning for a $250,000 bond issue. It passed, and the money was used for construction of the Cowen to Webster Springs, Diana to Webster Springs, and Point Mountain roads.

His son, Ernest V. Morton, followed in his footsteps and practiced at various places around the state, and grandson "Jack" Morton has been practicing in Webster Springs for sixty years. He became a legend for rarely losing a case either as prosecutor or defense attorney. One time at the end of a trial, the defendant broke away and jumped head first out the third floor courthouse window. He broke both legs, and didn't go any farther except to jail

Jack lost one race for prosecutor. "Dad didn't take sides in a coal mine strike," said daughter Cathy, who teaches at Webster Springs Elementary School and lives in the house that her great grandfather designed and built in 1909. "He took the position that the law was the law, and the result was that both sides got mad at him."

An icon in West Virginia political circles was Hans McCourt, who served seventeen years in the Legislature, including ten years as chairman of the Senate Finance Committee. He was president of the Senate in 1971-72. "He was politically powerful for two reasons," said retired judge and legislator Albert 'Boonie' Sommerville. "One was by virtue of his position as chairman of the Finance Committee. The other was that he was a very strong willed person."

"Hans McCourt was the consummate politician," said Jack Morton. "Although gruff in a way, he was likeable, had a quick wit, and was accommodating. He got along well with people."

The Charleston Gazette referred to him as "the gentleman farmer" because he lived on a farm on the Back Fork. John Morgan, retired State-house reporter, recalled one time when the Senate was debating an egg bill that Hans stood up and clucked like a chicken.

His enduring legacy as a legislator is "The Million Dollar Bridge," also called "The Bridge to Nowhere," which was built over Elk at Clifton Ford below Webster Springs in 1973. "The Bridge to Nowhere" was an obvious appellation because it sits in a remote area, but the "Million Dollar" designation is less defensible. Records at the Department of Highways in Charleston show that the bridge actually cost about $450,000. But calling it "The Half Million Dollar Bridge" wouldn't have had the same resonance.

McCourt envisioned the bridge as the first phase of a project that would eventually include a road up Elk from Sutton to Webster Springs. The road hasn't been built yet, although it is still talked about, and the Department of Highways held a public meeting as recently as 1998.

The story is told that one day Governor Arch Moore called Hans into his office, and asked for his help in getting three bills passed. "When I see equipment sitting at the bridge site, you'll get your three bills passed," Hans supposedly replied.

Hans and his wife, Georgie, died the same day on August 3, 1992. Georgie died at Webster County Memorial Hospital, and Hans died seventeen hours later at St. Joseph's Hospital in Buckhannon. They are buried above the Back Fork.

Randy White, former Webster Springs mayor and present state senator, believes the "up Elk" road will eventually be built, although he gives himself some leeway. "I think it will be built in my lifetime," he says, "but I'm counting on a fairly good record of longevity in my family."

Randy was elected to the House of Delegates in 1996, 1998, and 2000, to the Senate in 2002, and served six terms as mayor.

- - -

Boonie Sommerville served four terms in the House of Delegates, and twenty years as a circuit judge. He is also a continent-trotting fisherman, and a coon hunter. But I know him best for the time we went looking for the elusive grave of a 116-year-old man.

Boonie had been squirrel hunting in a remote area above the Right Fork of Holly, and told me that he came upon this grave. I immediately thought, there lies the oldest man who ever lived on the Elk drainage, and I asked directions. He shrugged in the manner of someone who recognizes a lost cause when he sees one, and volunteered to take me there.

We bounced over logging roads and deer trails for what seemed like days, and finally topped out on a ridge that divides the Right Fork and Left Fork drainages. I saw the cemetery, and my excitement grew.

But the grave wasn't there.

There were probably twenty graves, but not of anyone who had lived almost as long as Moses. We considered the possibility that the tombstone had been stolen, but there was no evidence of that. Maybe Ancient One had been moved elsewhere, but there was no evidence of that either, and evidence is of some importance to a judge and a writer.

We continued to search, and in doing so I came to know intimately, in a manner of speaking, all the occupants of this cemetery on the high ridge in the woods. All except one. The 116-year-old man. May he rest in peace wherever he is.

Boonie served ten years in the West Virginia House of Delegates, including four years as chairman of the House Judiciary Committee. In 1967, he was dubbed "freshman legislator of the year" by *Charleston Gazette* editor and political columnist Harry Hoffmann. The two became close friends, and would solve the world's problems over a drink in Boonie's office. "I'd invite him to stop by after a session," said Boonie. "I always thought he had the best grasp of the big picture of any political columnist I ever knew."

Boonie left the legislature in 1977 and was elected judge in the 14th Judicial Circuit, which includes Braxton, Gilmer, Clay, and Webster Counties. He was elected twice more before retiring in 1996.

One judicial moment that he recalls with great clarity was when two Clay County men sued each other over a coon dog trade. One sued to get his money back, and the other sued to obtain the remainder of the money he felt he was owed. At a defining moment in the trial, one of the plaintiff's pants fell down, and he in effect "mooned" the jury. But he won the case.

Boonie has fished in Quebec, Ontario, Montana, Wyoming, Colorado, Chesapeake Bay, Florida, the Gulf of Mexico, Newfoundland,

Alaska, the Aleutians, and every stream around Webster Springs. In July 2003, he fished for sockeye salmon in the Bering Sea surf off Unalaska Island on a trip with George Gillespie and Clyde See, and tangled with a burly sea lion.

The sea lion tried three times to take away the large salmon that Boonie had on, and on the third try succeeded, swimming away with the lure and the salmon. "He must have weighed a thousand pounds," said Boonie.

In September 1997, he was fishing for King salmon in Alaska's Kenai River when tragedy struck. His companions in a twelve-foot rubber raft were Joe Talbott of Webster Springs, and Don Skidmore, a Webster Springs native who was a hunting guide in Alaska. The raft was swept under a fallen tree and all three were dumped into the river.

Boonie was able to grab the raft and hold on. Joe made it to the shore, although to this day he doesn't remember how. Don was washed downstream. "The last I saw him, he was being swept around a bend," said Boonie. His body was found two months later washed up on a sand bar.

- - -

For sheer perseverance, no Webster County politician can match Sheriff Given. He has run so many times for the State Senate, House of Delegates, and Congress that he has lost track, although he believes he holds the record for elections lost. But he has won some, too. His five terms in the House of Delegates are the most ever for a Webster County legislator.

Sheriff was never a sheriff. His career, other than running for office, was as a partner with two brothers in the Given Construction Company. But his father, Hansford Given, was once a candidate for sheriff, and as a small boy his son accompanied him on the campaign trail, and people began calling him "Sheriff." The name stayed with him.

"Sheriff was a tireless campaigner," said Boonie Sommerville. "Nobody worked harder at it. One time he put stucco on a church at Boggs, free of charge, and he won every vote in the Boggs precinct."

A lesser known side of Sheriff is that he played football on the Cowen High School teams of the 1930s that lost only one game in three years.

- - -

Charley Dodd has seen many Webster Countians come and go.

He opened a funeral home in Webster Springs in 1933, and held over seven thousand funerals in the county. His combination hearse and ambulance when he started was a 1929 Paige, a large luxury car, and his first funeral was that of a woman from Parcoal.

In 1937, J.C. Hurt became Charley's partner, and the funeral home was known as Dodd and Hurt for the next forty-seven years. Dodd sold the business to John Reed in 1984, when it became Dodd and Reed. Charley worked at the funeral home until 1989, and continued with a separate business, Central Funeral Supply, until he fully retired in 2002.

- - -

Webster Springs was a mecca for doctors, primarily because of the presence of Pardee and Curtin and its outlying empire of mines and mills. Bergoo native Gordon Hamrick told the following story about James B. Dodrill, one of the early Pardee and Curtin doctors:

"Grandfather Adam J. Hamrick lived on Leatherwood Creek about two miles above the mouth, and he had a number of mules. When one of the doctors was called to an outlying farm, he would make his way as best he could to Adam J.'s farm and requisition a mule to carry him to his destination.

"One day Doctor Dodrill was called to see an ailing patient at a farm on top of the Gauley Divide, and he came to my grandfather's farm, got a mule, and as he was riding away, he turned his head and said over his shoulder, Call my wife and tell her the last you saw me I was headed up the mountain on Adam J.'s ass."

J.M. Cofer came to Bergoo from Spruce, the West Virginia Pulp and Paper Company town. He was sturdily built, and had large, strong hands. Bill Triplett remembers as a teenager going to Cofer for an infected knee. "He took a spoon and scooped out the infected part," said Bill. "I've never had anything to hurt like that did, but my knee healed quickly."

Leroy Crislip, a retired teacher, recalls going to Cofer. "He gave me a shot for something," said Crislip, "and when he pinched my skin to insert the needle, the pinch hurt far worse than the needle."

Ed Hunter, who came to Webster Springs in 1933, was a company doctor at Barton and Parcoal, and also had an office in Webster Springs. Later he practiced in Richwood. A son, John Hunter, of Carmel, Indiana, is retired from Dow Chemical Company, and remembers incidents from his father's practice.

"One time Dad worked on a fellow who came to the office with a bad head wound, and the following conversation ensued:

"What in the world did you get hit with?" Dad asked him.

"A catrock," the man replied.

"What in hell is a catrock?"

"Oh, it's a big rock that has a low place in the top that we feed the cats out of."

"Two men met Dad at his office late at night after they had been in a fight and both had been cut. As Dad sewed up the cuts, he said, What in the world were you all doing? One of the men replied, We were just having a weenie roast."

"One time Dad went to a house in a remote part of the county to deliver a baby. The husband was very nervous, so Dad told him to carry water from the spring and fill up a wooden tub in the house. Dad's main intent was to give him something to do. Days later, Dad saw the man on the street and he asked dad how he was doing. Dad said that he had just come from delivering twins. The husband replied, My God, Doc, who carried the water?"

(above) Webster Springs circa 1914
(below) circa 1930

In the Slaty Section

Dry Bed near Blackhole Run

Dry Bed near Chimney Rock Run

A Whittaker Falls panorama

Ken Yufer fishes the Mill Pool

Ghostly mill walls at Bergoo

The Elk Canyon above Curtin

Mike Surbaugh canoes Upper Elk

Back Fork (left) enters Elk

A refreshing leap Down Elk

Elk in the Cat Hole Canyon

The Sutton Dam straddles Elk

The heavily fished Mouth of Birch

The End of the World in Clay County

Evening in the Big Chimney area

~ Fifteen ~

The Wildcats

Webster Springs Athletics

Webster Springs High School began in 1910 with one teacher, R. Moore Dodrill, who was paid one hundred dollars a month. He taught what was called a "preparatory course" in a large room upstairs in the back of the Rink Theater. The high school was built in 1913 and the first graduating class was in 1914.

The first touchdown was scored in 1923 in the first year of football. Simpson Hamrick took a long pass from Blair Nichols and ran for the score to start a 25-0 win over Gassaway. The Wildcats won one game, lost two, and tied one that year. The coach was Marshall DePue.

Simpson Hamrick was born on Red Oak Knob on the divide between Leatherwood and Bergoo Creeks. Twenty-four years after his signature score, his sons, George and Paul, played on Webster Springs High School's only state championship team.

In the 1920s, playing away from home was a test of endurance. Consider this account of a game at Summersville, author unknown: "How were we to get there? Elbon Cogar offered the use of his International solid tired truck, and the team set out at daybreak, hoping to make it in time for the game, and in spite of mud and mire they did, tired and dirty, but with plenty of the good old Webster spirit. However, they were a bit dejected when they started the return trip, for Summersville won the game by a score of 92-0.

"It was getting late and cold when the truck made it groaningly into Twin Churches that night on the way home. After playing football and actually pushing that truck out of miles of mud holes, the tired lads were forced to spend the night grouped around a campfire, chilled and hungry. At daylight they finally persuaded a farmer to use two teams of horses to pull them on to Craigsville, where they arrived at noon. From there it took them until late that same night to reach Webster Springs."

Webster Springs played its home games at Duffy's Field, which was located on the south side of Elk at a locale known as "the Golden Shore." Around 1926-27, the Wildcats were playing Richwood, whose dominant player was said to have taunted the Webster Springs players. On one play he was driven

Simpson Hamrick

out of bounds into a swampy area, and his head was held under water by a Webster player who had to be forcibly pulled away from him.

Less contentious and more prosperous times were ahead. In 1947, the Wildcats won all nine of their games and were declared state Class B champions by the West Virginia Athletic Board of Appeals, which had put a new rating plan into effect that year. It was the only state title in the history of the school in either football or basketball.

George Hamrick, a 6-3, 190-pound junior end, was named to the Class B All-State team. In 2003, George and his brother, Paul, both of whom live in Florida, visited me while they were staying at their cousin Jack Hamrick's camp on Birch River.

All-Stater George Hamrick

Naturally I asked about the 1947 season. George described their single wing attack as "run right, run left, run up the middle, and punt." But they averaged twenty-nine points a game, so they didn't punt too often. Paul, the backup quarterback, was called "Little George" because he was a skinny five foot six and weighed 105 pounds. "I learned to get rid of the ball quickly," he said.

Paul was starting quarterback in 1948, and in the

final game of the season against Sutton he caught a pass from George for a touchdown. In the single wing offense, the quarterback was as likely to catch a pass as an end or running back. The ball was snapped to either the tailback, fullback, or quarterback.

George and Paul had played their freshman year in 1945 at Cowen, a coal-hauling railroad town. They told about a game played in the snow when coal dust was used to line the field. George also recalls the Cowen basketball coach, Forest White, telling him in practice, "Hamrick, you couldn't jump over a snuff can." "That was probably true," George said.

- - -

Brent Cool, the 1947 quarterback, remembers the hard times that preceded the title-winning year. "The seniors on that team started out together in 1944," he recalled. "It was a terrible year for football at Webster Springs. Our coach had been a professional football player. He was a no nonsense person who demanded a lot of his players. We had numerous guys who left the team because of what we had to endure and the terrible season we were having. In fact, for one away game, we only had eleven players suited up.

"We lost every game and scored only once. That was when I intercepted a pass and made it to the three yard line before being tackled. It took us four straight-ahead plays to get the touchdown, the only one for the year. I got along with this coach and I do believe that some of our success later was due to his physical training." The player who scored the lone TD was sophomore fullback Bill Hosey, who now lives in Ohio.

The coach in 1944-45 was Eddie Kosko, a Grant Town, West Virginia, native who starred in football and basketball at West Virginia Wesleyan College, and later played professional football with the Philadelphia Eagles.

Philip Cooper, retired Webster Springs postmaster who played end on the 1947 team, remembers the emphasis on physical conditioning that Kosko brought to the 1944 and 1945 teams. "We could have crossed the Sahara Desert without water," he said.

The 1945 team won three games and lost five, including a 27-7 loss at Burnsville in the final game of the season. Cooper remembers it as "the tomato game." "We were pelted with tomatoes, even though they won."

Russ Porterfield, a Richwood native, returned from World War II in late 1945, and resumed coaching at Webster Springs, where he started in 1939 at age twenty-three. He coached the basketball team in the second semester, and the football team at the beginning of the 1946 season.

Returning and prospective players for the 1946 football team

The 1946 team won six games and played scoreless ties with Gassaway and Richwood, setting the table for the championship year. "Interest in the team began to soar," said Cool. "We had numerous guys who wanted to be part of this success story. It was one of the biggest turn-around events of my life." Brack Davis, a senior, recalls that the Wildcats missed two field goals in the scoreless tie with Gassaway. "I can remember that," he said, "because I missed one of them."

Porterfield liked to squirrel hunt, and the story is told that at Monday practices, which consisted of running laps around the field, he would hold two or three boys back and they would go squirrel hunting with him. The boys weren't chosen as a reward for a good game. They were chosen because they knew where the squirrels were.

Porterfield told his players not to go squirrel hunting on game days. One time the lure of the woods was too strong for lineman George Davis, and he went anyway and got peppered with buckshot. But he played that night, carefully hiding his wounds from the coach.

Porterfield was a stern taskmaster. If, for example, a player didn't catch a pass that he thought should have been caught, the offending player immediately came out of the game and had to run a lap around the field.

"I've often thought about the way he coached," said Boonie Sommerville, who was a manager on the 1947 team and later played . "He wasn't strong on fundamentals, but he was a motivator, and he was even-handed in his discipline."

"He was a credit to the coaching profession," said Richard Smith, high-scoring halfback on the 1947 team (90 points) and an outstanding basketball player as well. "I never knew him to raise his voice in anger to any of the players. He was a good role model, and I feel fortunate to have played under his charge."

The Wildcats won all nine of their games, outscoring their opponents 262-20. They weren't scored on through the first five games, but in the sixth game the Wildcats not only gave up their first touchdown but trailed Richwood 7-6 at halftime in front of the home fans. "It is easy to remember the look on Coach Porterfield's face," said Brent Cool. "It was almost like shellshock." But the Wildcats dominated the second half and won, 41-7.

The Wildcats continued winning in the fall of 1948. They won their first four games before playing to a 12-12 tie at Richwood. *The next afternoon,* they traveled to Greenbank and lost, 39-7, on a warm, sunny day. Nobody remembers why two games were scheduled within eighteen hours.

In an oddity, Webster Springs had a player in consecutive North-South games in Charleston, but for different teams. Richard Smith was chosen to play for the South in the 1948 game, and the South won, 25-7. George Hamrick was chosen to play for the North in the 1949 game, and was named captain, and the North won, 14-9.

- - -

Brent Cool, a Diana native, attended Glenville State College, West Virginia University, and the University of Arizona. He served twenty-seven years in the Air Force, retiring with the rank of colonel. In Vietnam, he operated the sensor and camera equipment on an RF4C reconnaissance plane, and flew 155 missions. His squadron's unique motto was "Alone! Unarmed! Unafraid?" He now lives in Charlottesville, Virginia.

George Hamrick received a football scholarship from West Virginia University and played a year of freshman football and basketball, then transferred to Marshall. He joined the Marines, saw action in Korea, and graduated from East Tennessee State in 1957. Now retired from the Schering-Plough Pharmaceutical Company, he lives in Maitland, Florida.

His brother, Paul, lives in Jacksonville, Florida, and is a regional representative for Turf Time, a firm that aerates golf greens and athletic fields. Paul is no longer "Peewee" of his high school days. He is almost six feet tall and weighs 190 pounds.

Joe Talbott scoring in 1947 game

Richard Smith was a West Virginia state policeman for twenty-six years, worked fifteen years for the Department of Highways, and then worked as a security guard for the Bureau of Public Debt, a branch of the U.S. Treasury Department. He lives near Parkersburg.

Russ Porterfield left Webster Springs in 1957 for Florida, where he presided over another impressive streak. His Baker County High School basketball team won sixty consecutive games over two seasons. He died in 1978 while on a fishing trip to Hawthorne, Florida.

Joe Talbott, freshman running back on the 1947 team, coached at Webster Springs from 1961 through 1966. In 1961, the Webster Springs Boosters Club raised money to build a swinging bridge over Elk to Baker's Island so the Wildcats could practice there.

Joe retired from the U.S. Department of Labor in 1988, and has since served three terms in the West Virginia House of Delegates from the 36th District, which includes Webster County and part of Nicholas County.

His brother, Bill, was quarterback on the 1952 team that lost only to Summersville, 7-6, on the Summersville field. "We had three touchdowns called back," Bill recalled. He practiced law in Webster Springs for thirty-nine years, including four terms as prosecuting attorney.

Joe and Bill met on opposite sides in a college football game. Joe played quarterback for West Virginia Wesleyan, and Bill was a flanker back for Potomac State. Potomac State won, but neither of the brothers remembers the final score.

- - -

There were some big moments for Webster Springs in basketball, beginning with the 1943-44 season when the Wildcats, led by center Dyer Griffith, went to the finals of the regional tournament before losing to perennial state champion Beckley.

At six foot four, Griffith was tall for his time, and good enough to receive a scholarship offer at WVU. But he was wounded in Europe in World War II, and was unable to continue with basketball. Ironically, Griffith and his coach, Russ Porterfield, met in Europe when their units were exchanging places at the front.

Four years later, the 1948 team pulled off a huge upset, defeating Beckley, 51-46, in the regional finals. George Hamrick scored a game high 19 points, Richard Smith scored 10 points, and Paul Hamrick scored nine.

Bob Wills, writing the next day in the *Beckley Sunday Register*, said that "a cool headed quintet from little Webster Springs unleashed a minor atomic bomb in Beckley last night, completely outclassing the highly favored Woodrow Wilson Flying Eagles."

"The previous night we watched Beckley demolish its opponent with a pressing defense," said George Hamrick, "and we were determined they weren't going to do that to us. I would throw the ball down the floor to someone breaking in from the right or left, and we beat the press."

The Wildcats lost to Huntington East, 70-41, in the opening round of the state tournament at Mountaineer Fieldhouse in Morgantown.

Hamrick remembers an unusual episode from the regular season. The team was returning from a game at Richwood on a chilly November night and saw lights on the riverbank where the highway crosses Gauley River. "We stopped, thinking there had been an accident," he recalled, "and then we heard the familiar strains of *Shall We Gather At the River*. A local church was holding a revival, and baptizing its new converts."

Hamrick graduated in the spring of 1949 with the distinction of having made the All-State teams two consecutive years in both football and basketball.

- - -

Another milestone for Webster Springs basketball was achieved by the 1966-67 team that upset heavily favored Monongah, 59-55, in the regional semifinals. Jim Marsh, who retired in 2003 as principal of Webster County High School, was the coach.

The Wildcats had a balanced team, with all five starters averaging in double figures, led by Ray Profitt's 17.5 average. The other four starters were George Criss, David Klee, Brad Morton, and Jack Holcomb. The sixth and seventh players were Carl Williams and Craig Curtis.

Monongah had two good forwards and an outstanding guard in Roy Murphy. The Marion County team carried a 20-4 record into the regional tourney at Elkins. Monongah led from the start, and was still ahead, 43-36, late in the third quarter.

"Our strong suit was our zone defenses," said Marsh, "but they weren't working well that night. We had used the zone press all year, but I was reluctant to do it in this game because of Monongah's speed and the ball handling ability of Murphy. Also, this was a ninety-four foot court, and we were used to playing on smaller courts.

"But being down seven, we had no choice, so we began pressing and it bothered them, not only in regard to turnovers but also it got them out of their half court offense somewhat. Anyway, the tide began to turn and near the end we were up 57-49 and went on to win 59-55. We beat Parsons the next night, 73-62, to win the regional.

"At the state tournament at Memorial Fieldhouse in Huntington against Huntington Vinson we got behind early and did not play well in any phase of the game, eventually losing 62-45. We finished 17-7. Vinson went on to win the AA title."

Marsh lives in Buckhannon, where he coached for twenty-six years before returning to work in his native county in 1997 as principal of the consolidated high school.

- - -

No "highlight film" of Webster Springs athletics would be complete without the story of the long underwear. A. James Manchin originated wrestling at the school, and coached wrestling, football, and track from 1957 through 1959. When the principal declined to give wrestling any financial support in 1957, Manchin bought T-shirts with numbers and the school name on them, and a dozen pair of long underwear that his wife, Stella, dyed Wildcat blue.

These "long johns" were the wrestling uniforms throughout the first year. One of Manchin's wrestlers, Phil Harris, won the state title in his weight class in the 1959 tourney at Parkersburg. It would have made headlines if Phil won the title in his long underwear, but by that time the Wildcat wrestlers were wearing regular uniforms.

Jim Marsh played two seasons of football under Manchin. "He was a motivator," said Jim. "He introduced a drill at Monday practices called 'the Kentucky Derby.' We'd sprint from the goal line to the ten and back, then to the twenty and back, and so on. Then we'd do the same thing back down the field. In total, we ran about the same distance as the mile and a quarter Kentucky Derby.

"I've never been in such good shape in my life, and one time I even won 'the Kentucky Derby.' I expected Coach Manchin to say something to me, but instead he chastised the other players because they let 'a big old boy' beat them in sprints."

Manchin later became secretary of state and state treasurer. He was serving in the Legislature from his native Marion County when he died in November 2003.

The 1966-67 Wildcats basketball team, from left: Brad Morton, Jack Holcomb, Ray Profitt, Dave Klee, George Criss, and coach Jim Marsh

Sixteen

The Choppers

Webster County Legends

Paul Criss was a blockhouse of a man at five foot eleven and two hundred and fifty pounds who was called "The Walking Sawmill" because he and his partner could cut and trim as many trees in a day as the mill could saw.

In the early 1920s, Paul and a friend, John Cochran, cut a daily average of 17,046 board feet of hardwood timber over an eleven-day period for Smoot Lumber Company because they wanted to make a little extra money. Their feat was said to have been more than three times the average production of the best woodchoppers.

Paul was a legendary figure in a county that puts great value on its woodchoppers, and, in his case, its beard shavers. He came up with the marvelous gimmick of shaving people with a razor-sharp axe, and this stunt greatly delighted not only audiences, but also Kelly Axe Company, which employed him for many years.

Paul traveled around the United States giving lectures at forestry schools, demonstrating Kelly Axe products, and performing in theaters. He was interviewed numerous times on radio and later on television. One of his feats was throwing two double-bitted axes simultaneously at two different targets. "I do it every now and then just to show off," he would say.

The *Charleston Daily Mail* wrote about this in Paul's obituary. "As he developed the act, two small flags were secured to two posts with rubber bands and the rubber bands were the targets. When they were cut, the flags fell. He did this act all over the country, including at the Roxy

Theater in New York. The element of danger was real, and a few years before he died he remarked that at the time he was absolutely sure of himself. Now, he said, he wouldn't walk across a stage with a sharp axe in his hand."

But the show-stopper came when his wife, Pearl Wilson Criss, would hold an apple between her thumb and forefinger on top of a block of wood, and Paul, emulating archer William Tell, would split the apple with a full overhead swing. Paul's oldest son, Hobert, who lives in Amherst, Ohio, confirmed that his father would perform this feat.

He isn't sure when his father started shaving people, but an article at the time of his death said the first person he shaved was Holt Hammons, the Webster Springs police chief, at the Mountain State Forest Festival in Elkins. "It was like being shaved with a razor," Hobert Criss said, "assuming the axe was good and sharp."

Paul was a native of Dorrtown on Elk at Webster Springs. He was an excellent swimmer and very agile for a large man. "He could turn three flips off the diving board into the upper Cat Hole," said his son. "One day we were doing something around the place, and the topic of swimming came up. It was late October and the water was quite cold," but Dad said, 'Let's hit it.' And into the river we went."

Paul was a fisherman, and for many years there was a carving on a tree below Webster Springs telling of a walleye he caught. It gave the year of the catch, and the length of the fish, and was signed "P. Criss." The year was in the late 1940s, but nobody remembers the length of the fish.

A daughter, Sarah Criss Ward, who lives on Elk below Webster Springs, recalls growing up at the Dorrtown farm. "My grandfather, Charley Wilson, did the farming mostly," she said, "because dad was traveling a lot for Kelly Axe by that time. But he would also work on the farm when he was home."

Hobert Criss believes his dad's first job in the woods was when he was nine years old. He carried water from a creek to dampen the tram road and make it easier to skid logs. Sarah Criss Ward has a picture of her father at age thirteen using a cant hook at Delphi, Nicholas County. He is described in the picture caption as "a skinny little boy," but that soon changed.

His strength was legendary, and he had the quickness that typifies the best choppers. It is said that he could pick up 95-pound bags of cement in each hand and hold them straight out. Once he carried four bags of feed out of a store in Webster Springs, one under each arm and one in each hand. Someone said, "Paul, can't you carry more than that?" "I could," he replied, "but I couldn't get through the door with it."

Paul Criss

Charles Atlas, who was billed in vaudeville days as "the world's strongest man," met Paul in Florida at a Kelly Axe show, and supposedly said, "Paul, *you're* the strongest man in the world. There's nothing you can't lift or carry."

Paul had a part in cutting the Mingo Oak, a legendary West Virginia tree. He, Ed Meeks, Upton Sears, Henry Rose, and Clyde and Virgil Hamrick, cut the giant white oak in 1938. A picture showed Paul lying in the notch that had been cut prior to finishing off the tree with a specially made eight-foot crosscut saw. The saw is now on the wall at the Pardee and Curtin Lumber Company office at Curtin.

The tree stood on Trace Fork of Pigeon Creek in Mingo County, and died over a period of three years of complications from old age. It was 576 years old, 145 feet tall, and its diameter at ground level was eight feet eight and three-fourths inches. The Mingo Oak still lives, in a way. Blocks of it are on display in the vestibule of the WVU Forestry School in Morgantown, and at the state museum in Charleston.

An even bigger tree at ground level was a yellow poplar cut by Pardee and Curtin on Big Run at Camp Four in 1938 and put on display on the Webster County Courthouse lawn. It was over twelve feet in diameter. But it kept slipping downhill, and was removed as a hazard after about a year at the courthouse.

Paul Criss was an entertaining storyteller, and his natural, easy-going manner and deep voice appealed to audiences. He always said he didn't want to offend anyone in the audience because he might want to come back sometime.

He was an advisor for the first woodchopping competition in Webster Springs when county agent Jack Burton started the Rhododendron Festival in 1938. It was suspended during World War II, and didn't return until 1960. Today it is a Memorial Weekend tradition on Baker's Island.

Bill Gillespie remembers as a young boy seeing Paul perform at the festival. Paul's appearance was an exhibition only, since the company he worked for, Kelly Axe, had put up the prize money. Years later, Bill wrote the following account:

"The question was, could he really chop as fast as the papers said? Well, a lot of people didn't know and so the suspense thickened. Finally, the chopping and sawing contests began and really good times were set. Clyde and Lester

Hamrick won the crosscut sawing by cutting a 20-inch poplar log in 42 ½ sec-
onds, and L.E. Cook of Glady Fork won the underhand chop by cutting a 16-inch
poplar in 49 seconds. And then it was Paul's turn.

"He hadn't entered the regular competition, as he was the world cham-
pion and no one wanted to chop against him, but he would give a demonstration.
Could he defend his reputation? The bets were about even, for and against.

"What a figure he cut as he strode to the center of the arena. Big, robust,
and confident, he really personified his nickname, Paul Bunyan. As he stepped
up on his log you could have heard a pin drop and then he nodded to the timers
and started. Chips flew four and five feet, and when the last one slowly slithered
across the grass, the timers all agreed on a time of 34 seconds. He had made
believers out of everyone, and as he strode back through the town that day, axe on
shoulder, and with confidence showing in every stride of his caulked boots, he was
a genuine hero."

Paul died in 1973 at age seventy-six. His wife, Pearl Wilson Criss,
died in 1988. They are buried in the Point Mountain Cemetery.

~ ~ ~

Arden Cogar, who succeeded Paul as the icon of Webster County
choppers, was cut of the same cloth as "The Walking Sawmill." He is not
as large, but at five foot ten and two hundred and five pounds he definitely isn't a small man, either.

He doesn't look that big in chopping pictures, because he is usually
bent over a block of wood. In person, however, he gives every appearance
of a compactly built athlete. Former Webster Springs basketball coach Jim
Marsh believes that Arden would have made a superb athlete because of
his strength and quickness.

Chopping came naturally to him. "I always liked to chop wood,"
he said as we sat in the living room of his home on the Back Fork on a
rainy day in January 2005, surrounded by trophies. One wall of the room
was converted from a bookcase to a trophy case. I said something about
them. "They're just trophies," he said, shrugging his sturdy shoulders.

We had just returned from visiting his birthplace on Desert Fork
of the Right Fork of Holly River, where he told me about chopping down a
large linden (basswood) tree when he was around ten years old. "I spent
three or four days at it," he said. "When dad found out, he made me help
him cut it into eight hog troughs. All told, I put two weeks of work into
that tree."

Arden's son, Jamie, now a lawyer in Charleston and an outstanding wood chopper in his own right, began at an early age too. Using a

small hatchet and barely out of diapers, he chopped down five freshly planted pines in the yard. Then he chopped off part of a door facing inside the house, and dividers between the bookshelves.

"It wasn't all at once, or anything like that," said his mother, Carol, and it wasn't something we ignored. If we saw him doing it, we made him stop, but we didn't make a big issue of it. I suppose, in a way, he was making his own footprints in the family chopping tradition."

Desert Fork is "out of the way," to put it mildly. We drove there from Route 20 in the Jumbo community, passing the site of the one-room Laurel Fork School where Arden and his four brothers and two sisters attended. It was a walk of about a mile and a half to the school over Laurel Fork Mountain. The school building had fallen down and someone had tried, unsuccessfully, to burn the boards.

There were around seventy families living on Desert Fork when Arden was growing up, but only a few remain now in the lower end of the stream, and none in the area of Arden's birthplace. Most of the land, including his homeplace, is owned by timber companies. But Arden owns seventeen hundred acres himself, most of it in Webster County.

The two-story house where he was born in 1934, and where his father was born, no longer stands, nor does the nearby smaller house where he grew up. Two white pines are lonely sentinels marking the spot.

"My father [Hans Cogar] would never leave," Arden said. "I talked to him about it, but I guess he was one of those hard-headed fellows. He just wouldn't move." His father farmed, worked in the coal mines, and in the woods. After he died at age eighty-one, Arden's mother, Nora Pugh Cogar, a Hacker Valley native, left Desert Fork to live with her children.

We stood in the drizzle on a day that was refreshingly mild for January. Arden told about places that were familiar to his childhood. "We made molasses there," he said, pointing to a collapsed out-building. "The cellar was over there. Mother always kept a well-stocked cellar. The Apple Butter Tree stood on that far hillside. Its apples cooked up good and made good apple butter. The Left Hand Cornfield [located on the left prong of Desert Fork] and the peach orchard were over there," he said, pointing across the little rivulet that is Desert Fork in its upper reaches.

He related the story of the mysterious death of Amos Tharpe. It is said that he was killed around the time of the Civil War, supposedly by three men who posed as Union soldiers. The reason they killed him is unclear. There is, or was, a rock marking his grave on Amos Fork of Desert Fork, which is named for him.

Arden Cogar competes in the standing cut

When Arden was growing up in the 1930s and 1940s, the Desert Fork drainage was a popular place for deer hunting because it contained one of the few herds left in the state. Deer never completely disappeared from that area, as they did from most places.

One of the early stockings took place in nearby Holly River State Park. "We always heard that the Holly River deer came from Michigan," he said. "If you killed a deer with a tag in its ear, that meant it came from the park. Another thing, they were bigger and darker than our deer."

Arden's uncle, John Cogar, had a hunting camp on Desert Fork, and as many as sixty hunters would gather there from far and wide and sleep in a barracks-like setting with top and bottom bunks.

During that period, the DNR did in fact bring in deer from other places, including Michigan, to "jump start" the feeble West Virginia population. Michigan deer are a separate sub-species from the Virginia whitetail, which is our native deer, and which remains dominant to this day, the Michigan deer notwithstanding.

Arden left the farm when he was eighteen to work in the woods. The first place was on Sugar Creek near Skelt. He has been working in the woods ever since, and retirement wasn't on the horizon when I visited him in 2005. "I have my health," he said. "I was never in a hospital overnight in my life, and I'm doing what I like to do."

For him, swinging an axe is not just for show. He has logged in many of the state's fifty-five counties. "Maybe a third of them," he told me over lunch at the Home Town Diner at Diana (a cheeseburger for me, homemade potato soup and cornbread for him). Interviewing Arden in a public place in Webster County is a lost cause. Everybody knows him, and everybody wants to talk.

On the way to Diana from Desert Fork we stopped to talk to Ronald Cogar, a young man who was standing by the road. "What's happening?" Arden asked. "The wild horse got out and I can't catch him," the young man replied. We heard the wild-sounding whinny of a horse up the hollow. They talked some more. "Well," Arden finally said, "so everything is under control?" "No," the young man replied with commendable frankness.

- - -

Arden's first chopping competition was at the Mountain State Forest Festival at Elkins in 1957, when he was twenty-three years old. He didn't win, but he returned in 1958 and won the underhand chop, the first of his hundreds of wins over the years in the U.S., Canada, and Australia. From 1966 to 1980 at the Forest Festival, he won eleven first places, three second places, and one fourth place.

Unfortunately for nostalgia's sake, Arden and Paul Criss never met in competition, partly because of their age difference and partly because Paul's job took him out of state much of the time. In 1959, Paul invited Arden to accompany him to Vermont for a chopping event. Paul wasn't competing, but he wanted Arden to meet his friends on the Kelly Axe circuit. Arden did compete, and won the underhand.

We were sliding down a long hill toward Desert Fork, following the fresh tracks in the mud of a log skidder, when a flock of wild turkeys crossed the road in front of us. "Look at the size of the beard on that one," Arden said, pointing through the rain-splattered windshield of his four-wheel drive pickup.

"There are many good choppers around," I said, "but your name is synonymous with wood chopping and Webster County. Why?" The question had absolutely nothing to do with turkeys, but given the steep hill and the slick road, I wanted my last words to form a question.

As we watched the turkeys depart into the wet, gloomy under-brush, he replied that it is probably because he appeared seven times on ABC's *Wide World of Sports*. As the name implies, the program went beyond the bounds of baseball, football, and basketball to cover such things as woodchopping competitions. He believes his name recognition soared because of those appearances.

Arden, the quintessential "good old country boy," would never say it was because he was the fastest chopper, but Bill Gillespie, who has emceed the Webster Springs Woodchopping Festival for over forty years, can and did say that. "Five clockings that he recorded in the 1970s still haven't been beaten, to my knowledge," said Bill.

Bill tells the story about Arden's first appearance in Australia, where chopping is a national sport. "His reputation had preceded him," said Bill, "and they scheduled him to chop on the afternoon that he got off the plane, still suffering from jet lag. But he won anyway."

He has won fifty-seven world titles, which are wins recorded in competitions that were billed as world championships and offered sufficient prize money to back up the claim. Primarily, those were held at Hayward, Wisconsin; Melbourne, Australia; Albany, Oregon; Vancouver, British Columbia; and Webster Springs.

The standing block is Arden's favorite and the event he has won most often. In his prime, he "owned" the standing block, which is setting a block of wood on end and chopping it in two, like chopping a tree.

I gazed again at the trophies in Arden's living room, barely able to take all of them in at once. They represented almost fifty years of swinging an axe in local, state, national, and international competition. But, he insisted, he'd still rather swing an axe out in the woods.

Arden Cogar in his chopping heyday (above left),
and visiting his birthplace on Desert Fork (above right)

Seventeen

The Back Fork

Elk's Alter Ego

The Back Fork of Elk begins modestly on Turkeybone Mountain in Randolph County near Pickens, and cascades toward Webster Springs, twenty-five miles away, through one of the finest hardwood timber growing regions in the world. A sign at Pickens advertises the village as "The Haven in the Hardwoods."

Few streams cascade as well as the Back Fork. It seems to be perpetually tripping and falling over itself, culminating in a series of falls about seven miles above Webster Springs that would have inspired Beethoven to rewrite his Fifth Symphony.

Sugar Creek and Little Sugar Creek flow through the upper reaches of the Back Fork from Turkeybone Mountain, while Coalbank Fork, Hewett Fork, and Flint Run come off Point Mountain. All have native trout populations, as does Big Run, which enters the Back Fork at the Randolph-Webster County line five miles below the headwaters.

On what began as a rainy and dreary day in late October 2003, I visited the headwaters with Don Gilkeson, a longtime friend who retired in 1996 after thirty-eight years with the Division of Natural Resources and the Department of Environmental Protection. Don and his wife, Doris, live on Elk between Curtin and Bergoo.

Doris once saw a mountain lion on Elk, but that sighting couldn't compete with the "Crossing Guard Bear" that she and her daughter, Debbie Gilkeson Minnich, saw on the highway near their home. The bear was standing on the yellow line, its paws upraised, while its two cubs crossed the road as their vehicle approached.

Don and I drove east on Point Mountain and dropped off toward the Back Fork near Waneta, a long ago coal mining community. On the way down, we encountered a flock of wild turkeys that walked in front of us with an air of sullen insolence, although their feathers were dampened from the rain and they appeared to have little to be insolent about.

Turkeys will feed in almost any kind of weather except prolonged cold and deep snow. Then they will stay on the roost for days or even weeks at a time. I mentally pictured Point Mountain in January, and wished them well. These were birds of the year, and of good size, but they had yet to endure a Point Mountain winter, which will test anybody's insolence.

The same can be said of Turkeybone Mountain, which got its name, somebody in an expansive mood once told me, because of the many turkey bones that littered the mountain after a particularly severe winter during which many of the birds died.

We came to the Back Fork at the mouth of Big Run, which begins a stone's throw from the Point Mountain Road and is aptly named. It is a large run that was tumbling swift and milky colored from the rain on the day of our visit, carrying with it the freshly fallen leaves of autumn.

We followed the Back Fork in a northeasterly direction to the mouth of Flint Run, which announces itself to the mother stream by tumbling over a large rock ledge in the manner of a gangly adolescent. We drove up Mud Lick Run and came out on the headwaters of the Back Fork near the Parting Springs Fire Tower on Turkeybone Mountain. The tower, the mountain, and Kumbrabow State Forest form a triumvirate that embraces the very head of the Back Fork.

Parting Springs is a community that no longer exists. Its name is derived from a spring that oozed out of the ground and parted, one flow draining into the Middle Fork of the Buckhannon River, and the other draining into the headwaters of the Back Fork.

The showers had ended, but the sky remained a vengeful looking gray, reminding us that we were wayfaring strangers in a remote land that is famous for its abundant precipitation. The most snowfall from a single storm ever recorded in West Virginia was fifty-seven inches on November 24-29, 1950, at the nearby village of Pickens, and the most snowfall in a season was three hundred and one inches at Kumbrabow in the winter of 1959-60. Pickens has an average annual rainfall of sixty-six inches.

We headed out the Turkeybone Road toward Pickens. Just beyond the former Luther Winkler house, at an elevation of 3,360 feet, is the well preserved one room Turkeybone School, which, if it hasn't already appeared in *Goldenseal* or *People & Mountains*, is a picture waiting to be taken by those who have a primordial urge to photograph old schools, barns, mills, covered bridges, haystacks, and sheep on high ridges. At the newspaper I traveled often with Larry Pierce, whose obsession was old barns. He always threatened to do a book of pictures of old barns, but I don't think he ever did.

Turkeybone School

Turkeybone Road is on the divide between Big and Little Sugar Creeks of the Back Fork, and the Middle Fork of the Buckhannon. The school sits below the road on the Back Fork drainage, and is one of more than two hundred small schools that once dotted the Randolph County landscape. This particular one was begun by German and Swiss settlers in 1893, and was called Turkeybone School No. 14 in the numbering of schools in the Middle Fork District.

Margaret Egleson Isch of Helvetia attended grades one through eight at Turkeybone, and graduated from Pickens High School in 1936. The farm on Turkeybone Mountain where she grew up was known as the Egleson farm for her grandfather, Noah Egleson, and her father, Edwin Egleson. In more recent times, it was known as the Isch farm for her husband, Ernest Isch. If a single starting point can be assigned to any stream, it can be said that the Back Fork begins on the Isch farm.

The hamlet of Pickens is on the Middle Fork drainage at an elevation of 2,770 feet. It is well known for its maple syrup festival, its school that contains kindergarten through twelfth grades, its tiny high school graduating classes, and for successfully resisting consolidation, which was a scourge like smallpox that spread a pall through almost every community in West Virginia at one time.

In 1989, there was a plan afoot to bus the Pickens students to schools at Mill Creek twenty-five miles away, but it met with fierce opposition from parents who didn't like the idea of their kids riding a bus over mountainous roads in winter. There are mountains in any direction out of Pickens.

I remembered attending the maple syrup festival and eating pancakes at the Pickens School, which I described to Don as "a red brick building." I'm sure he had seen it many times before, but he didn't say anything out of politeness, because it turned out the building is made of wood and is painted white.

I rode in embarrassed silence toward the head of Little Sugar

Creek, with perhaps a touch of the sullen insolence that had character-ized the turkeys we saw crossing the road. We passed through the Casto Settlement at the very head of Little Sugar, and drove along Fork Ridge that separates the drainages of the Sugars, Big and Little.

A detour brought us to the Dave Low Gap, named for Dave McClanahan, who lived nearby on the Back Fork. Arden Cogar (see The Choppers) once caught a twenty-four inch rainbow trout at the Dave Hole where McClanahan lived.

It was sprinkling rain again and a breeze was ruffling the few leaves that remained. Below us, the Back Fork ran in a deep and forbid-ding canyon. Upper Elk and its drainages are partial to canyons, I thought absently.

Dropping down, we came to the Back Fork where a logging road crossed the stream. We were about two miles into Webster County, and the occasion called for lunch. We sat in the truck and ate. I had a glorious peanut butter sandwich lavished with nectarine marmalade that Doris Gilkeson had made, and I ate happily and admired the river in front of us.

There is an inviting pool above the crossing where trout must surely live. Nature agreed in principle because the sun came out for the first time that day and gave its blessing to the pool and the coppery beech leaves that clung to the mother tree at the upper end.

Sam Knotts, who lives at Pickens and is a fishing guide on the Back Fork, told me that Back Fork trout aren't as particular as their cousins across the mountain. "Elk has more hatches," he said, "although we do have them on the Back Fork too. But attractor flies do better on the Back Fork. Besides that, it's a more pristine stream, and there isn't as much fishing pressure."

We returned to the low gap and dropped down onto Little Sugar just above where it joins Big Sugar near Skelt, and soon came to the meeting place of Big Sugar and the Back Fork, about ten miles above Web-ster Springs. In the spring when water flows are good, this is

Sugar Creek (left) enters Back Fork

one of the most appealing river settings in West Virginia, or anywhere.

Nearby is the site of a historic survey marker denoting where four land grants from the 1780s came together. Around 1916, a concrete monument with a stone on top replaced the poplar tree called for in the original survey of land given by the Commonwealth of Virginia to brothers Thomas and Joseph Pennell.

Don and I admired the rendezvous of Sugar Creek and the Back Fork. "You took my picture here one time," he said quietly. I mentally searched my checkered newspaper past, which included an occasional stab at photography when a real photographer wasn't available.

"Why?" I inquired, fishing for something that would jog my fading memory.

"I was taking a water sample," Don replied. "You took my picture and wrote a story."

'Who did I come here with?" I asked, still fishing.

"Me," he said.

I could think of nothing further to ask.

Don said he had a clipping of the picture and story at his home, but later he couldn't find it and I was buoyed by the possibility that it was his memory, not mine, that had departed, as migratory birds depart in autumn.

The rain had given way to blue sky and white clouds that were piled high toward the heavens, and it was not a place to mourn the loss of memory. There was a breeze and a slight chill from the water as I placed my notepad on a rock. "Memory gone," I wrote, leaving a blank space that could be filled in later when we determined whether it was Don's memory or mine.

The dreaded clipping eventually surfaced. It was from *the Charleston Gazette* of July 9, 1975, and told about the threat posed to the Back Fork by sediment from mining and timbering, particularly on Sugar Creek. There also was the picture of Don I had taken. Reluctantly, I filled in the blank space.

- - -

In May 2004, I returned to Skelt with Bob Hines, who lives at Jumbo. Bob and his wife, Nancy, showed me a picture of Skelt in its heyday, which was around 1900. A large number of houses stood along the Back Fork. The railroad bed is still visible where a logging train came down from Pickens.

The name Skelt originated with William 'Skeltie Bill' Cogar, an early resident of the Back Fork country whose ancestors came to America from Germany. They spelled their surname Koger, which later became Coger or Cogar. There is a Skeltie Bill Reunion held each year at the Jumbo Community Center. Skeltie Bill and his wife, Mary Bender Cogar, are buried in the Sugar Creek Cemetery.

An appealing landmark at Skelt is the Church in the Wildwood. This little church didn't inspire the song, *Church in the Wildwood,* but it easily could have because of its remote setting on the Back Fork, its little cemetery, its wood stove, and its ancient pump organ that still plays, if slightly off key.

The Church in the Wildwood

It was built in 1926 as the Sugar Creek Methodist Church, but in the 1970s became non-denominational. Susie Arthur, who with her husband, Jim, lived downstream at what is still known as the Arthur Bottom, first started calling it the Church in the Wildwood.

Services are held on Saturday evenings in the milder months. "It's impossible in the winter," said Anna Cogar Wolfe. Anna and her sister, Ruth Cogar Clark, are the only two people still living in Skelt. They were born there, moved away, and came back in 2001. Their father, Brant Cogar, had a store, post office, grist mill, blacksmith shop, and barbershop in Skelt.

I seized the moment and decreed that the church will be the official seat of worship for the new state of Middle of Nowhere, which was born on the headwaters of Elk but has since been expanded to include all five hundred and thirty seven square miles of the Elk drainage above Sutton Dam, and anything else that we wish to include. In the latter respect, we are like Mussolini in his apologia for fascism. We share his thirst for empire.

Bob Hines and I drove up the Back Fork to his camp where Point Mountain Run drains out of Big Swamps. Bob is not a fisherman, but he didn't disagree with my guess that a nice brown trout was probably lurking under one of the two rootwalls where the river flows on the opposite side from his camp.

He is a deer hunter, and there were the heads of three very nice bucks on the wall. One of the deer was wearing a hat. "Do you observe that often in deer around here?" I asked in a moment of embarrassing silliness. Bob gave the perfect answer: "Only as the weather gets colder."

Apple trees bloomed in the yard. "Are the apples used for making applejack?" I asked, continuing my search for the elusive nectar. But even as I asked, I doubted if anyone still makes applejack in these unenlightened times in which we live. "No, they're sour, but deer and bears seem to like them," Bob replied. He pointed to broken limbs in the trees where bears had visited to eat the apples.

Bob's next door neighbor in the remoteness is Joe Talbott, the Webster Springs resident and state legislator who has had a camp there for twenty-five years. "My problem with bears," said Joe, "is that they eat my Chinese chestnuts. They climb the trees and either bite off the limbs or ride them down and break them." I silently thought that if I found anything that would attack, eat, demolish, and otherwise wage unrelenting war on Chinese chestnuts, I would give them a medal.

- - -

The major landowners on the Back Fork are Coastal Lumber Company on the headwaters, and Pardee and Curtin on the lower end. The upper edge of Pardee and Curtin's six thousand acres is the Arthur Bottom below Skelt. Farther downstream is a series of appealing falls that led to my introduction to Jumping Boy.

One splendid day in late June 2003, I visited the area with Dee Curtin, president of Pardee and Curtin. We crawled through rhododendron to reach one of the falls, which was as yet unnamed. The state flower was blooming so profusely all around us that it was almost annoying. But Dee was inspired by the prolific bloom and decreed that the unnamed falls would thereafter be known as Rhododendron Falls. I feel a certain parental affection toward it, since I was present for its christening.

We saw an oddity there, or at least I hadn't seen it before except in pictures. A large trout surfaced at the base of the ledge, its dorsal fin protruding from the water like a miniature version of Jaws, and then it leaped in an attempt to clear the falls. It failed on that and another jump, but it nicely imitated life, which is an endless succession of mostly failed attempts to surmount barriers.

Dee and his wife were at the same falls in 2002 and saw a trout trying to jump the cascading water. It may be a primordial urge to move upstream, or Jumping Boy may have come into the Back Fork from a colder tributary, and was instinctively seeking to return to the cooler water. Jumping Boy was a very handsome fellow, either a brown or a rainbow. It was difficult to tell with the bright sunshine glistening on the drops of water he brought with him out of the pool.

The largest falls on the Back Fork is Big Falls, which is located above Jumping Boy's lair and below the Arthur Bottom. It is a series of four falls, the last and biggest one cascading into a rounded emerald green pool framed by hemlocks. I made a mental note to swim there some day.

One time Cheryl Kinderman and a friend were camping on the riverbank just above Big Falls, and during the night it rained heavily and they were awakened by the Back Fork running through their tent. "We were lucky we weren't swept over the falls," recalled Cheryl, who grew up on the Back Fork at Webster Springs and now lives on Old Field Fork at the head of Elk.

In descending order from Big Falls are Perch, Rhododendron, and Bridge Falls. The bridge that gives the latter its name is the Pardee and Curtin Bridge, which was built at the site of a former railroad trestle. Below the bridge are Laurel Run, Sawmill, and Boy Scout falls in the vicinity of Breece, a logging town that no longer exists. A railroad once ran from Breece to the top of Point Mountain and down Baltimore Run to the Pardee and Curtin mill at Bergoo.

A spur line crossed the Back Fork between Perch and Big Falls to gain access to the timber on the north side. When Dee and I visited, we found spikes that had been driven into rock to anchor the tracks, and we envisioned ponderous Shay engines spraying water as they forded the stream and gave the name Splash Crossing to the site.

- - -

A Back Fork icon is the Big Sycamore about five miles above Webster Springs. The tree, a seedling when Michelangelo began painting the ceiling of the Sistine Chapel in 1508, is in poor health.   It suffers from wood rot fungus, a common affliction of aged trees.

Big Sycamore has been harmed in other ways as well. A windstorm broke off part of its crown, ice storms have broken its limbs, and its roots are being severely compacted by the hundreds of visitors who come annually to see and photograph it.

Also over the years, thoughtless people have hacked away at the trunk cavity until they managed to squeeze inside. In 2001, someone built a fire in the hollow base that burned a considerable part of the inner trunk, thus putting the tree at further risk.

Big Sycamore was once the largest sycamore in the nation, and is

The Big Sycamore

still the largest sycamore in West Virginia. Two hemlocks, one about thirteen feet in height, grew from a cavity on a large lower limb, but in 1992 the limb broke from the weight and came crashing down.

Following are Big Sycamore's vital statistics:

Overall height: 139 feet.

Height to first limb: 86.5 feet.

Crown spread: 100 feet.

Circumference: 24.7 feet.

Estimated age: 500 years.

The Big Sycamore bottom is owned by Pardee and Curtin, and is leased to the DNR. The company, the state agency, and Main Street, a volunteer Webster Springs group that promotes the downtown and surrounding area, have developed Sycamore Park, including a new bridge over the Back Fork, and a picnic pavilion. The bridge replaced one that was severely damaged by vandals a few years ago.

- - -

In 2004, as we approached The Warm Season, I walked up from the Pardee and Curtin gate on a perspiring day and swam at Big Falls, thus fulfilling the promise I had made a year earlier. I can't say the water was cold, nor can I say it wasn't, because hypothermia set in the moment I entered the icily idyllic setting, and I felt nothing after that.

I stayed in the water long enough to confirm that the depth of the pool in the center is over my head, and although I swim well I'm not a polar bear. So I thought it best to grab the nearest ice floe and paddle out while I could still move my arms and legs.

But it was a pleasant day, and I was in a generous and forgiving mood. As I toweled off with my bright red and well-traveled Colonial Williamsburg T-shirt, I named Big Falls the official swimming pool of the state of Middle of Nowhere.

Big Falls of the Back Fork

~ Eighteen ~

The Voyageurs

Boating on Upper River

Iwent to the Webster Wildwater Weekend in early April 2004 on a day that began miserably, with rain and cold. Even less comforting was the sight of snow at the higher elevations around Webster Springs. But a fire burned brightly in the large fireplace in the picnic pavilion on Baker's Island, and since most of the boaters had already put on their wet suits and were oblivious to the cold, the fire was left to us lesser mortals to enjoy.

Elk flowed nicely after a day or two of rain, and seventy-six boaters took part in the day's race, which began at Curtin Bridge and ended at Baker's Island. The winners were Jess and Chara Whittemore of Friendsville, Maryland, who won the men's and women's divisions, respectively.

I had lunch with Ken Stockwell, pastor of Methodist churches at Webster Springs, Miller Mountain, and Curtin, and a native of Ivydale, Clay County. He told me about fishing Elk as a boy, and about catching a twenty-nine inch walleye north of Ivydale. We ate hot dogs from the concession stand and talked about the movie *The Passion of the Christ*, about mutual acquaintances, and of course about fishing.

By the time the contestants came into view around the bend above us, sweeping like a small armada toward the buttressed bow of Baker's Island, the rain had stopped and the temperature had moderated. I saw a smiling golden retriever among the race watchers. The dog appeared to be pleased with the improved weather. But then I remembered that golden retrievers smile all the time regardless of the weather. I will argue that where two or more people are gathered outdoors anywhere on earth for any reason, a golden retriever will be in their midst, smiling.

It turned out that Smiling Dog was River, a five-year-old golden retriever who came to the race with Shawn and Bobbie McClung of Alderson. Shawn was among the boaters, and Bobbie and River were spectators, as I was.

I learned later that golden retrievers are the result of breeding Russian shepherds with bloodhounds, and I wondered if River knew of her European or perhaps Asian ancestry. In any event, she was a delight, and there, as the boaters flashed past, I conferred sainthood on her under the authority given me by the state of Middle of Nowhere. She smiled broadly.

She joined Abby, the yellow lab whom I had previously met on the headwaters of Elk, in sainthood. Abby and I had both smiled that day as we watched Ed Maguire catch a native brook trout on the Crooked Fork of Elk.

My hosts at the Whitewater Weekend were Mike Surbaugh and Jim Casey of Horizon Line Adventures, the Webster Springs outfitters with whom I have fished several times. Horizon is the primary sponsor of the April affair.

All of Elk from its start to below Webster Springs is attractive to boaters when the flows are good, but the most popular stretches are these:

Camp Four to the Twin Bridges below Bergoo (approximately seven miles; sufficient flow is especially desirable in this stretch because it is smaller water than farther downstream).

Twin Bridges to Webster Springs (an eight-mile stretch for the more ambitious boaters; includes the canyon section in the Curtin area).

Webster Springs to Sandy Beach (twelve miles of Class III water and the most remote setting on Elk below Elk Springs).

Sandy Beach to The Pines (slightly milder water than the above Down Elk leg, and less than half as far).

The top-rated rapids are the PX Rapids at Parcoal, three miles above Webster Springs, where coal miners once crossed to reach the Pardee and Curtin mine. The PX Rapids are Class Four to Class Five in high water. Boaters are especially wary of a "slot" where the current funnels down and goes through an opening that tends to pull them into extreme turbulence.

The Cherry Falls Rapids are formidable as well. Cherry Falls nestles against Webster Springs on the upriver side of town, and is fiercely protective of its unincorporated status. It is named for T.R. Cherry, who came to Webster County in the 1870s and built a mill that was powered by water from the falls.

Cherry was a New Englander, and eventually returned there, although he lived in Buckhannon for a time after leaving Webster County. He once drilled for salt sulfur water with the intention of competing with the Webster Springs water, but this venture never panned out.

His legacy is the falls which bears his name. Like at Whittaker Falls, there is a series of ledges, with the lower one being the most prominent. It stretches all the way across the river, and is enough of a drop that some boaters elect to portage around it, although there is a "coffee table" (milder water) in the middle that others sneak through.

Mike Surbaugh's "favorite" ledge at Cherry Falls, or at least the most memorable, is the third one, where he was bounced out of his raft. "It reached up and grabbed me and wouldn't let go," he said. I once was a passenger on that particular raft, which I called "Old Blue" for its Easter egg blue color, and in recognition of the seemingly thousands of coon dogs named Old Blue. But I was fishing, not whitewater boating or coon hunting, and we definitely weren't running Cherry Falls. I saw to that early on.

Following the 2005 Webster Wildwater Weekend, I asked Barney Lilly how he performed. "I finished upright," he replied. That hasn't always been the case, thanks to Cherry Falls. "I had a good swim there once," he explained. "I attempted to run the final ledge on the right side, which probably wasn't a good idea, and the hydraulics pulled me back and held me. I had to exit the boat, but that turned out okay. In a few seconds I was standing in water that was only knee deep."

Barney lives in Charleston, is retired from Columbia Gas Transmission, and is one of the organizers of the annual Good Friday trip on Birch River at my home. Barney's daughter, Suzanne Simmons, won the women's division of the 2005 Webster event. The men's winner was Bryan

Jim Casey (left) and Mike Surbaugh

Mascio of Morgantown.   There would have been some fantastic times posted if the race had started a couple of hours later than it did. A hard rainstorm in the Elk headwaters the previous night raised the river a foot and a half, but the full extent of the rise didn't reach the race course until after the boaters had finished.

It was on Birch, or rather as the boaters were coming off the river, that I first met Mike Surbaugh and Jim Casey. Jim is a native of the Pittsburgh area who came to Webster Springs in 1979. He manages the Webster Springs Public Service District's sewer plant below Webster Springs, from where he can walk out the door and see the unglamorously named Sewer Plant Rapids. They are generally considered to be the second most challenging because of their steep gradient, just a curl or two of water behind the PX Rapids, with Cherry Falls third.

Mike is a science teacher and wrestling coach at Webster County High School who migrated to Elk about eight years ago from Mars, for all I know. "I'm from all over," he told me in response to my standard newspaper question. If I had interviewed Winston Churchill, my first question would have been, "Where are you from?" One day I visited Mike at the high school. It was noontime, and I found him sitting outside gazing at the sky. I wondered if he knew something the rest of us didn't about strange little people and tiny spaceships and canals with Class Six whitewater. "No," he said, "I was just watching balloons. It's a class project."

Certainly there is nothing otherworldly about his view of rivers. "Being on a river in a boat is like being a part of nature," he said. "It's primitive. Five hundred years ago it was the only way to travel." I agreed, and I had a bizarre feeling that he had been here five hundred years ago, although he looks much too young.

The Back Fork of Elk is a nearby alternative if main Elk in the Webster Springs area is running too high, but it is popular on its own merit as well. Boaters cite its backwoods setting and the moderate Class II (usually) water. A favorite run is the six miles from the Pardee and Curtin Bridge to Webster Springs. Farther up the Back Fork, the four miles from its junction with Sugar Creek down to Big Falls is a very scenic run. The falls tend to "sneak up" on boaters who aren't familiar with the water. Scouting the run ahead of time, or asking an experienced paddler for advice, is recommended.

"In general, the Back Fork isn't too demanding," said Phil Smith, a Charleston resident who joined the West Virginia Wildwater Association in 1968, not long after its inception, and first paddled Elk in 1972. "I always tell people that I have 100,000 miles on my boat." He is one of the pioneers, with Barney Lilly, of the Good Friday outing on Birch, and is retired from Dodge Reports, a news service for construction companies.

One of the most adventuresome of Elk boaters in terms of trying different waters is Turner Sharp, a Baltimore native who now lives in Parkersburg. He is truly a modern day voyageur. "My goal," he told me, "is to see as much of West Virginia by water as possible, and especially anything on the Elk drainage."

He has run Old Field Fork from its Crooked Fork tributary to the start of Elk, but the last time I asked he hadn't yet run Big Spring Fork. "It's on my list," he said. He has also run the Slaty section of Elk (the start of the river), Leatherwood Creek at Bergoo, the Back Fork of Elk, the Right Fork of Holly, Birch River, and Leatherwood and Sycamore Creeks in Clay County, among a long list.

Surprisingly, at least to me, only a few boaters run the scenic and isolated Slaty section. "You've got to run it when it's up," explained Mike Surbaugh, "but on those occasions everything else is good, too." Turner Sharp told me about a trip on the Slaty section on May 10, 1997, when he and his fellow paddlers, Hunt Charach and Jeff Hilbert, were "treated" to drizzle, sleet, and snow all the way to Whittaker Falls. Later, traveling over the Highland Scenic Highway, they encountered six inches of snow at the higher elevations.

"It turned out to be one of the prettiest times I have experienced on this highway," Turner said. "Occasionally the clouds would break and the sun would highlight the emerald green colors of the Greenbrier Valley in all its spring splendor far below, while we were driving in wintertime conditions."

(Hunt Charach, a Los Angeles native who "adopted" West Virginia when he was driving through the state on his way to college, died of cancer in 2000. He was the U.S. Public Defender for the state's southern federal court district, and was an accomplished guitarist and whitewater boater).

Turner pointed out a unique aspect of running extreme upper Elk in spring. "The dry bed has flow, of course, but you can return later and hike the same river bed in its dry condition. There's nothing impressive about the dry bed, perhaps, but it is interesting nonetheless."

One of the oft-told stories of boating on upper Elk is of the time Susan Klimas' kayak traveled the first mile and a half of the Slaty section, but without her. She was tossed into the water by a large wave on Old Field Fork near the start of Elk while boating with Turner and Mike McClanahan. Mike paddled about a mile and a half down the Slaty section, looking for the missing kayak, but failed to find it. Susan returned later in warmer weather, in another kayak, and discovered the craft "hiding" behind a rock, and lodged against a tree. She carried one boat and towed the other down the railroad track to where Elk meets the Dry

Branch Road, a distance of about three miles.

I wasn't familiar with the boating potential of the two Clay County tributaries mentioned above, and I asked Turner to describe them. He did so, starting with the final four and one-half miles of Leatherwood Creek:

"The whole area is crisscrossed with pipelines and seemingly they all cross Leatherwood Creek. I did a limbo move [squeezed underneath] two of them, portaged two, got hung up on one that should have been portaged, bounced off rocks on two, scraped over four and probably paddled over a dozen more. The low gradient and good visibility on this creek made it more of an aggravation than anything dangerous.

"The take-out is one-half mile down Elk on the left descending side under the WV 16 bridge at Hartland. It is possible to drive to a spot underneath this bridge, but do not be surprised by a braying donkey that hangs out there. She is not lonely; she thinks you are going to feed her."

On running Sycamore Creek from Indore to Elk:

"This is one of the prettiest Class I creeks that I have paddled. Amazingly for a small creek, we had no strainers [trees in the water] to walk around, just a couple to duck or avoid on one side or the other. The banks in most places were lined with hemlock and rhododendron, with several sections of low cliffs. The scenery did include its fair share of trash along the banks, but although this is also oil and gas country we did not have any trouble with pipelines crossing the creek."

(Water levels on Elk can be obtained on the Internet at the West Virginia Wildwater Association website. Readings are from the USGS gauging station at the Clifton Ford Bridge, which is located eighteen river miles below Webster Springs. The gauge measures water flow and depth. Depths of five feet or better at the site are considered good for upper Elk boating generally).

Nineteen

Down Elk

Through Cat Hole Canyon

Elk gathers the waters of the Back Fork at Dorrtown, an unincorporated residential area adjacent to Webster Springs and named for long ago lawyer and congressman Charles P. Dorr. Centralia and the upper end of Sutton Lake are twenty-three miles away. To get there, the river flows through a deep gorge that I have named Cat Hole Canyon.

I initially thought the Cat Hole had something to do with felines until Dave Simmons, who lives at Dorrtown and owns Country Woodworks, gently informed me that it was named for the large catfish that are caught there. Not only that, but there are two Cat Holes, upper and lower, which would have greatly enhanced the feline aspect, had there been one.

Catfish are still caught in the Cat Holes, but walleyes, which were once found Down Elk in large numbers and record size, have largely disappeared below Webster Springs since Sutton Dam was completed in 1961 and stopped their upstream spawning migration. Or at least that is the theory.

Jim Marsh, a Dorrtown native, told me that his father, also named Jim, caught many large walleyes, including one of over thirty-five inches, which would have been a state record. He caught this fish at the Fall Hole at Dorrtown in the late 1940s or early 1950s on a Pikie Minnow, everybody's favorite lure of that era. In my early fishing days I regarded a perch colored Pikie Minnow with a mysticism normally reserved for Eastern religions.

Jim senior was primarily a night fisherman, and he preferred rainy nights. "He would hear it raining in the middle of the night and get up and go fishing," said his son. The July 1945 issue of West Virginia Conservation magazine had a picture of Jim senior and his son, who was a very small boy at that time, with a string of walleyes that ranged from seventeen to thirty-two inches.

Sampson Green, who lives on Grassy Creek of the Right Fork of Holly River, grew up on Cave Run on the Down Elk section. He remembers that walleyes congregated in a pool at the swinging bridge above Clifton Ford. "You could shine a light into the water and it reflected off their eyes like pinpoints of light," he said.

Walleyes were once found in the Hotel Bottom Hole at Webster Springs, now called the Hoover Hole, and also in the Bullion Hole of the Back Fork of Elk in front of the present Tom Cogar logging office. The Bullion Hole was named for a family that lived nearby. Jimmie Bullion played on the first Webster Springs High School football team in 1923.

The most famous catfish of Cat Hole Canyon was outlined on a sycamore tree at Skidmore Bottom below Webster Springs. It was a very large fish and was caught either at the Bridge Hole, the Skidmore Bottom Hole, the Sand Hole, the Round Hole, or the Bear Hole, all deep holes in the vicinity of Skidmore Bottom.

When Jerome Dean was a small boy accompanying his father on a fishing trip, he dropped their seven-cell flashlight in the Bear Hole. "I remember seeing it going down until it was just a glimmer of light, and then it disappeared," said Jerome. His father, Cal Dean, a superb poker player (see Company Town), no doubt knew it was time to "fold" the flashlight hand.

Bill Gillespie, Jim Brown, and I visited Skidmore Bottom in March 2004 on a day when the river was running a chalky white from snow-melt in the headwaters. We looked at every sycamore tree under heaven, and couldn't find the outline of a fish on any of them, not that we really expected to after all these years.

But I did see where Jim fell in the river in January 2002. He was wading across to look at a timber sale, lost his footing, and slid with quiet dignity beneath the icy waters. He had a walk of about a half mile to his vehicle, and his clothing was frozen stiff by the time he got there. He must have looked like a penguin on an ice floe.

Skidmore Bottom is named for John Skidmore, who was president of the Webster Springs National Bank, and died in 1907. He is buried in the lower end of the bottom, where the only sounds are the wind in the trees and the flow of Elk. I could not imagine a more undisturbed place, unless it would be a garden that needs hoeing on a hot day in August.

At one time, about fifteen families lived across the river from the bottom. The crumbling remains of swinging bridge piers are still visible. Skidmore agreed to build a school if the county would build the bridge, and for many years kids trooped across the swaying structure to attend the one-room Skidmore School, which still stands on the Down Elk Road at Skidmore Crossing where the Midland Railroad crossed.

Farther downriver is the Puzzle Hole. Mary Marsh Babbitt recalls visiting the Puzzle Hole School as a small girl when her father, Richard Marsh, taught there. The one-room school was located on the south side of the river. Those who lived on the road side walked over a swinging bridge to the school.

Some of the children brought their lunch in pint bottles, flat like a whiskey bottle, which they probably were, filled with coffee and crumbled cornbread. "One little boy caught a Junebug, pressed it in a book, and gave it to me," she recalls.

"We lived at Dorrtown, and my father would bring kids home with him, perhaps two or three at a time. That was in 1934, and for some of them it was the first time they had seen electric lights or automobiles."

- - -

On a warm, sunny day in July 2003, when the river was running with a decent flow, but not threatening, we fished a five-mile stretch of Down Elk. I say "not threatening" only because the water wasn't at the Class Three stage that it is capable of in the canyon. Any water at any stage deserves respect.

Because of low water, we bypassed the two Cat Holes, and I was secretly thankful that we also bypassed Dead Man's Island, the chilling name given to a place below the Skidmore Bottom where a drowning victim or two have washed up.

We began fishing at Sandy Beach, just below the Puzzle Hole. Eva Carpenter, her daughter Mary, and Mary's husband, Bill Sandy, live across the river from Sandy Beach, their house accessible only by a swinging bridge. But the beach is named for sand, not for the Sandys.

We fished with Mike Surbaugh and Jim Casey of Horizon Line Adventures. The "we" were my nephew, Rob Johnson, his sixteen-year-old son Travis, and myself. The river was clear, the sky was an azure blue, white cumulus clouds were piled haphazardly like underwear in a dresser drawer, and the fishing was decent for a warm day in mid-summer. Rob, Travis, and I caught perhaps twenty smallmouth, the largest of which was about fourteen inches long.

Our first catch came at the Blue Hole just below Sandy Beach. I'm certain there is a Blue Hole on every river in the world, and upper Elk has at least four of them. There is one in the Slaty section near the start of the river, one at Blackhole Run a few miles downstream, the one we fished below Sandy Beach, and another two miles above the Clifton Ford Bridge.

First Fish at the Sandy Beach Blue Hole was a smallmouth of about twelve inches, which set the tone for our catches that day. All of them were in that general size range. The locals who fish Down Elk in mid-summer say the bigger bass are caught at night on surface lures, which is the way it usually happens.

Because of the swift current, parts of Elk in Cat Hole Canyon are difficult to fish thoroughly from a boat. In that respect, it reminds me of New River in the Gorge. But fishing strategy was not of pressing concern to Travis, my nephew's athletic son. He had heard of Webster County, but had never heard of Webster Springs, and knew of Elk only as the river that comes into the Kanawha at Charleston, his hometown.

But he knows food. The previous evening we had returned from fishing on Birch River, and Rob grilled thick steaks on the patio. Teenagers have no defined parameters for mealtimes, and Travis hadn't eaten all day. When I asked him why, he had no idea. But the parameters had been defined by that time. He periodically broke away from a baseball game on television to inspect the sizzling steaks, his eyes mere slits that glowed like charcoal in the gathering darkness. Saliva dripped from his tongue.

The next morning, he discovered Webster Springs over an egg and bacon sandwich at the Subway Restaurant, and announced that he was well pleased with his new find. I had no problem with his earlier scant knowledge. Rob and I fished the Strange Creek Eddy of Elk in Braxton County in summer 2003, and on my next trip up Elk I mentioned this to a few people until I grew weary of explaining where, what, and why Strange Creek was. They did, however, chuckle when I told them what Rob said about a raspy-sounding frog we heard. "It has a person in its throat," he said.

Our outing at Strange Creek was memorable for two reasons. One, the river was clear, which it rarely is, and, two, we saw an incredible variety of fish. We saw white suckers, redhorse suckers, largemouth bass, Kentucky spotted bass, smallmouth bass, rock bass, carp, gizzard shad, and probably other species I'm forgetting.

Travis took to Down Elk with the assurance of a teenager, riding one of Mike and Jim's sit-on-top kayaks. His only previous experience

The author (left), Travis, and Rob Down Elk

had been that spring when he and Tommy Polites, a fellow soccer and baseball player at Capital High School, wrapped Rob's sit-on-top around a rock in Birch at my home.

I'm convinced that kids must jump off rocks for the same reason that walleyes must migrate upstream. Following the primordial urge, Travis sailed off a large square rock at the Chestnut Bottom Hole. A later platform was the Bee Run Rock at the former Arthur Miller farm.

Our day ended at The Pines just below Tackle Box Rapids, where Geary Weir lost his tackle box and all its contents at some unfortunate moment in the past. "We were both grabbing for it, and almost got it, but not quite," said Mike Surbaugh. I was on the verge of telling of the time I lost my tackle box and assorted other items on Elk at Frametown, but I was tired after a day of sun and water and was feeling physically and mentally incapable of explaining where, what, and why Frametown was.

- - -

Down Elk is swinging bridge country. There are seven of these structures from just above Sandy Beach to the Clifton Ford Bridge, and six of them are the only access to the Elk River Road by families who choose to live in the isolation of Down Elk Across Elk. I call them the Swinging

Bridge People.

I drove Down Elk from Webster Springs a week after our fishing trip and walked across one of the bridges to visit Eva Carpenter, daughter Mary, and Mary's husband, Bill. Evie, as she is known, was peeling Early Transparent apples, and I detected a whiff of apple pie in the oven.

The peelings, and apples with bruises or other imperfections, went into a bucket to be fed to the deer that come into their yard. Early Transparents are good for apple sauce and pies, she said, and I nodded sagely. Later, over coffee and a piece of pie fresh from the oven, I nodded sagely several times.

I asked about the bridge, which is their third one. They told me that the original washed away in 1975. They were returning home in the middle of the night and decided to cross, even though floodwater was lapping just under the planking and their only light was a dim flashlight. "I told them the bridge would be gone by daylight, and that if we wanted to cross we'd better do it quickly," said Evie. She was right. At dawn, there was only space across Elk where the bridge had been. The second bridge went to its watery reward in 1985.

Bridge III is a handsome work of art that spans the river for three hundred and twenty-five feet, with an approach of ninety-six feet on the house side. Its river span is longer than that of the so-called Million Dollar Bridge at Clifton Ford.

- - -

Rob and I returned Down Elk on the first day of August 2003 to fish with Mike Surbaugh. "Wear good wading shoes," Mike advised. "We're going to do a lot of walking." I'm partial to low water, but I find the first fifty miles of Elk difficult to wade because I'm convinced it is where rounded rocks go to spawn and die.

Charlie Heartwell calls them "bowling ball rocks." In his experience, the only river more difficult to wade is the Savage in Maryland, where rounded and jagged rocks are combined. Jerome Dean says that in high water in Elk you can hear the rounded rocks rolling along in the current like the sound of the little men bowling in The Legend of Sleepy Hollow.

In December 2003 Rob and I walked in the snow on the riverbank above Bergoo and thought of people we'd like to send running barefooted over the snow-covered rounded rocks. It wasn't a pleasant thought at the Christmas season, but secretly I began compiling a list and took great delight in it.

The fishing was slow on our August trip. Perhaps Rob needed an uneventful outing, because two days earlier he had been bounced out of a raft on New River by a huge wave. I told this story to Gary Jarrell of Fisher Auto Parts, and he topped me, as people tend to do. He said that he fell out of a raft on the New, and the domino effect took four other people with him.

Above the Clifton Ford Bridge, where the river channel narrows on the left, we saw an extraordinary sight. A wild turkey hen sailed across and lit on the opposite bank. She stood there, a lonely and mysterious bird. Then turkey poults began to flutter across the channel until it seemed the sky was filled with them and the sun darkened. The rear guard consisted of three or four hens who were the last to cross.

We came to the home of Dana and Kathleen Clutter. Dana, a retired coal miner, is known far and wide as "Down Elk Dana." We heard his lawnmower whirring, and his coonhounds barking, and we stopped and talked. I said I would like to return another day and meet the coonhounds.

- - -

Rob caught a smallmouth of sixteen inches near Dana's home. But it was getting late. The sun had given way to shadows on the river, and only the hilltops still clung to the late evening sunshine. The Clifton Ford Bridge, also known as the Million Dollar Bridge, looked every penny of it in the half light.

I hooked what felt like a decent-sized bass just before we left the river, and had it on for about five seconds before it shook loose, a happy ending for both of us. I have no interest in keeping fish, and less interest in unhooking them as the day wears on.

Mike seemed to be just warming up, and it was cause for concern. He loves rivers, and in fact he and his wife Julie were married on the riverbank in front of their Webster Springs home. He canoed upriver from Baker's Island, she canoed downriver from the upper end of the Hoover Hole, and they met and paddled to the bank, where Judge Boonie Sommerville performed the ceremony. Julie asked the neighbors to turn their dogs

The Clifton Ford Bridge

loose for the occasion, and one of them celebrated its freedom by curling up on the long flowing train of her wedding dress.

Mike had fallen in love also with Elk, and he had made a pact with God. "I told God that if he would let me enjoy being out on the river, I'd be forever grateful," he explained to me, "and I would settle for catching only one fish per day."

I felt humbled to be fishing with a man who had bargained with God, and with another man, my nephew, who has never been mistaken. "I thought I was mistaken once," he confided to me that day on Elk, "but I was mistaken."

Mike caught the one divinely sanctioned fish below where we saw the turkeys. Then he caught an unsanctioned second fish below Clifton Ford, and I felt obligated to remind him of his pact. He replied that, yes, he'd forgotten about it in the excitement of catching two fish. But soon he caught a definitely unsanctioned third fish, and I rather pointedly suggested that it was time to go home.

But then I thought, "Who am I to judge someone else's arrangements with God?" The Apostle Paul speaks sternly about judging our neighbor, especially if he is sitting in the same boat with us and catching fish, has impressive shoulders and arms, and coaches wrestling. But it was late, the sun was gone, and I was becoming very judgmental. When you lose the sun, you've lost the heart and soul of an evening, I thought rather sanctimoniously.

Back home, Rob and I grilled steaks and I gradually became more tolerant of everything. The miserable rounded rocks were only a distant memory the following morning when we went fishing down Birch. I came upon a box turtle, not quite of adult size but a very nice, bright-eyed young fellow perched on top of a flat plastic motor oil can. He twisted his head sideways to hear every word I had to say. He never interrupted me or tried to top my stories. With fitting ceremony, I named him to an important cabinet post in our fledgling state of Middle of Nowhere.

The organization of the new state has proceeded well. Neil Boggs, the former host of NBC's Meet the Press, came all the way from New Mexico to insist that we have a state question, as New Mexico does, so we selected the only four words ever uttered by deer hunters: Got Your Buck Yet? They run the words together, as in gotyourbuckyet. Neil immediately and excitedly recognized the language as Mayan, which anthropologists know as a lost civilization in Central America.

The West Virginia Legislature has agonized for years over whether to make English the official state language, but the state of Middle of Nowhere didn't agonize for a minute. It adopted Mayan as its official language. Two hundred thousand deer hunters can't be wrong.

- - -

I returned Down Elk another day to visit Dana and Kathleen Clutter and the coonhounds. Dana told me he was born across the river at what was known as "the Wilson patch" for long ago residents Charley and Fannie Wilson. He attended the Salisbury School, which was located at the present Elk River Pentecostal Church. In the late 1930s, there were sixty-three children attending the one room school.

Dana and Kathleen ticked off names they could remember of families who had kids attending there: Salisbury, McCourt, Miller, Hall, Brady, Tenney, Clutter, Anderson, McElwain, Evans, Cogar, Brooks, and Fisher.

Clifton Ford, downstream of their home, is named for Dana's great great grandfather, John Clifton, an early settler. Dana has lived at his present location since 1953, and worked thirty-three years in the mines for Island Creek and Pardee and Curtin.

I was properly introduced to the coonhounds, who greeted me with excited barking as if I were treed. I have been barked at, snarled at, yapped at, regarded sullenly, or slobbered on by every breed, size, and shape of dog known to mankind, and I always prefer coonhounds, especially those named Old Something or Other.

While the dogs barked and slobbered, I thought of coon hunting stories, especially one. Dana has a reputation in this regard, as does Boonie Sommerville. One day, so the story went, Boonie walked into the barbershop at Webster Springs, and Dana was there. Naturally they began swapping tales, and Dana told about one of his dogs that would stay at a tree all night, and all the next day, if necessary.

All eyes turned to Boonie. The snipping scissors grew silent. "I had a female dog who was soon to have pups," Boonie began. "I went hunting on Old Lick Run, and she wanted desperately to go, so I took her with me. But during the night, she disappeared. I looked for two or three days, and couldn't find her. Two weeks later, I returned for a final try and went all the way out a long ridge. I heard faint barking, and followed the sound. I came to a big sinkhole with a poplar tree in the middle. A coon was sitting on the highest limb, and there in the sinkhole was my dog, barking treed. Not only that, but she'd had her pups in that sinkhole, and they were all barking at the coon too."

Twenty

Elk in the Center

Carpenter Country

Upper River comes to Braxton County at Centralia, or rather Braxton County comes to Upper River. One quarter mile below the mouth of Laurel Creek, the backwater of Sutton Lake at summer pool stage merges with the untamed waters of Elk. It is fifteen miles from that eclectic mix down to Sutton Dam, the monolithic slab of concrete that was completed in 1961.

Above Centralia all the way to Clifton Ford is the final canyon of Elk, and it is deep and isolated. I have fished and camped there several times. One time my nephew, Rob, then a teenager, was with me when a violent electrical storm descended. We were not far from where Solomon Carpenter was born under a rock cliff, and we found a rock cliff of our own to take shelter under and ride out the storm.

Centralia, which was once one of the largest voting precincts in Braxton County, has dwindled down to a precious few. The exodus culminated with the building of the dam, when many people were required to move, but Centralia had already seen its heyday.

In the early 1900s, there were three band mills, fifty-three houses, a company store, hotel, theatre, saloon, church, grade school, high school, two fraternal lodges, restaurant, post office, freight depot, blacksmith shop, and grist mill.

Hap Sizemore, who has lived at Centralia since 1923, attended high school classes in the company store building. Prior to that, classes were held in the Methodist Church, where the Odd Fellows and Rebekah Lodges also met.

The theatre was a three-story building where silent movies were shown, and boxing matches were held. Pearl Holden Shamblin, mother of Frances Skidmore of Caress, played the piano for the silent movies in the 1920s. Next door to the theatre was the saloon, with a hotel or boarding house above it, which was a common alliance in the early lumber towns.

The economic centerpiece was Davis Lumber Company, and today a few people still call the hole of water where Laurel Creek enters Elk "The Company Store Eddy." Davis Lumber owned 13,943 acres in the Centralia area, and one of its legendary saw logs was from a black walnut cut on Gulf Run above Centralia that measured over eight feet in diameter.

But logs come and logs go. Glenda Diggins Loyd of Gassaway told me about her father, W.T. Diggins, and a partner, assembling a very large stack of prime logs at the mouth of Laurel, but the 1918 flood washed them all away.

The large walnut cut by Davis Lumber would bring enough money today to make a substantial down payment on a house. I was having lunch in Webster Springs with Bill Gillespie and Jim Brown of Gillespie Forestry Services, and while we were waiting for the roast beef special I asked them how much money this one tree would be worth at present prices.

If it was growing in a field, they calculated, it would probably have produced a 12-foot log, and yielded 5,808 board feet of lumber, which at today's prices would bring approximately $23,232. If it was growing in a preferred location at the edge of the woods, it would probably have produced three short logs that would have yielded 11,860 board feet worth $47,440 today.

I marvel at fanciful names that Indians are said to have given rivers, but Walnut River, which is the name the Delaware Indians (or perhaps the Miami) gave to Elk, may be fitting in view of the above. It is also said that the Shawnee called Elk the Tischilwaugh, or Tiskelwah, meaning "river of plenty fat elk."

There is a third version. In his book, *Play of a Fiddle*, Gerry Milnes quotes Ernie Carpenter as saying that his great great grandfather, Jeremiah Carpenter, "gave Elk River its name after killing a large elk along the river." The family tradition is that Jeremiah fashioned a boat out of the hide, and used it to transport the meat back to his cabin.

- - -

Unless a more persuasive case is made to the contrary, it appears that Centralia is the community closest to the geographic center of West

Virginia. At the very least, the name Centralia counts for something, being a made-up English word for center. Nearby Flatwoods claims the title with a sign on Interstate 79, but it may not be as close as Sutton, the county seat, and Centralia may be closer still.

The West Virginia Blue Book defines the center as being located in the Elk River Wildlife Management Area. It gives coordinates, as well as mileage from Flatwoods, Sutton, and Centralia. Flatwoods is six miles away, Sutton is four and three-quarter miles away, and Centralia is four miles away. There is, or was, a wildlife clearing in the Elk River WMA that is the epicenter, according to local lore. I once stood there and felt good about being in the center of everything.

The West Virginia Geological and Economic Survey came out of a 2003 controversy over the highest point in the state relatively unscathed (see Lofty Beginning), and it's staying out of this one. It says the state's borders are too irregular to determine an exact center. But the data in the Blue Book probably came from them.

In the course of writing about the geographic center, I spoke with Cliff Wilkie, a former Braxton County surveyor. At that time, he was working in Maryland but living in Ohio. Then, out of the blue, in November 2004, I received a letter from Cliff. He was the newly designated Geodetic Surveyor for the City of Albuquerque, New Mexico. He told me he had given thought to the "trials, tribulations and concomitant humor of attempting to establish the centerpoint of an amorphous and completely randomly placed pile of dirt called a State."

To underscore his point, he included an article written by Fred Roeder, the unofficial historian of the New Mexico State Surveyors Association. The article appeared in *Benchmarks*, a publication of the association. A portion of it follows:

"The U.S. Geological Survey has long published a list of approximate geographic centers and probably regretted it. Part of the difficulty is that there is no generally accepted definition of 'geographic center,' nor is there a satisfactory method for determining it. A State or any other political or geographic entity may have as many geographic centers as there are definitions of the term.

"It may be defined as the center of gravity of the surface, or the point at which the surface would balance if it were a sheet of uniform thickness and weight. As can be imagined, if topography is to be considered, mountain ranges would tend to shift the point of gravity, just like a hammer balances near its head.

"Another method might be to ignore the irregularity of surface and balance the outline of a projected area on the shell of the spheroid, of the geoid, or of

any other reference surface that mathematics can invent. An area could also be projected onto a plane surface and its center be computed. This would yield as many different centers as there are projections."

The article accomplished two things for me personally. First, it compelled me to rise and give a standing ovation to the West Virginia Geological and Economic Survey for opting out of the issue of the West Virginia center. Secondly, through it I learned that Castle Rock, South Dakota, claims to be the geographic center of the fifty states of the United States; that Rugby, North Dakota, supposedly marks the center of the North American continent; that a frigid spot of ground in the Siberian uplands near the Arctic Circle is the geographic center of the Russian Federation, and, to give ultimate closure to the matter, Iskenderun, Turkey, lays claim to being at the center of the entire landmass called earth.

- - -

Elk between Centralia and Sutton is Carpenter country. The story of Jeremiah Carpenter, thought to be the first permanent white settler in what is now Braxton County, continues to fascinate, as do the stories of his descendants.

The centerpiece of the Carpenter legend is that Solomon Carpenter, the firstborn of Jeremiah and Elizabeth Hamm Carpenter, was born under a rock cliff on Camp Run of Laurel Creek of Elk River in present day Webster County. Whether Jeremiah and his wife had gone to the rock to escape from Indians, which is the popular version, or whether they simply arrived there in their wanderings is a question that is not likely to be answered.

Information on the early Carpenters, especially Jeremiah and his son, Solomon, is frequently contradictory, which isn't unusual, given that over two hundred years have elapsed since Jeremiah settled on Elk near present Centralia.

According to family tradition, Jeremiah was born in Augusta County, Virginia, in 1755, and some accounts say that at a young age he was captured by Indians and lived with them for several years. The same tradition holds that he was the son of William Carpenter, who was killed by Indians on the Jackson River in Virginia in 1764. It may have been at this time that Jeremiah was captured.

Most accounts say that Jeremiah and three of his brothers served in the Revolutionary War, and that Jeremiah took part in the Battle of Point Pleasant in October 1774.

The year of his arrival on Elk isn't known for a certainty, but the strong likelihood is that he came there between 1780 and 1790. Family genealogies show that he bought a considerable amount of land on Elk and Holly Rivers in that period.

In 1785, he married Elizabeth Hamm at Alderson, Greenbrier County. Whether they came to Elk before or after their marriage isn't known, but according to John D. Sutton's *History of Braxton County and Central West Virginia*, they settled at the Samuel Skidmore bottom across Elk from the present day Baker's Run Campground at the upper end of Sutton Lake.

Jeremiah's brother, Benjamin, and Benjamin's wife, Ruth Jeffers Carpenter, settled about four miles downstream at the mouth of Holly River. It was a fateful move, because in 1792, traditional accounts say, both were killed by Indians.

The birth of Solomon Carpenter under the rock cliff is generally believed to have occurred soon afterwards, but there is a problem with that. His death record at the Braxton County Courthouse says that he died on November 13, 1866, at age eighty-four. If the age is correct, that means he was born in 1782. The 1860 Braxton County census gives Solomon's age as seventy-seven, which, adding six more years, essentially agrees with the death record.

One version of the circumstances surrounding his birth is that around the time of the death of Benjamin Carpenter and his wife, or perhaps a few months later, Jeremiah and Elizabeth fled up Laurel Creek to escape another Indian threat, and took refuge under the ledge where Solomon was born.

The story takes a radically different twist in *Tale of the Elk*. Bill Byrne wrote that Jeremiah and his wife "came across the mountains before the Revolutionary War" and took up abode under the rock ledge. "Within a very few days, a son was born to them, and to him was given the name Solomon." The Byrne version has Jeremiah and family staying there for "a number of years." Byrne said the rock was located near the mouth of Camp Run "at the edge of the creek bottom."

But the Solly's Rock of popular perception today is located about three-quarters of a mile upstream from the mouth, and on a steep hillside perhaps a hundred feet above the run. Peter and Elizabeth Silitch and I went there in November 2004 on a gray day that threatened rain.

The cliff overhang is of impressive size, and we could envision someone taking refuge there, especially if the possibility existed that they were being chased by Indians. But to accept that the Carpenters stayed there for more than a short period of time with their newborn son requires a leap of faith. And whether it is the real Solly's Rock, as tradition says, is another question without an answer.

While Peter was photographing the rock, visitors stopped by. They were brothers Daniel and Carl Bean of Cowen, who grew up about three miles away on the White Oak Road near Erbacon. Daniel is a retired school principal in Webster County, and Carl is a retired railroader. We discussed the legend, and came to no particular conclusions, except that, as legends go, it is a very good one. On the way home, Peter, Elizabeth and I unanimously chose Solly's Rock as official rock of the new state of Middle of Nowhere.

We also found the perfect choice for state stump. It is a large, crumbling white oak stump from a tree that grew in front of the cliff, and could have been there over two hundred years ago when Solomon was born.

Later, we embraced Laurel Creek, although not necessarily the one we visited, as the new state's official creek. This will please everybody, since there seems to be at least one Laurel Creek within a mile of wherever anybody happens to be at any given time.

On the last day of March 2005, Peter and I returned to the traditional Solly's Rock to look for other possible candidates nearby. We found an impressively honeycombed rock closer to the mouth of Camp Run and not far above the run, where, we judged, two or three people could have taken refuge for a short time. We didn't encounter any of the rattlesnakes that are said to inhabit Camp Run. The story is told that the wife of a Trout Unlimited member accompanied her husband there on a fish stocking trip, and either stepped on or almost stepped on a large rattler, and that others have encountered rattlers as well.

The traditional Solly's Rock is firmly embedded in local lore, perhaps correctly. On our way back down Laurel Creek we stopped to visit Vincent Williams, who has lived there all his life. He believes the traditional rock is the right one. He said an elderly man named Carpenter, who lived at the mouth of Camp Run in the 1930s, recalled seeing the remains of split oak timbers that had been placed in front of the rock as a sort of wall.

Although the story surrounding the birth of Solomon is full of uncertainties, the place of his death is fairly well documented. It is given on his death certificate as Franklin Township, which today is Holly District, Braxton County, and includes the Centralia area. An act of the West Virginia Legislature on July 31, 1863, divided Braxton into four townships: Clay, Lincoln, Washington, and Franklin. The townships were changed to districts in 1873.

To complete the puzzle of the lives of Jeremiah and Solomon, nobody knows where they are buried. It is generally accepted that Jeremiah died around 1832, and John D. Sutton wrote that Jeremiah and his wife Elizabeth were buried at the Skidmore Cemetery "not far from where his cabin used to stand."

The Skidmore Cemetery was started as a family burial plot around 1800, and later became a community or neighborhood cemetery It was the largest of six cemeteries moved when Sutton Dam was built. It contained 211 graves, but only about thirty percent of them were marked with inscribed stones or monuments. Many remains were reinterred in the Braxton County Cemetery on Airport Road.

I visited the Braxton County Cemetery on a sunny day in November 2004 that wasn't as warm as it looked. A cold breeze ruffled my jacket collar and tugged at my cap. I didn't find a marker for Jeremiah, but there were many graves marked simply "Unknown."

One of the marked graves caught my eye. It was that of Solomon Carpenter, 1745-1810. The dates indicate he was probably the brother of Jeremiah and the namesake of the man born under the rock cliff. Family genealogy confirms that Jeremiah had a brother named Solomon.

Virtually all of the other graves in what is referred to on the Army Corps of Engineers relocation map as "Block E" are "Unknowns." Jeremiah, the first permanent white settler on Elk in Braxton County, and his son, Solomon, may be among them.

- - -

Solomon Carpenter of rock cliff fame was the father of William 'Squirrely Bill' Carpenter, a legendary oldtime riverman on Elk. Sutton newspaper publisher J. Holt Byrne wrote of Squirrely Bill that "during his lifetime his chief vocation was hunting and fishing, and at either he reportedly had no equal in the entire section from Webster Springs to Charleston."

He was born in 1828, the fifth son of Solomon and Mary Elizabeth Knight Carpenter. In addition to being a hunter and fisherman, he was also a raftsman and builder of canoes and johnboats, a family craft that continued for two more generations. The Carpenters built johnboats of serious length. A picture that accompanies this chapter shows a johnboat that is obviously quite long, although not all of it can be seen in the picture.

Squirrely Bill was small of stature, but it is said that he could propel a canoe or johnboat with more ease than any of his contemporaries. He would take orders from Sutton merchants, float to Charleston with two or three companions, and return with the merchandise, pulling the boat over the shoals.

His fishing haunts were from Wolf Creek to Stony Creek on the lower end of present Sutton Lake. He was also a trapper of great renown. When I visited Goldie Carpenter Aillio, his granddaughter, at her Clarksburg home in December 2004, she told about her grandfather falling in the river one icy day with a knapsack full of traps on his back.

Squirrely Bill died in 1921 at age ninety-three, and is buried in the Town Hill Cemetery at Sutton. There is still a Squirrely Bill presence in Sutton. A muzzleloading rifle that once belonged to him is owned by Joe Greene of the Greene-Robertson Funeral

Squirrely Bill Carpenter
(photo courtesy of Goldenseal magazine)

Home. The story goes that Henry McElwain obtained the rifle in a trade with Squirrely Bill, who received a hog or other farm animal, and money.

"My grandfather, William McElwain, inherited the gun when his father Henry died," said David McElwain of Sutton, a retired teacher. "The McElwains were among the first settlers in Sutton, arriving around 1812 and settling in the bottom below the mouth of Granny's Creek, where six generations of McElwains have lived, and where I grew up."

There is a second Squirrely Bill rifle. Don Douglas of Clarksburg, a great nephew, has an ancient percussion cap rifle that he believes belonged to Squirrely Bill. In the manner of those weapons, it is long and heavy, and must have required considerable effort on the part of the diminutive Squirrely to lift it, aim, and fire accurately. But apparently he managed quite well, given the stories of his hunting exploits.

Shelt Carpenter, one of Squirrely Bill's sons, was also a well known man of Elk River. He guided fishermen and entertained them around the campfire with fiddle tunes and stories. A story in *the Clarksburg Exponent* following Shelt's death in 1937 called him "the mountain philosopher."

Politically, Shelt was a strong Democrat, but he would help friends

Squirrely Bill's muzzleloader

of opposite persuasion, at least up to a point. "In one election," his daughter, Goldie, told me, "he worked all day for a Republican friend who was running for a county office. Then at the end of the day, he voted a straight Democratic ticket." Asked why, Shelt explained, "well he didn't need my vote." Whether this meant he thought his friend was going to win anyway, or, conversely, going to lose anyway, is unclear.

Shelt died at age seventy-five, and was buried at the Kitzmiller Cemetery near the present Bee Run Boat Dock. This cemetery was one of the six moved when the dam was built. Shelt and his wife were reinterred at the Braxton County Cemetery. His homeplace on Elk above Sutton is now covered by the waters of Sutton Lake.

Goldie Aillio, who was ninety-one years of age at the time of my visit to her Claerksburg home, is the last surviving member of the Shelt and Mary Ann Carpenter family. She was born at the homeplace in the house that she believes was built by her grandfather, Squirrely Bill. A path led up the mountain to the Bee Run School that she attended.

She recalls a "shanty town" across the river in the vicinity of Stony Creek where workers lived who were cutting timber for the chemical plant at Sutton. A railroad ran up the south side of Elk to transport wood to the plant. The plant had a contract to manufacture wood alcohol for the War Department in World War I, but the war ended just as the first batch was being loaded for shipment.

Like most of the Carpenters, Goldie plays a stringed instrument, in her case a five-string banjo. Playing oldtime fiddle tunes was a Carpenter tradition for five generations, beginning with Jeremiah and continuing through Ernie Carpenter, Goldie's brother. In *Play of a Fiddle*, Gerry Milnes wrote that they were "perhaps the best known old time fiddling family in the state, and perhaps in all of Appalachia."

One tune they all performed was Shelvin' Rock, which Jeremiah is said to have composed to commemorate the birth of his son, Solomon, under the rock cliff. A 1986 album of Ernie Carpenter's music, entitled *Elk River Blues*, includes Shelvin' Rock.

Another of their tunes was called Camp Chase, for the Union prisoner of war camp in Ohio. Supposedly it was played by a Confederate prisoner called Devil Sol Carpenter to gain his freedom after the camp commander had made that offer "to the best fiddler in camp." Whether the Camp Chase fiddler was a direct descendant of Solomon Carpenter of rock cliff fame isn't known, but the latter had a son, Solomon, born around 1840, who saw military service in 1861 in the home guard in Braxton County.

- - -

If present Sutton Lake is haunted by memories of its colorful past as part of Elk River, the railroad trestle over the lake is a more recent nest of the occult. In the 1970s, the crew of a coal train came out of the tunnel on the Centralia side of the lake to discover to their horror that the trestle was on fire. They decided their best choice was to continue across, and they safely reached the opposite side, although several loaded cars behind them wrecked. Four cars went into the lake, and are still there. The cause of the fire remains a mystery.

The trestle continued to exact a toll. Retired railroader Harold Carpenter, a descendant of Solomon, was fishing there and got a lure caught in his scalp that had to be cut out. I was fishing under the trestle one day when a train came across and an egg size lump of coal hit me on top of the head, drawing blood. The trauma and the bloodletting may have exorcised the haunting, because later in the day I caught a bass that weighed over four pounds.

Shelt Carpenter and daughter Goldie in an Elk johnboat

Twenty One

Elk Through Braxton

Sutton Dam and Below

The view from the top of Sutton Dam was impressive. "It's a long way down, isn't it," said a teenage boy who smiled as he walked by me on a frigid day in March 2004. I smiled and nodded. We were standing two hundred and ten feet above Elk River. Downstream, the white cupola on the bell tower of the Braxton County Courthouse stood out even in a snow squall.

Four of the dam's five sluice gates were open, shooting out water in spectacular fashion. Somewhere in there, I thought, are contributions from Old Field Fork, Big Spring Fork, Blackhole Run, Bergoo Creek, Leatherwood Creek, Back Fork, and dozens of other places I had visited in the process of writing *Upper River.*

I especially thought of Parting Springs on Turkeybone Mountain at the very head of the Back Fork, and I assumed its waters were down there in the mix at the base of the dam. If so, they would arrive at the mouth of Elk in Charleston in twenty-one hours. I had just read that in a Corps of Engineers manual.

I think about such things, and I tend to bore people with trivia questions about them. My nephew's sons and daughter have learned the entire history of Babe Ruth and the 1927 Yankees through my maddening trivia obsession. They have also come to the realization that there has been no good music written since Beethoven died in 1827, and that Geronimo was under-appreciated by the U.S. Army.

But Keith Ann Nuckles of the Corps of Engineers at Sutton Dam was equal to the occasion when I looked up from the manual and asked her when the water we could see spraying from the sluice gates would arrive in Charleston. "In its own good time," she replied.

We both marveled at another statement that leaped out from the manual. It said that in the September 1861 flood, the flow of Kanawha River into the Ohio at Point Pleasant was so strong that the Ohio ran *upstream* as far as thirty miles.

I once heard a university professor on a book tour say he would fail a student for asking a hypothetical question, but I will ask one anyway. Suppose that a flood of 1861 magnitude would occur again *and Sutton Dam wasn't in place*, what would happen at Charleston? The answer, according to the manual, was that forty percent of it would be under eleven feet of water.

The 1861 flood was the flood of record at Sutton, cresting almost thirty-seven feet above normal, according to data reconstructed by the Corps of Engineers. In December 1861, retreating Confederates burned all but four or five houses in Sutton, completing a dismal three months for the town.

Sutton Dam, finished in 1961, might have been Clendenin Dam, which was the original choice of the Corps of Engineers. But the corps decided that the Clendenin project (actually upstream at Queen Shoals) would be too expensive, and it turned to Sutton for the taming of Elk.

Because of its close proximity to the river, Sutton was flooded several times in the first half of the twentieth century, including huge floods in 1918 and 1932. Before the Midway Hotel walls were paneled over, there was a water line high up in the dining room from one of the floods.

Sutton, the most centrally located county seat in West Virginia, is named for John D. Sutton, who gave an acre of ground for a public square. He came to his namesake town from Alexandria, Virginia, in 1809, after an earlier trip he had made to look at land his father had bought on Elk and Granny's Creek. His father, also named John, later joined him and lived with his son until his death. Father and son are buried in the Skidmore Cemetery on the town's south hillside overlooking the Elk Valley. A single bevel top monument marks their graves.

Braxton County Courthouse

The town was called Newville, or Suttonsville, before it became Sutton in 1836 when Braxton County was formed. Town records were partially destroyed by the 1861 fire, and the village was reincorporated later, perhaps around 1883.

The original courthouse was built in the mid-1800s, and the present one around 1886-87, becoming the town's first brick building. It has been added to since, including major additions in 1938 and 2000.

Courthouses have adopted the custom of placing artillery pieces on their grounds. My brother Bob always said they were used for putting down taxpayer revolts. Oddly, the weapon at the Braxton County Courthouse is a 75-mm Japanese gun. It was obtained soon after World War II, but nobody around today remembers the details. The U.S. Army Artillery Museum at Fort Sill, Oklahoma, identified it as the Japanese weapon when I sent them photos.

In 2002, the Braxton County Commission had the gun sand blasted and repainted, and its wooden spoke wheels replaced. During that time, a controversy arose over the nationality of the weapon, but the matter was put to rest when, in addition to the museum's verdict, the sand blasting revealed Japanese writing on the breech. The Japanese gun replaced a stubby little cannon, its nationality unremembered, that was sacrificed in one of the World War II scrap metal drives.

- - -

Two businesses identifying with Sutton are Braxton Motor Company and the Midway Hotel. Generations of Braxton Countians grew up believing that God in His infinite wisdom created heaven, earth, and Braxton Motor, and not necessarily in that order.

The company was started in 1916 by A.L. Morrison and others, and in 1923 was bought by Lester and Henry Gerwig, and Frank Marlow Sr. They built the present building over a six-year period, moving into it in 1929.

Despite the "Motor" part of the name, Braxton Motor hasn't sold cars (Fords and Mercurys) since 1949. When the company was incorporated in 1950, there was some discussion about deleting "Motor," since they were selling furniture, appliances, hardware, and building supplies, but not cars. But tradition won out and the company name continues as Braxton Motor.

A ramp, that has since been enclosed or boarded over, was visible inside the store for many years, and served as a reminder of the car days. Frank Marlow Jr., retired manager, said the ramp was used to drive cars to the second floor paint shop. Long gone are the gasoline pumps that stood on the sidewalk in front of the building.

Also gone is the Braxton Motor Restaurant, which was located in the present hardware section. Amanda Gerwig, who came to Sutton from Exchange, Braxton County, and was quite the businesswoman for her time, owned the restaurant. She moved it to the Midway when she bought the hotel in the 1930s.

The Midway began in 1894 as the Elk, and became the Midway after Gerwig bought it. The name reflected the fact that Sutton was the midway point for the West Virginia Transportation Company buses that ran between Clarksburg and Charleston.

"The arrival of the buses was a big event," recalled Suzy Nuzum, Amanda Gerwig's granddaughter. "They carried freight as well as passengers. I remember boxes being unloaded and stacked on the sidewalk in front of the hotel."

Buses were often parked overnight in a building that was constructed by Braxton Motor and rented to West Virginia Transportation. The building is now used by Braxton Motor for storage, but is still referred to as "the bus garage."

The Midway dining room was a culinary haven. One of its distinctions was a "Family Table" where Sutton businessmen gathered to eat lunch. In a way, the Midway also fed the fish in nearby Elk. "We would take the old bread in the evening and feed the fish from the bridge," said Suzy Nuzum, who was born at the hotel.

In the late 1930s and early 1940s, the DNR closed Elk to fishing

Elk River Bridge at Sutton, circa 1900
Photo courtesy of Sutton Feed and Hardware

from present Sutton Dam to below the bridge, designating it as a spawning ground for bass and other fish. Watching and feeding fish from the bridge became quite an attraction.

The bridge was built in 1930, replacing an earlier suspension bridge. Retired Braxton County school teacher David McElwain recalls riding the ferry that took automobiles across Elk during construction of the 1930 bridge.

- - -

I owe my introduction to the outside world to Juergens Drug Store. Juergens and Walker Drug stood across from each other on Main Street, and the first ice cream cone I ever ate was at Juergens on a trip in from the country. I remember that the coldness of the ice cream gave me a headache.

The drug store pioneers were E.L. Juergens and Alfred Walker. The latter obtained a position with Juergens in 1892, and a few years later became a member of the firm that was known as Juergens and Walker. They were partners in the Sutton Bottling Works, which bottled soda pop and delivered it with horse and wagon. The partnership continued until Walker's retirement in 1928. At some point the two drug stores became separate entities. Alfred Walker was the first president of the West Virginia Pharmaceutical Association when it was formed in 1907.

Alfred's son, Albert, who owned Walker Drug from 1941 until his

The same scene today

Sutton Bottling Works
Photo courtesy of Nell Kiddy Crisman

death in 1962, was a pilot with the American Expeditionary Force in France in World War I. His daughter, Nell Kiddy Crisman of Phoenix, has a picture of her father with his airplane.

Hugh Elliott was the last owner of Walker Drug. He bought the business after Albert Walker's death and ran it until his retirement in 1995. Willard Moore, who later had a restaurant in the Walker building, found a yardstick from the drug store days that advertised: "Use Juergens Tar and Wild Honey for Coughs, Colds and Hoarseness. Use Walker's White Healing Salve for Cuts and Sores."

To walk into the Walker building is to walk back in time. It has a massive front door with a beveled glass pane, huge ceiling fans, and ceiling fixtures that once held gas lights. In the basement was a hand-dug well that preceded the days of "city water."

Hugh Elliott recalls one early morning when he and the town policemen, Gale Barrett, were conversing in the back of the store when a man walked in and wanted to buy the front door. "He was very persistent," said Hugh, "although I kept patiently explaining that it wasn't for sale. Then, right in front of a uniformed policeman, the man declared that he would "come back some night and rip it off."

Although there hasn't been a Walker Drug in Sutton since 1995, the name continues in the neighboring town of Gassaway. Carl Walker Sr., Albert's cousin, established a drug store there, which, after his death, was owned by his sons Carl Jr. and Steve until bought by the present owner, Frank Grindo, in 1979.

- - -

One of Sutton's historic old churches is now the Landmark Studio for the Arts. The Methodist Episcopal Church South built the Gothic Revival structure in 1896, and later it was occupied by the Presbyterians and Southern Baptists. Retired Sutton banker Roy 'Butch' Cutlip and his wife, Janie, were married at Landmark when it was a Presbyterian church.

In 1984, the building took on a new use, becoming home to the Hillbilly Players, a local theater group. Today, Landmark is host to a variety of events, including plays, musical events, film festivals, and art shows.

The original Sutton High School, built in 1906, held its baccalaureate services at what is now Landmark. The old school barely escaped the wrecker's ball in the 1970s when it was scheduled for

Landmark Studio for the Arts

demolition, but alumni, including Metropolitan Opera singer Suzanne Fisher, rallied in its support. It was spared demolition, and is now part of Sutton Elementary School. Suzanne was a 1922 graduate of Sutton High School. She made her debut at the Met in 1935 in Madam Butterfly, and remained there until 1943, singing in both the U.S. and Europe.

Burnsville native William Kidd, who became a federal judge in West Virginia, was also instrumental in saving the school. His daughter, Suzie, attended elementary school there. " I remember him saying that he didn't want them to take Suzie's school," said his daughter, who now lives near Albany, New York.

- - -

Elk reaches a geographic apogee at Gassaway, where the river makes a large bend. At the top of that bend is the northernmost point on the river. It has gradually climbed there from its beginning at Slatyfork. From Gassaway, Elk turns southwest and continues in that general direction to Charleston. In the early 1900s, Elk was the avenue of transportation between Sutton and Gassaway: a steamboat called The Good Ship Gassaway carried passengers between the two towns.

Everywhere you turn in Gassaway, the ghost of Henry Gassaway Davis hovers. The town is named for him, as are Davis Elementary School and Davis Presbyterian Church. Davis, a Baltimore native, was

Henry Gassaway Davis

Elk Street in Gassaway in the early 1900's

an empire builder whose passion was railroads. His first job was as brakeman and conductor on the Baltimore and Ohio, and eventually he bought his own railroad. He also became a U.S. Senator from West Virginia, and in 1904 was the running mate of Alton B. Parker, the Democratic nominee for president who lost to Theodore Roosevelt.

Davis came to Gassaway in 1904, or rather his railroad did, after he bought the Coal and Coke, formerly the Charleston, Clendenin and Sutton. From 1904 until 1987, trains rolled through Gassaway. A daily reminder of the town's past is the depot, a Romanesque Revival structure that was built in 1914 of brick and locally quarried stone.

One of the Italian immigrants who came to Gassaway with the railroad was Luigi Nardella from Fugi, a village in southern Italy, who arrived in the United States as a teenager. At New York's Ellis Island he signed up to work for a railroad builder. That particular firm happened to be building the Coal and Coke in West Virginia.

After the railroad was completed, he remained in Gassaway, married Filamena Torchi, and worked for the Coal and Coke and B & O. He was a hostler, or one who services the engines in preparation for their runs. He died in 1978 at age ninety-four.

Sons Angelo and Carl still live in Gassaway. Angelo was a railroader, and Carl worked in construction and was mayor of Gassaway for six years in the 1990s. During World War II, he worked in a shipyard as a welder, and later taught welding in Braxton County schools.

In railroad mileage, Gassaway is located about halfway between

Gassaway Depot

Charleston and Elkins, and was a natural location for the Coal and Coke's repair shops. Elkins is eighty-two miles away; Charleston is ninety-one miles away. The story is told that before Davis bought the railroad, he pointed to the broad Elk River bottom and said, "This is where my shops will be." Then he went to Charleston and bought the railroad. The Coal and Coke lasted until 1918, when it was sold to the Baltimore and Ohio.

Passenger service into Gassaway ended in 1951, but freight service continued for another thirty-six years. The last freight train ran on April 29, 1987. Orvin James, the conductor, recalled that the train went from Gassaway to Dundon, where it picked up loaded cars from the Clay County coal mining village of Widen, and returned to Gassaway.

The town of Gassaway bought the depot from CSX in 1989 and is renovating it as a railroad museum and visitor information center. "Everybody in Braxton County, either directly or indirectly, at one time had a family connection to the railroad," said Alan Boggs of Gassaway, whose grandfather, Robert Boggs, was a conductor for the Coal and Coke and later the B & O.

There is still a train presence in Gassaway. In 1988-89, Summersville businessman Bill Bright bought sixty miles of track that CSX planned to abandon, including forty miles on Elk. The track was upgraded, and named the Elk River Railroad. The Gassaway yard is one of the Elk River Railroad's parking lots for cars that come off the CSX system.

The Hotel Gassaway, later called the Valley, was a symbol of Gassaway as a railroad town. The three-story hotel, with its distinctive gambrel-style roof, was built in 1905 by A.J. Williams. It is said that President Woodrow Wilson and his wife once stayed there.

Doyle Boggs, a railroader and father of Braxton County delegate Brent Boggs, started his career as a clerk at Gassaway. He remembers calling sleeping train crews at the Valley to get them up for their morning runs.

He also remembers as a youngster going to the depot in the night to see the train bearing presidential candidate Wendell Wilkie come through. "The train stopped briefly," he said, "but otherwise there was nothing to see."

Another Gassaway hotel of renown was the Lincoln, which was opened in 1923 by Lillie Brewster and attracted diners from far and wide until its closing in 1968. The Lincoln was famous for serving three family style meals a day at a long table.

- - -

The Bank of Gassaway was founded in 1905, the same year as the town, by Henry Gassaway Davis. The original bank is now the Gassaway Public Library, which retained the bank vault as part of the library's décor when a new bank was built in 1996. The old vault now stores books instead of money. "Kids are impressed that it was something that once contained lots of money," said librarian Brenda Hickman.

Jim McQuain, chief executive officer of the Bank of Gassaway, told me the history of the eagle that sits in the lobby. It was ordered from Italy in 1907 by the niece of C.E. Hannah, the first bank president. Originally it perched on top of the bank, and later was moved out front and sat on a pedestal. Now it's in the lobby at the present location. "We thought it had been out in the weather long enough," said McQuain.

The Sutton counterpart of the Gassaway eagle was a stuffed bear that stood for many years on a shelf in the lobby of the Home National Bank. Later it reposed on the front porch of longtime bank cashier A.L. Morrison on South Stonewall Street, facing Elk River.

When Home National was bought by City National in 1992, CNB assistant vice-president and regional manager Jeff Lilly discovered that Home National had its own personalized currency at one time. Ten and twenty dollar bills were issued by the Federal Reserve with Home National Bank printed on them. A few longtime customers still have these bills.

- - -

There were many businesses that closed during the Great Depression of the 1930s, but Pletcher Pontiac GMC *opened* in Gassaway because of the Depression. In 1933, George Pletcher and his son, Ralph, came from Weston, where their garage business had gone under, and rented space at 732 Elk Street. Today, seventy-two years later, the Pletcher name is still over the door.

Myrtle Hamilton, a relative, had told them that Braxton County needed good mechanics, and that the garage on Elk Street was for rent. George rented the building from the Bank of Gassaway, and moved his family there, beginning the Pletcher presence.

George died in 1934 after infection developed from a cut on his hand. Ralph bought the building the next year, and, in 1937, started selling cars. Upon Ralph's death in 1948, his wife and their oldest son, Ralph Jason, became partners in the business, an association that would continue into the early 1980s. Ralph Jason's brother, Noel Jon, better known as Skeeter, continues in the business today.

He was called Skeeter by mechanics at Pletcher because he would run off from home and go to the garage, where he would crawl under cars and hide when his sister, Marium, came looking for him. The mechanics called him "skedaddler," or one who runs away. Eventually, skedaddler became Skeeter.

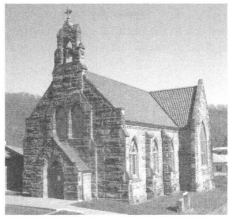

Skeeter and his nephew, Ralph Jason Jr., are familiar figures at Pletcher Pontiac today. Ralph Jr. and Skeeter's son, Jon, represent the fourth generation of Pletchers in the firm.

St. Thomas Catholic Church

Two grand old structures in Gassaway are the St. Thomas Catholic Church and the Davis Memorial Presbyterian Church, both of which were built by Italian artisans who were employed in the building of the Coal and Coke Railroad.

St. Thomas was built in 1906. Its benefactor was Richard Kerens, a St. Louis native and railroad associate of Henry Gassaway Davis. The church was named for Thomas, the disciple of Jesus, although the name also honors Richard Kerens' father, Thomas Kerens.

Davis Presbyterian Church

St. Thomas was constructed of an outer wall of locally quarried stone and inner wall of wood and plaster. The interior architecture is best described as neo-Richardsonian for the influence of New England architect Henry Hobson Richardson, whose style is reflected in many great railroad stations and other structures built by railroad men. The high, curving ceiling resembles an overturned sailing vessel.

Henry Gassaway Davis followed with Davis Memorial in 1908. It was also built of local stone. The church was a contribution to the town, and also a memorial to Davis' wife. The ornate pews, light fixtures, pulpit, and inside doors reflect, in style, their benefactor's Scotch Presbyterian heritage. Two Bibles, enclosed in glass and open to the Book of Psalms, date back to the beginning of the church. The ceiling is high and curving, like at St. Thomas, but with greater use of massive beams.

- - -

Frametown, which resides on Elk nine miles below Gassaway, is named for James Frame, one of four brothers who came to Virginia from England in the late 1700s. James migrated to present day Frametown from the Birch Village area, built a grist mill on the south side of the river, and was a justice of the peace.

Lee Hall, one of the early merchants, also had a grist mill, and a blacksmith shop, and sold ice from Elk. He sawed it out in slabs, packed it in sawdust, and it would keep into the warm weather months. This was a common practice before refrigeration came along, and particularly at remote northern Canada fishing camps.

Another early Frametown merchant was Austin Long. He gave away plates with the months listed around the edges, and in the middle the lettering "Austin Long, General Merchandise, 1909." In recent years, a friend bought one of the plates at a local yard sale.

We know about the cattle drives of the Old West, but less familiar are the turkey drives of Frametown. I learned about them when I visited James and Janice Hall in February 2005. James was a schoolteacher and after that had a store at Frametown for twenty-six years. His wife taught school for thirty-seven years.

The turkey drives occurred in the late 1920s and went from Elmira to Frametown. James, an Elmira native, took part in two of the drives as a young boy. The destination was the B & O Railroad at Frametown, where the turkeys were slaughtered, packed in barrels, and shipped to Baltimore. The slaughtering, plucking, and dressing took place in a large building and was done mostly by local women.

"We drove about a thousand head of turkeys on each drive," said

James, "staying overnight at a farmhouse along the way. The turkeys would roost on rail fences, and it was necessary to stay with them until they had all gone to roost. By the same token, we had to be up early before they came off the roost, otherwise they would scatter in all directions."

The first drive was a financial success for Abel James, the Frametown merchant who bought the turkeys and sold them to a large meat processing firm. But the second drive went awry. The weather turned warm and the turkeys spoiled in the railroad car during shipment. Abel sold his store to cover the loss, but he was undaunted. He rode throughout the community on horseback buying and selling furs, and later returned to the store business.

Bill James, a Frametown native, was depot agent for the B & O at Frametown for a time. He remembers the passenger train designations: No. 36, which arrived from Charleston in the morning, and No. 35, which returned to Charleston in the afternoon. The eastern destination was Grafton, where the main line ran east and west.

Train stations dotted Elk from Charleston to Gassaway at one time. One of the more refreshingly named was Shadyside, which was located at the mouth of Coon Creek above Frametown. Prior to the Civil War, a large grist mill, called the James Boggs mill, stood on Elk at Shadyside near where Art and Randy Duffield now live. Timbers that were used to divert water to the mill are still visible, as is a long rock wall that was a part of the raceway.

The surname James is a common one around Frametown, and the persistent legend is that one of the clans was related to the outlaws Frank and Jesse James, and that Frank James may have been in Frametown at one time. Most of the stories associate Frank's appearance with the robbery of the bank at Huntington, West Virginia, in 1875, although revisionist history now claims that neither Frank nor Jesse were involved in that robbery.

- - -

Farther downriver, the legend of Strange Creek has become enshrined in West Virginia folklore. It involves a surveyor named William Strange, who became lost at the mouth of Holly River below Centralia. According to the legend, his skeletal remains were found many years later on what is now Strange Creek. He had carved his epitaph on a tree:

Strange is my name and I'm on strange ground, and strange it is that I cannot be found.

There are other versions of his dying message, but the above gives the essence of them. There are also different scenarios as to where his remains were found. Some accounts say it was on the head of the creek near Dille, while others say it was farther down, or even at the mouth. In any event, Turkey Creek, which it was then named, became Strange Creek, and I'm sure will remain that as long as the world stands and fanciful stories are appreciated.

I wrote a chapter in *River on the Rocks* on the legend of Strange Creek, and my research led me to conclude that, yes, there was a surveyor named William Strange, and that, yes, he became lost in 1795 and was never found. That is, he was never found unless we accept the legend of the skeleton and the carving.

The village of Strange Creek was once called Savagetown for brothers Jesse and William Savage, who came from Ohio and founded the Elk River Iron Company around 1874. Their furnaces on the hillside above the present village are still visible.

The brothers mined ore near where the furnaces were located, brought limestone from across Elk, and "cooked" the mixture with charcoal. Although the Elk watershed in Braxton County isn't traditional limestone country, a report by the Geological and Economic Survey in 1915 said there was a thin seam of limestone gravel on the north side of Elk, the only limestone seam found in the county. Somehow, the Savage brothers knew of it.

The product that came out of their furnaces was pig iron, which by definition is a crude hunk of metal that comes out in the shape of a pig, if we let our imaginations work. Some of the "pigs" weighed as much as a ton.

The Savages had counted on the railroad coming to Strange Creek to take the iron to market, but it was another twenty-five years before that happened. So they were left to transport the ore down Elk in specially built boats. From Charleston, they continued down the Kanawha and Ohio Rivers to the steel mills at Ironton and Portsmouth, Ohio.

Strange Creek Furnaces

But there were many problems associated with "running the river" in boats laden with iron, and the operation lasted only five or six years. However, the brothers did create a village, and although it no longer bears their name, the story of the iron furnaces endures, as does the legend of William Strange.

Twenty Two

The Signature Fish

Elk's Homegrown Muskies

I heard it said so often that, sadly, I grew up half believing that muskies "as big as a crosstie" exist in Elk River. Well, maybe, but a crosstie for standard gauge railroad track is eight and one-half feet long, which equals 102 inches, which is 41 inches longer than the longest Elk muskie I've ever seen claimed in print.

That was the supposed 61-inch fish that Old Sol Nelson gigged in the End of the World section in Clay County (see Bill Byrne). But there are plenty of muskie tales to go around, and they would fill a book much larger than this one, because Elk in Braxton and Clay Counties is muskie, or musky, or muskellunge country, or maskinonge if you want to sound Canadian. The name, in fact, originated in Canada with the Ojibway Indians.

Elk formerly held the state record, and who's to say it won't again, although impoundment muskies live in a less challenging environment and are likely to grow bigger. At this writing, both the length and weight records were held by fish caught in Stonecoal Lake. Neighboring Stonewall Jackson Lake has potential state record fish, too.

But so does Elk. Kevin Yokum, a Division of Natural Resources fisheries biologist, saw an Elk muskie in the summer of 2003 that he believed may have been longer and heavier than the Stonecoal fish, both of which he helped weigh and measure.

He and other DNR and Division of Environmental Protection personnel were electro-shocking to collect fish for tissue analysis, and the muskie, momentarily stunned, came out of the water in a great leap. "It was over fifty inches for sure," said Kevin, "and it was a heavy fish."

Harold Wilson related the story of Ted Stout, who lived at Frametown, hooking and losing a muskie in the lower Frametown eddy in the 1970s that would have held the length record even today. The fish got away as he was bringing it into the boat with a gaff, but it was severely injured. A week or so later, other fishermen found the dead fish under willow bushes. It measured fifty-two inches from the nose to dorsal fin. The remaining several inches were missing.

The most famous Elk muskie was the former state record holder that weighed forty-three pounds and was fifty-two and one-half inches long. It was caught on March 26, 1955, by Lester Hayes Jr. at the junction of Birch River and Elk at Glendon, Braxton County. It held the weight record for forty-two years, and the length record for forty-eight years.

The Mouth of Birch is heavily fished. I suspect it is the most heavily fished place on Elk with the exception of Whittaker Falls after a trout stocking, or possibly the mouth of Big Sandy Creek at Clendenin. Gary Tawney of Newton, Roane County, told me about catching and releasing a thirty-six inch muskie while fishing from the railroad trestle at the Mouth of Birch, and, soon after that, raising a muskie that "made the mud boil" as it swirled at the lure.

Gary's son, Cole, was featured in a *Sunday Gazette-Mail* story by John McCoy in February 2005. Although only thirteen years old, he had caught seventy-one muskies in four years at the time of the article. One was a thirty-two inch fish that he caught and released at the Mouth of Birch.

The 1955 record-setter may have been a descendant of a muskie written about by John D. Sutton in his *History of Braxton County and Central West Virginia*. Prior to the Civil War, Sutton said, a muskie grabbed a small boy by the leg while he was wading at the Mouth of Birch. The boy would have drowned, according to the account, but was rescued by others who were nearby.

The predatory instincts of muskies are well known. It is said that they will attack one another if there is no other prey handy. But hands or feet dangling in the water will do. Todd Mollohan, proprietor of the Century Inn at Sutton, and Butch Barton were fishing in the upper Frametown Eddy, and Butch was dangling his bare feet and legs in the water over the side of the boat. A very large muskie swirled in the vicinity of his feet, which he kept out of the water the rest of the day and probably thereafter.

One time Todd bought a new rod and reel, and went to the Foodland Eddy above Gassaway to make a few casts and get the kinks out

The Sugar Creek Eddy

of the line. On his second cast he caught a thirty-six and one-half inch muskie. It was a prompt and proper introduction to Elk muskies for the new outfit. Todd thanked the fish for straightening out the line, and released it.

One of the famous muskie eddies in Elk is Sugar Creek between Gassaway and Frametown. In the 1950s, kids from Gassaway would swim just above the Sugar Creek Church, sailing out into "the old swimmin' hole" on a wire or rope swing. One day they noticed a large muskie cruising nearby, seemingly watching them. It was like in the movie *Jaws*. This happened more than once, and they soon decided against swinging out and dropping into the deep water.

Bill McMorrow, a retired state trooper who lives at Pinch, grew up on Elk in the Frametown area, and he recalls his great uncle, Andy Given, showing him large fishing hooks that had been broken by muskies
.

My most unforgettable muskie moment, perhaps because of the setting, came when I was fishing with Don Hamric, the Glendon postmaster and legendary muskie fisherman, above the Mouth of Birch on the railroad side. The water is deep there. Large rocks, probably from long-ago railroad construction, are just underneath the surface.

I was working on my reel, which had malfunctioned. Don and I always seemed to be plagued with malfunctioning reels. Meantime, Don's canoe drifted into the rocks. The classic green canvas canoe would have been right at home on the cover of an L.L. Bean catalog, and I loved to fish from it. As Don idly swished a lure in front of the canoe, a huge muskie swirled up and lunged at it. That was the only time I ever knew Don to become excited. But the fish quietly sank back into the depths around the rocks. Certainly it was the largest muskie I have ever seen in the water, and perhaps its ghost is still there.

I saw one of near comparable size when I was fishing with Jim Wetzel at the Interstate 79 bridge near Sutton. It rolled up three times but didn't strike. Soon afterwards, I caught a two and one-half pound smallmouth that I quietly released without comment, given the size of the muskie we had just seen.

But my favorite fish story from that particular bridge was when Bill Jett hooked "a large fish" and fought it all over the river. "I was sure I'd hooked a state record something," he told me, and he was right. It was a state record folding lawn chair. "It had sediment and other debris on it," said Bill, "and it must have weighed eighteen pounds." I asked the inevitable question: "Did you have it mounted?"

On another trip I made with Don Hamric above Glendon, he hooked a large muskie that did an interesting thing. It sank to the bottom in about three feet of water and lay there, motionless. We could see the lure protruding from its jaw.

"You've got it hooked pretty good," I said, in the absence of anything else to say.

"But it hasn't done anything yet," Don replied.

When it did, this time it was Don's reel that malfunctioned. The fish took off and the line broke with a snapping, zinging sound that reverberated around us. Don had the most casual approach to fishing, and just about everything else, of anyone I've ever known, which is why I liked to fish with him. Serious fishermen can be seriously boring. On this occasion, he merely shrugged his sturdy shoulders (he played high school football for the Gassaway Elks) and said something about needing to get the reel fixed. I don't think he ever really did.

- - -

One time Don was fishing with his twelve-year-old grandson, Doug White, at the Interstate 79 bridge over Elk at Frametown, and Doug had his thrifty heart set on catching a muskie. He had just bought a Hula Popper with his hard-earned nickels and dimes.

They were catching a few bass, but Doug wasn't going to be satisfied with anything less than a muskie. He reached in his tackle box and brought out the shiny new Hula Popper and threw it under an overhanging bush. It would be the only throw he would ever make with that lure. The river opened up, as the saying goes, and a muskie they estimated to be over forty inches grabbed the lure, went down, and dived under the boat. The line snapped.

Don expected Doug to be heartbroken at losing the big fish, but he had a more pressing concern. "Oh, darn," he said, "there went my three dollar and thirty seven cent Hula Popper." Doug now lives in Swansboro,

North Carolina, and is a representative for Pfizer Pharmaceutical Company.

Don's favorite lure was a Lucky 13, and they seemed to appeal also to Doug's dog, Bouncer. After Don's death, Doug called home one day and suggested that they preserve his grandfather's wooden Lucky 13s for mementos. Doug's father, Herb White, dipped them in a preservative and hung them on the deck to dry. He heard a yelp, and there came Bouncer with a lure in his nose.

Herb and his wife, Ann, took Bouncer to veterinarian Ross Young's office and waited their turn. Jim Gumm was there with his hunting dog. "Look," said Jim, pointing to Bouncer, "I'm teaching my dog to hunt, and Herb is teaching his to fish."

Another time it was Ann's turn to head to the doctor. She and Herb were fishing at dusk, and a Hula Popper from an errant cast struck her on the head. "Oh, gracious, I think you just caught something," said Ann. "Is this the catch of the day?" asked the doctor in the emergency room at Braxton County Memorial Hospital.

- - -

"Old school" muskie fishermen Galvin Reynolds and Everette Dean once had a muskie hooked that Galvin, at least, believed would have broken the state record that the Mouth of Birch fish held at that time. Galvin lived at Gassaway and worked in the meat department at the A & P Store. Everette lived at Strange Creek and was a carpenter.

The rule of thumb is that you catch one muskie for every eight hundred casts. Galvin knew the odds and had his own way of dealing with them. He tried to reach eight hundred casts as quickly as possible. "Sometimes I'd get out of the boat, walk up to the road, and hitch-hike home," said his son, Earl, a retired railroader. Earl still remembers his father's sacred counsel like it was being played on a broken record: "You've got to keep your bait in the water."

The possible record muskie was hooked by Everette in the Tate Creek Eddy above Villanova. He had bought a new rod and reel and remarked as they set out that "I'd like to catch a muskie today that would tear this outfit up." He almost got his wish. At the very least it tore up the landing net.

The fish came across a log and took the lure. Everette had it on for several minutes, although it seemed longer than that, and eventually brought it to the boat, where it lay exhausted. But they didn't have a gaff hook and their landing net was too small for such a large fish. They both knew that.

But they also knew they had to do something.

"Try to net it," said Everette.

"I'll try," said Galvin.

There is something about a landing net that sends even an exhausted muskie into renewed frenzy. In seconds the fish had broken the net handle and was gone, leaving the lure still clinging to the net. Neither Everette nor Galvin said a word for a long time. The next day, Galvin went out and bought the biggest gaff hook he could find.

Galvin's presence on the river may have brought good luck to others. Johnnie Dean of Chapel Route, Gassaway, was fishing near Galvin one day behind the U-Pak Store and caught a forty-six inch muskie. But working with Galvin, as Jerry Burrows did at the A & P Store for many years, brought only bittersweet luck. Jerry hooked a large muskie in the Barbershop Eddy above Gassaway that sawed his 30-pound test line on a tree limb to the point that it stripped the swivel and swam away.

When I was writing for *the Charleston Gazette*, I didn't necessarily have to go looking for muskies. Sometimes they came to me. One day the receptionist called and said there was a man out front with a big fish. It was Doctor Jim Boggs, a surgeon at Charleston Area Medical Center and founder of the Big Otter Clinic on Interstate 79. The fish was a forty-six inch muskie he had just caught in Elk in Clay County.

That was a *few* years ago, as I calculate time, and I wondered if the good doctor had caught anything comparable since then. Well, almost, he said when I called him in 2004. He told me about catching a forty-one inch muskie below Villanova, and there was a story involved. There always is.

He and Doctor Jack Chambers were drifting through the eddy, and the muskie apparently saw the lure coming and raised out of the water, or at least its head came out of the water, and the lure literally dropped into its mouth. The fish threw the lure, but got hooked under the jaw, and was landed.

As a fisherman, Doctor Boggs will be remembered as "the Crazy Crawler man." A Crazy Crawler is a stubby lure with paddles, or wings, protruding from its sides. It sputters along the surface. The "Crazy Crawler" doctor caught a five and one-half pound smallmouth below Villanova on the lure, as well as the above muskie.

- - -

There is a perceived decline in the number of muskies being caught in Elk in recent years, but that doesn't necessarily mean there are fewer muskies. Elk still has the perfect cover, perfect gradient, and a paradise of forage fish that made it a great muskie stream in the first place.

The gradient, or rate of descent, averages less than four feet per mile over the final one hundred miles between Sutton and Charleston, and logs are scattered everywhere like an aquatic pick-up-sticks game. If pileated woodpeckers are attracted to dead trees, muskies are attracted to logs.

As to forage, which is a euphemism for anything that is eaten by something else, Elk is the world capital. The richness of upper Elk in tiny aquatic life that feeds its trout population has its counterpart in the large forage fish of middle and lower Elk.

I wrote in an earlier chapter about my nephew and me fishing the Strange Creek Eddy and seeing a remarkable variety of fish species, including gizzard shad and redhorse suckers, two favorites of muskies. There are five species of redhorse in Elk, the most common being the golden. If I do nothing else with the remainder of my life, I'm going to write a novel and call it The Golden Redhorse. Or form a band of that name. Or open a restaurant. The possibilities go on. For starters, we chose the golden redhorse, commonly known as sucker, as the official fish of the new state of Middle of Nowhere.

Muskies are known as moody fish, but aren't we all. Bud Toms, who lives on Elk below Gassaway, described muskie moodiness perfectly: "Some days you might raise four or five, and other days you'll doubt there is such a fish." Kevin Yokum suspects the moodiness may mean only that they aren't hungry. "They might feed for twenty minutes and catch a large redhorse and not feed again for two or three days," he said.

Elk isn't fished as much as it once was because many fishermen are going to the lakes such as Stonecoal and Stonewall Jackson, where muskies were introduced. In the words of ESPN baseball announcers when a batter strikes out and walks away, "That's more beer for us." Meanwhile, Elk's muskies are homegrown. They were born there. They own water. They pay taxes. They buy my books.

"It's easier to get a boat in and out of the water at the lakes," said Kenny McCord, who works in the meat department at the local Kroger Store. I like to corner him in front of the hamburger counter and announce in an imperious voice, "The muskies aren't biting today." He always replies, "I don't care," and I can't think of anything more to say.

Kenny once caught a forty-two inch muskie in Elk, but his most vivid recollection is of the time he was fishing above Gassaway with Danny Mick and raised a muskie that was longer than the end of the boat. "It was one of those lazy follows," he said. "It drifted up and followed the lure, but didn't strike. I brought the lure around the boat, the muskie following, and as he passed the end of the boat, he stuck out on both sides. He was a very big fish."

- - -

I thought about the variety of fish in Elk, which led me to think about Stuart Welsh, who works in the Cooperative Fish and Wildlife Research Unit at West Virginia University. Stuart visited my home on Birch River in 1995 when he was surveying the darter population in Elk and Birch.

Darters are small fish of the group that fishermen generally lump together as "minnows." In a way, they are the canaries of freshwater streams. Canaries were used long ago in coal mines to detect the presence of deadly methane gas, which quickly killed them. Along the same line, darters are among the first small fish to disappear when there are adverse changes in habitat or water quality.

When I contacted Stuart in November 2004, it was to gain confirmation of something I'd always heard, which was that Elk has an unusually high diversity of fish species. True, he said. "Regionally, the Elk has the highest diversity of fishes, with over one hundred species. This diversity, although unknown to most people, has enormous ecological value and deserves recognition and protection."

He provided a list (see Fishes of Elk River) that includes household names and those that are unknown outside such a list. For example, there are seventeen species of darters. The most elusive is the Eastern sand darter, which is found on lower Birch and is perhaps related to an ostrich. At the approach of the diver, it burrows into the sand. The saddest story is that of the Tippecanoe darter because it is on this earth such a very brief time, and then is gone, like a vapor. It grows to about an inch long, and in its only breeding season turns a joyous bright orange color.

I've written about catfish in Elk that have reached weights of sixty-five pounds. On the other end of the scale is the stonecat, a relative of the mad tom, another small catfish found in Elk. Stonecats are tiny, live only in fast water, and are voracious predators, so be careful on days that they feed, if we can figure out when that is.

Stonerollers are on the list, and we all know them. We see their nests of small rocks in the riverbed. They roll stones while nesting or looking for food. And I might as well say it and get it over with, they gather no moss. Stonerollers are related to the familiar horny head chub, the fish with "horns" on its head.

The most ephemeral of Elk fish is the ghost shiner. It is found only near the mouth of the river in the Mink Shoals area, and has no color, therefore its spectral-like name. It would have made a great character in the 2002 book, *Elk River Ghosts, Tales & Lore*, by Mack Samples.

In addition to its diversity of fishes, Elk is home to twenty-nine species of mussels, including three that are federally endangered. Some are clinging to their bivalve lives, as it were, because of various sediment-causing activities that adversely affect mussel populations.

The old bridge over Elk at the lower end of Gassaway owes its life to mussels. When a new bridge was built in the 1990s, the Department of Highways planned to drop the old bridge into the river and pull it out. But the DNR was aware that a mussel bed was located below the bridge, and it protested that removal of the bridge in such a traumatic way would result in the crushing of many mussels, a protected species.

So the bridge remains, symbolizing a victory for wildlife diversity. Its approaches have been removed, leaving the main portion standing alone in the river, a rather odd sight. The metaphor about crossing that bridge when you come to it isn't applicable in this case. But it doesn't appear to be in the way of anything, and probably most people have gotten used to it. Someday it might even become a tourist attraction. The organizers of the state of Middle of Nowhere recognize it as the bridge that flexed its mussels, and proudly named it the official state bridge.

- - -

In October 2004, I visited Mark Shafer, president of the Elk River Musky Club, at the sporting goods department at Shafer's Truck Stop near Clendenin and admired the gallery of muskie pictures on the wall. All but one of the fish were caught in rivers or lakes other than Elk, but regardless, they're the same awesome looking fish.

The only Elk catch was one of the larger ones. It was a fish of forty inches that was caught at Queen Shoals by Tim Callison, who makes lures under the trade name Big Chimney Baits. The Queen Shoals Eddy has produced many fine muskies over the years. In the long ago, it was a favorite fishing haunt of Governor William MacCorkle, who would ride the train up from Charleston to fish there.

Clendenin historian Henry F. Young wrote in his 1985 book, *Tall Tales*, about two exceptional fish that came from Queen Shoals, although neither was a muskie. One was a sixty-five pound mudcat, or flathead catfish, that lodged in the water wheel of a grist mill, and stopped the wheel. Young said it was the largest fish he'd ever seen taken out of Elk. This may have been the mill owned by "Uncle" Dan Snyder, a legendary miller at Queen Shoals.

The other fish was a forty-four inch paddlefish, also known as spoonbill catfish, although they are not related to the catfish family. Writing in *West Virginia Wildlife* magazine, Dan Cincotta called them "throwbacks," or primitive fish of prehistoric ancestry. They are known by their long bills, and by the fact that they feed on plankton, or tiny animal and plant life.

The Elk River Musky Club holds five tournaments each year, all catch and release. Only one of the five, the Carl Norman Memorial, named for the club founder, is restricted to Elk. In 2004, eighteen fishermen participated in the Elk-only tourney and raised nine muskies. Although none were caught, it was a decent showing for the stream of legend.

In September 2004, Mark was fishing in the Sugar Creek Eddy in Braxton County and lost a fish that he estimated to be in the mid-forties range. It might have been the same fish that his cousin, Richard Shafer, caught in January 2005 at Sugar Creek. It was forty-seven inches long and was released.

- - -

Elk is also known for large walleyes, and on the final day of December 2004 Jerry Rose of Procious, Clay County, caught a walleye near his home that weighed eighteen pounds four and one-half ounces, a new state record for weight. John McCoy wrote about it in the *Sunday Gazette-Mail*:

"The walleye weighed nearly 19 pounds on the certified scales of a nearby grocery store. Because Rose wanted to release the fish, however, he kept it tethered to the dock for four days until a DNR representative could arrive to verify its size for the record books.

"Biologist Kevin Yokum placed the walleye's weight at 18 pounds, 4 ½ ounces - down more than 10 ounces from its original weight, but still nearly half a pound heavier than the former record.

"After having the fish's weight certified, Rose released it. "I'm a firm believer in catch and release," he said. "The walleye was a big female, full of eggs. I wanted to give her a chance to spawn."

Walleyes are gone from Elk above Sutton Dam, and the lake strain of walleye that is stocked in Sutton Lake doesn't migrate upstream to extent that river walleyes do. At this writing, the DNR was considering stocking river walleyes at both Sutton and Summersville Lakes in the hope that they will follow their primordial urge and head upstream. To which we will all say, God Speed.

Twenty Three

The Roman Road

Elk In Clay County

Elk leaves Braxton County at Duck or Villanova. The post office on the north side of the river is called Duck, and the former railroad stop on the south side is called Villanova. Over the years, many visitors have mailed letters and cards from the Duck P.O. to show their friends in far-flung places that, yes, there is a Duck, West Virginia.

I once wrote that Duck was named for an abundance of ducks that floated around the mouth of the creek, but I've forgotten the source of that story, and I've personally never seen a duck there. The naming of Villanova goes back to the Roman Empire, if we want to take the grand view. It was called Villanova, or *new village*, by Italian immigrants who built the railroad. One of the earliest to make the Romanesque connection was C.R. Remage, the principal and only teacher at Gassaway High School in its first year, of 1912.

The original post office was located in the Nottingham Store at Villanova, and remained there until the mid-1990s when the U.S. Postal Service built a new post office on Duck Creek. "But it has always been called Duck Post Office, even when it was at Villanova," said former postmaster James Nottingham.

James and his wife, Vida, live on Horse Ridge near Villanova . The Braxton-Clay County line runs through their house. "If I'm snoring too loudly," says James, "my wife gets up and goes to Clay County."

When James was a teenager, he and other boys went camping on

Elk below Strange Creek, driving there in a 1948 Plymouth. They swam across the river and raided Wilbert Nottingham's corn patch. "We stuffed ears of corn in our swimming trunks or whatever we were wearing," said James, "and returned to our campsite. We shucked the corn and boiled it in a big pan, and discovered that it was field corn, not sugar corn. But we were hungry and we thought it was good anyway."

The nine miles from Villanova to Ivydale was my favorite small-mouth water when I was fishing Elk obsessively, partly because the effects of Sutton Dam water releases weren't as severe that far down. I also liked it because it includes the End of the World section that conveys a sense of impending doom that fits my warm and sunny disposition.

The best day of bass fishing I ever experienced was in the Groves Creek Eddy above the End of the World. I fished it often, borrowing a boat from Dwight Cadle. On that particular day, it seemed I caught or lost or raised a fish every third or fourth cast. I've thought about it often, and I can only conclude that the stars and planets were in perfect alignment.

Opal McMorrow Ramsey, who lives at Villanova, grew up at the mouth of Groves Creek at a settlement called Ira. Ira was a "flag station" on the railroad, meaning if anyone wanted to board the passenger train, they would "flag it down." The outgoing mail was hung on an L-shaped hook, and the train slowed enough so that a crewman could retrieve it.

As a young girl, Opal rode the family horse from Groves Creek to Swandale, a Clay County lumber mill town, to sell garden produce. "We called it going peddlin' to Swandale. It was an all day trip. I took an ear of corn for the horse's lunch, and I would buy a can of Vienna sausage for myself at the Swandale store."

Opal's father, Willis McMorrow, worked in the Blue Ridge Coal Company mine that was located at the nearby community of Paddy. Opal and her husband to be, Jim Ramsey, walked across the bridge at Groves Creek in 1934 and went upriver to Villanova to be married by the Reverend Hebert Metz.

"I remember the bridge well," said Paul Sirk, an O'Brion Creek native, "and I never cared for it. "It went down, and then up to a middle pier, and then down again." But the worrisome bridge was not to last. There was a huge ice jam in Elk in 1935, and when the ice went out it took the bridge with it.

When I visited Opal in November 2004, her sisters, who were also visiting, told me about attempting to cross Elk in a johnboat above the mouth of Groves Creek when the river was high. They were swept over the long shoal, and a railroad crew heard their screams and came to their rescue. The sisters who shared that adventure were Edna McMorrow

Butler, Mary Etta McMorrow Duffield, and Rosalea McMorrow Miller.

I had a harrowing experience at the Groves Creek shoal when I was fishing there with Gordon Swartz, a state trooper friend, and we were caught in a violent electrical storm. I shared many deer hunting adventures with Gordon, but none were as memorable as the Groves Creek storm. Malevolent streaks of lightning flashed in the darkness, illuminating the bank on both sides. Thunder crashed with a fury seldom seen except among rioting fans at World Cup soccer games, and I was convinced the apocalypse had arrived and we were cornered on water in a metal boat.

- - -

We are indebted to Ellis Friend, father of photographer Ferrell Friend, for preserving the history of Ivydale, the community on Elk about halfway through Clay County. His *Reflections on Ivydale* were first published as a series in *the Clay Free Press*, and later in *Hickory and Lady Slippers*, a project of the Clay County High School Art Department.

He wrote that Andrew Friend came from Braxton County and settled in what is now Ivydale in 1835. The town was surveyed by Jack Ice, and named for his daughter, Ivy. The first storekeeper was Melvel Friend, and the first school was located on the Cornelia Friend property.

My introduction to the term "log tide" used to describe a flood sufficient to float a log raft came from reading Ellis' stories. He made many raft trips, but was best known as proprietor of the Ellis Friend General Store in Ivydale for forty years.

He wrote about being part of a crew that took a log raft to Charleston in 1898 when he was fourteen years old. The crew spent the night at Dulls Creek at the home of the Reverend Levi Reed, who had a store 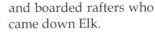 and boarded rafters who came down Elk.

During the night, a storm blew in, bringing snow, sleet, and ice. Their raft, a large one, containing one hundred and thirty-five logs, was coated with ice when they pushed off for Charleston the next morning. Bucking a heavy wind that was

Ivydale Bridge under construction, circa 1901

blowing upriver, they

reached Charleston late in the day. Ellis' account of their arrival follows:

"We began trying to land just about opposite where Bigley Avenue begins, although at that time there was no Bigley Avenue. It was mostly corn fields. When we began trying to tie up, we found that our cable had frozen in ice so that it was almost impossible to bend or handle.

"The river banks had also frozen in ice, making it hazardous, so we fought the raft on down to just about where Spring Street Bridge is now located. Still we couldn't land. It looked very much as if we might go out into the Kanawha River in a few minutes.

"Suddenly our pilot yelled 'Lay'er over to the right, boys. See that pocket boom ahead.' He said he would try to put her in there. We were tearing down bucket lines and breaking small boats loose from shore. I don't think I have ever heard so many ropes snapping and breaking in my life. To our great surprise, the boom held. The raft began slowing down and our pilot grabbed the cable, leaped ashore and took two half hitches around a water birch, bringing the raft to a standstill. If we had stripped the boom and it had not held, we would have gone out into Kanawha River."

- - -

Bridges divide rivers into "chapters." The next chapter below Ivydale is the Dundon Bridge, which heralds the river's approach to Clay, and is the gateway to Widen, the former Elk River Coal and Lumber Company town. Many people have told me they were going to write a book on Widen, but I believe the field is still wide open. However, in 1979 the Clay County High School Art Department published *Widen: An Appalachian Empire* that presents an excellent overview of the town's history.

Buffalo Creek enters Elk at Dundon, and is the fourth largest tributary. It is forever enshrined in local folklore as part of the name of the Buffalo Creek and Gauley, the railroad that ran from Dundon to Widen. The charter called for the railroad to go all the way to Gauley River, but as it turned out it stopped at Widen.

The railroad was twenty miles long and crossed Buffalo Creek seven times. In 1963, the BC&G made its final coal-hauling run from Widen to Dundon. There have been many suggestions that it be resurrected as a tourist attraction, but that hasn't happened.

Ferrell Friend was a sophomore at Clay County High School when the Dundon Bridge was built in 1928. He had a summer job driving a flatbed truck on the project, and he became the first person to drive a vehicle over the nearly completed bridge.

In its time as headquarters of the Widen empire, Dundon boasted a large and well-stocked company store, boarding house, ice house, two-room school, railroad shops, office building, band, baseball and softball teams, and a community building with meeting rooms, stage shows, movies, and Sunday School.

Dundon is believed to have been named for the man who led a party of Virginia surveyors into the area prior to the Revolutionary War. According to a 1958 article in *the Clay Free Press*, uncovered by Clay County historian Jerry Stover, Virginia wanted its western boundary to extend to present day Elk River, then called Tischilwah, and hoped the survey would influence England's decision (the Ohio River was eventually chosen). Surveyor Captain Dundon and his men came on horses and pack mules to a ridge above Elk, from where they also saw the creek that is now called Buffalo.

Their surveying and mapping included 100,000 acres that were later awarded to William Wilson for his service as a military leader with the Virginia militia. This same tract is believed to have eventually evolved into what in modern times became known as the Elk River Coal and Lumber company tract.

The *Free Press* article (author unknown) also said there was a well-hidden silver mine on present Lilly's Fork of Buffalo from which the Shawnee Indians extracted ore and fashioned items that would be traded for other goods on their return to their winter home in late fall from their summer encampments in the Dundon and Swandale areas.

J.G. Bradley, founder of the Elk River Coal and Lumber Company, lived at Dundon. Neil Boggs, who became an NBC newsman, grew up there, and delivered *the Charleston Daily Mail* to Bradley's home. "He was very businesslike but friendly," Neil recalls. "He would bring his card to the door to be punched when I collected, and he always had a quarter ready. He was always dressed in a suit. If he didn't have the suit coat on, at least he had on a vest and tie."

The Dundon Bridge played a major role in the saga of the Centennial Log Raft. Dick Frame, commander of American Legion Post 33 at Gassaway, conceived the idea of building a raft and running it down Elk to Charleston as part of the 1963 West Virginia Centennial observance. His father, John M. Frame, had been a rafter on Elk.

Poplar logs were cut on the Elk River Wildlife Management Area, assembled at the present Kroger parking lot between Sutton and Gassaway, and the raft was launched in May 1963. A picture of it passing under the railroad bridge at Gassaway hangs on the wall of the Century Inn at Sutton.

The raft reached the Dundon Bridge on the third day, where it struck a pier on the right descending side and split apart. The two halves were floated separately to Clay and reassembled. But this took time, and meanwhile the river flow had dropped, and it was September before there was sufficient water to resume the trip. But eventually the raft did reach Charleston and tied up behind the Civic Center. Pete Samsell, then director of the DNR, headed the welcoming committee. The thirty-two logs were later auctioned off and bought by a sawmill owner for about $2,000.

-   -   -

Clay County was organized in 1858 and named for statesman Henry Clay, who is perhaps best known for uttering these seven words on the issue of slavery: "I would rather be right than president."

The town of Clay was first called Marshall for U.S. Supreme Court Chief Justice John Marshall. In 1863, the West Virginia Legislature, flexing the muscles of a newly formed state, changed the name of the town to Henry, for Henry Clay. In 1927, the town's name was changed for the third time to Clay, its present designation.

The town is well fortified. Its old courthouse on the hill, built in 1902, is guarded by a 155 mm howitzer, affectionately known as "Long Tom" because it had a range of over 25,000 yards. "Long Tom" was the mainstay of American artillery in World War II and Korea.

It was raining in April 2004 when Ferrell Friend and I walked around the massive gun. We learned from Paul Parsons of VFW Post 4419 that Senator Robert C. Byrd had obtained the weapon for the county in 1996 from a federal armory in Pennsylvania. "We thought about asking for a small tank," said Parsons, "but we couldn't find space."

The rain continued as we climbed the steps to the old courthouse. It was familiar territory to Ferrell, who was deputy county clerk from 1936 to 1942. He introduced me to chief magistrate Jeff Boggs and assistant Vickie Gency, who occupied the office where he once worked.

Ferrell and I were colleagues at *the Charleston Gazette*, and I have fished Elk many times with him, or rather he paddled and I fished. He always said I ruined good fishing trips by wanting to fish all the time. A photographer by profession, he has probably taken more pictures of Elk than anyone else in the world.

We walked down the hallway and talked with magistrate Mike King and Clay County historian Jerry Stover. Mike told me about the time in the 1980s when he and his brother-in-law, Buck Nieberg, set out to canoe from Clay to New Orleans. "We camped at Nine Mile Creek on the Kanawha River," Mike related, "and set out in fog the next morning, hugging the left bank. It was a good thing, because out of the fog loomed a string of barges being pushed by a tugboat. We'd probably have rammed the barges if we had been out in the river.

"We contacted the tugboat captain on radio and told him where we planned to go. There was a long pause, and then he replied, You can't be serious. We looked at the foot-high whitecaps on the Kanawha and decided that we weren't serious. We tied up at Point Pleasant, called home for somebody to pick us up, and then walked to a Kentucky Fried Chicken restaurant, bought a bucket of chicken, and ate it all."

Buck Nieberg, Mike's companion on the adventure, is a retired policeman and lives in Dunellen, Florida.

The old Clay Courthouse

Jerry Stover, president of the Landmarks Commission and Historical Society, is a retired Clay County art teacher. One of the classes he taught was on Appalachian culture, which led to the *Hickory & Lady Slippers* series. "My students decided to do a book," said Jerry, "and it wound up being thirty-two books."

We climbed the stairs to the second floor courtroom, where ghosts of Clay County's judicial past must surely gather to talk over old times and old trials. One they would talk about would be the Booger Hole trial of 1917 when a mob showed up at the jail intent on lynching a man and his son who were accused of a murder on Booger Hole Creek, a tributary of Rush Fork of Big Otter Creek. The county prosecutor coolly talked them out of it.

One of the lawyers in Clay's past was Henry Davenport, whose story is an interesting one. He arrived in Clay in 1894, fresh out of law school, intending only to stay for a week and do some fishing, but he stayed for twenty-five years. Around 1943, Davenport wrote *Tales of the Elk and Other Stories*, which has often been confused with Bill Byrne's book because of similar titles, but which on its own is a delightful collection of anecdotes.

Clay County and Murray Smith were synonymous for fifty years. Murray, a native of Roane County, was hired by the Clay County Bank in 1938 as bookkeeper and remained there until his death in 1986. He became the bank's fifth president in 1965, and was still president at the time of his death.

He first came to Clay in 1924 when Chilton Bobbitt, Clay County High School principle, invited him to attend school there and play football, which he did from 1924 to 1927.

Murray was a tireless promoter of Clay County. He would call reporters at *the Gazette or Daily Mail* and say that "There's a story up here you may be interested in." I was always interested, because his stories were always good ones. My favorite was the one about a moonshiner who lived on a remote ridge near Clay and made the good stuff for fifty years before being caught.

At his hearing in federal court in Charleston, he captivated the judge and lawyers with his courtly backwoods mannerisms. The charges were dropped, in return for which he promised that he would never make moonshine again. "But I miss it every day," he told Murray and me when we visited his home. "I loved to make moonshine."

I've tasted moonshine only once, and it raised the hackles on the back of my neck, in a nice way. A friend and I took refuge under a bridge when we were trout fishing on the North Fork of Cherry River in Nicholas County and a rain came up. He produced a flask, the contents of which came highly recommended, and it did seem to make the rain go away, more than once.

Murray's crowning moment of glory as a promoter came in 1966

Murray Smith, banker and promoter

when he invited the New York Stock Exchange to move to Clay. The stock exchange had threatened to leave New York because the city was talking about increasing by fifty percent the transfer tax on stocks. Murray's offer to the NYSE made headlines around the country.

"At the time," said his daughter, Elizabeth Smith Miller, "I thought, how embarrassing. I didn't realize that it was only a joke." Now one of her proudest possessions is a picture of her father standing on Main Street in Clay beside a homemade sign that proclaims "Wall Street."

There is a shelf at the Sauk Center Public Library in Minnesota dedicated to Murray, who visited there during bankers' conventions and gave the library several West Virginia books. In one correspondence, he signed it "Your friend from Jumping Gut, West Virginia." Jumping Gut is the name of a tributary of Elk in Clay County.

- - -

On Groundhog Day 2005, Ferrell Friend and I had a late breakfast at Tudor's Biscuit World at Clay Crossroads, admiring the pictures on the wall that cover a lot of Clay County history. Prominent, too, were front pages from *the Clay Free Press*, including one that carried a large picture of Ferrell and a story on the publication of *The Quicker the Sooner*, the book I wrote about him. At least I admired the history on the wall. Ferrell seemed more interested in breakfast.

We drove down Elk, stopping first at Dundon. I walked a short distance up the BC&G tracks looking for the opening of the Dundon mine, which was one of the first mines begun by the Elk River Coal and Lumber Company. Its coal was known as "Dundon Red Ash," a reference to the high iron content that, when burned, left a reddish ash. The marketing slogan was "Dundon Coal Makes Warm Friends and Keeps Them Warm."

At the lower end of Clay, another bridge crosses Elk and leads to the community of Pisgah. Near there in 1899, the Methodist Chautauqua built an eighty-room hotel on Mount Pisgah's lofty height. It isn't clear from old accounts how long the hotel was open, although it is believed to have been open for only a short time. In any event, it burned in 1912.

Elk was running green and "joyful," a word used by Peter Silitch to describe Birch River at my home. Near Elkhurst, a swinging bridge leads across the river to the site of a mill and train depot known as Yankee Dam, where New York "Yankees" supposedly settled in the 1800s and built a dam from the south side of Elk to an island about midway across the river (J.R. Schoonover, Hickory & Lady Slippers, 1997).

According to Schoonover's article, they erected a water mill that furnished power to run an axe handle factory, button factory, and blacksmith factory. A fire destroyed the buildings soon afterwards, and Daniel Schoonover rebuilt the mill for grinding corn and wheat. It was washed away in the record 1861 flood (see Elk Through Braxton). The mill was rebuilt for a second time by Hiram Lewis and used as a grist mill.

Elkhurst, just below Yankee Dam, was a coal mining community and railroad stop that was named for the river and for the wooded hillside above it, called a "hurst" in Old English. The Schoonover article said a group of men from Nova Scotia built a sawmill there and named it Elkhurst.

I walked across the swinging bridge to the former site of Yankee Dam. The bridge is a work of art compared to most such structures, but even so I was astounded to learn that cars were once driven across it. Rocky Legg, who lives on the railroad end of the bridge, told me about seeing a large muskie near the bridge.

Nearing Procious, I told Ferrell of the several times I camped on the island at the upper end of the Procious Eddy. Benny Vaughan had a store there, and we would borrow a boat from him or a neighbor. But until the day of our visit, I didn't know the history of the Procious Post Office.

I discovered from the very helpful lady there that it was established in 1884 and was named for the first postmaster, Adam Procious, a Union soldier from Pennsylvania who, with his wife, Elizabeth Furlong Procious, boated down the Allegheny and Ohio Rivers to Point Pleasant, then up the Kanawha and Elk Rivers to the mouth of Twistabout Creek. He bought land on the head of the creek, and established the post office at his home. Mail was delivered by horseback once a month and placed in a trunk until patrons asked for it.

In 1894, after the railroad was built, the post office was moved to Elk at Camp Creek, and in 1933, with the building of West Virginia Route 4, the post office was moved again, this time to the present community of Procious.

The largest Elk smallmouth I ever saw was caught by a young boy at Procious. I was driving by and saw him bringing the still-flopping fish up from the river. My recollection is that it was twenty-three inches long and weighed five pounds.

Twenty Four

Bill Byrne

Let Me Sleep, Let Me Dream

I was introduced to Bill Byrne's book, *Tale of the Elk,* when I was visiting Charleston lawyer and Sutton native Bob Kelly at his office in the Kanawha Valley Bank building. He walked over to a bookshelf, took down a hardback the color of a rich red wine, and handed it to me. "I think you will enjoy reading this," were his approximate words.

He thought right. I have told enough people to fill a room even at a historical society meeting that *Tale of the Elk* is an entertaining book that ages well. Ironically, it wasn't a smashing sales success when first published in book form in 1940, but later reprints caught on, and the book has since developed a cult following.

Bob Kelly, too, was a man of Elk River. He had a camp above Ivydale, and, like Byrne, was a writer. In 1961, he published *Tales, Trouts and Tigers*, an engaging book about his hunting, fishing, and travel experiences, and followed it in 1973 with *More Trails on Six Continents.*

Europe, Asia, Australia, South America, Africa, and North America were Kelly's haunts. Between publication of the two books he returned to Africa four times. But his heart always belonged to Elk, and particularly to his camp. He wrote that "there is no best time to be on the Elk River."

Byrne's book, *Tale of the Elk*, began as a series of articles in *West Virginia Wildlife* in 1927-1931, and that was probably all he ever envisioned for his Elk stories, except that he later arranged them in order, made some revisions and additions, and they were published collectively in *the Brax-*

ton Democrat in 1933.

It wasn't until three years after his death that *Tale of the Elk* came out in book form. D.N. Mohler, president of Charleston National Bank and Byrne's son-in-law and executor of his estate, initiated the 1940 publication.

Charleston Printing Company printed 1,000 hardbacks that sold for $2.50 per book. The investors, in addition to Mohler, were H.B. Davenport, Bob Kelly, and Carl Andrews, the latter the mayor of Charleston. A 1960 hardback reprint by Mountain State Press revived the book. I called it "a welcome reprint of a golden oldie" in a review. Still later, a paperback version came out.

Byrne's camp in Clay County shares equal billing with the book. For one thing, a place called End of the World has a mystique of its own. Supposedly it was named by log rafters who came around a bend and saw only steep cliffs rising on the left descending side. To them, the most appropriate appellation was that they were viewing the end of the world.

The bend is almost exactly a mile long on the railroad. Bill James of Frametown, a retired railroader, said there was always a "slow" order for trains on the End of the World bend. Retired state trooper Bill McMorrow recalled the advertising slogan of a Gassaway taxi firm of the 1940s: "We'll take you to the End of the World and back for two dollars."

In 1892, Byrne and two associates bought fifty acres at the mouth of Jumping Gut Creek. Later, Byrne bought out the associates, sold the timber, and in 1911 converted a house left over from the logging days into a fishing camp. After giving the place two or three names that didn't seem to fit, he decided to call it simply The Camp At the End of the World.

From a writer's standpoint, Byrne had struck the Mother Lode. In addition to having the End of the World and Jumping Gut at his doorstep, he also had the nearby creeks of Waters Defeat and Twist and Shoot. He wrote about such local characters as Old Sol Nelson, quoting them in their native "tongue." Old Sol, a.k.a. Uncle Solomon Nelson, was a central figure in End of the World tales, as was Connard 'Coonrod' Eagle, a part Cherokee who lived on Snake Creek.

Old Sol was involved in the story of the largest muskie that anyone ever wrote about on Elk, at least involving fish of theoretically possible size. Byrne gigged the fish between the End of the World and Jumping Gut shoals. It got away, but about a year later Old Sol gigged it and it supposedly measured sixty-one inches. He identified it as the Byrne fish by a white spot in the middle of its back where Byrne's gig had struck.

Solomon Nelson came to Clay County from Pendleton County in

the period 1840-1850, and was known far and wide as "the Fiddler of the Wilderness." In this context, Byrne struck a responsive chord with me when he said that to his uneducated ear, all oldtime fiddle tunes sound alike. My favorite is "Granny Will Your Dog Bite?" because of the catchy title, but I couldn't pick it out of a lineup if I was being tortured.

Old Sol was the great grandfather of Reverend James Duffield, who lives on Rush Fork of Big Otter Creek. When Duffield was a teenager, he and his mother, Sarah Duffield, spent a night at

W.E.R. Byrne

Byrne's camp as guests of Peck Byrne (W.E.R. Jr.), who read to them the story of the Wild Boar of Jumping Gut from one of his father's articles.

Byrne had found the skeletal head of the boar in a tree, and asked Old Sol about it. Sol said that his dogs and the boar fought in a rhododendron thicket along the cliff above the End of the World, and all three fell or jumped over the cliff and were mangled, hence the name Jumping Gut. The boar's head was displayed inside Byrne's camp for many years. He wrote that it had a "gargoyle" look.

A more scholarly explanation was offered by Karen Hutchens, who lives at the End of the World. She pointed out that "gut" is an Old English word that means, among other less savory definitions, "a narrow waterway or small creek." Jumping Gut is certainly that, and it "jumps" over rock ledges on its way to Elk.

Roger Vaughan, who grew up on Elk above Ivydale, said Waters Defeat was called that because a log rafter named Waters splintered his raft there and was "defeated" in his intent to reach Charleston. The origin of the name Twist and Shoot eluded my best efforts.

- - -

In February 2004, I visited Bill Mohler, grandson of Bill Byrne, at his home in the South Hills section of Charleston. Mohler retired in 2002 after practicing law for fifty-two years, and in a sense he followed in his grandfather's footsteps. He was a trial lawyer, as was Byrne, and he appeared in courtrooms in Sutton, Clay, Webster Springs, and Charleston, all his grandfather's old haunts.

He accompanied his grandfather to the End of the World camp on several occasions as a young boy. "He wore me out," said Mohler, who was about ten years old at the time. "I paddled the boat for him in the long End of the World pool, and I'd even have to bait the damned hook [minnows and crayfish]. I didn't like fishing for a long time after that."

Byrne wrote about catching a muskie and taking it to a store just above the mouth of Groves Creek to be weighed. Twenty years later, around 1934, Mohler remembers walking up the railroad track to the Groves Post Office with his grandfather to get the mail at the same store.

"It was a small building, almost like a camp," said Mohler. "On the way, we crossed several railroad trestles. My grandfather would point out various kinds of trees and shrubbery. I remember that he pronounced an elm tree as *ellem.*"

At first, the only access to the Byrne camp was by train. The Coal and Coke Railroad ran up Elk by the time Byrne established his camp in 1911. By the early 1930s, a highway was being built on the other side of the river and would become the Elk River Road.

Once the road was completed, Mohler accompanied his grandfather on the drive from Charleston to the End of the World bottom. They

The Camp at the End of the World

would stop at Clay Crossroads to visit Byrne's friend, Naaman Shelton, who had a service station there. A little building that still stands in the middle of the crossroads was part of the station. It now houses a community FM radio station.

"When we arrived opposite the camp," said Mohler, "grandfather would honk the horn and George Washington Webb would come over in a johnboat and bring us across the river." Webb, a retired coal miner, and his wife, Becky, lived in the camp as caretakers, and were still living there at the time of Byrne's death.

"Webb farmed the property," said Mohler. "He had pigs, chickens, a cornfield, a mule named Kate, and a tobacco patch. He made twist chewing tobacco which he and my grandfather would chew." An earlier caretaker was Annis Nichols, who lived there with his family soon after Byrne established the camp. Annis was the grandfather of my neighbor, Dreama Nichols Young.

One of the pictures in the 1940 edition of *Tale of the Elk* is of Byrne and a granddaughter, Barbara Reeves Mohler. Byrne is sitting in a canoe with his arms outstretched, either measuring a mythical fish for the benefit of the photographer, or reaching for his granddaughter. Barbara now lives in Charleston near the Jay Rockefeller house on Barberry Lane. I hoped she would remember the name of the photographer, but she didn't. She was too young at the time.

Another granddaughter, Sandy Brown of Gallipolis, Ohio, lived at her grandparents' home at 1422 Quarrier Street from 1923 to 1936, and was at the End of the World camp many times. Bill Byrne liked buttermilk, but some don't. "Grandfather had a standing offer at camp of a nickel to anyone who would join him in a glass of buttermilk," Sandy recalled. But she doesn't remember anyone ever taking him up on it.

In 1959, Bill Mohler bought the End of the World property from the Byrne Trust, and still owns it. The Byrne camp no longer exists, the only remaining structure being a stone cellar. But Mohler built a camp across Jumping Gut from the original.

- - -

Except for the Civil War, Byrne probably would have been born in Sutton. His parents, Benjamin and Mary Holt Byrne, lived there, but Benjamin was a member of the Virginia Convention that passed the ordinance of secession, and he was in Virginia when the war started. He voted against secession twice, but remained loyal to Virginia.

He was able to bring his family from Sutton to Virginia, and Bill Byrne was born on October 26, 1862, at Fort Defiance, a crossroads community ten miles north of Staunton that is big enough today to have a high school and an Exxon station.

Benjamin was first an enrolling officer in the Confederate army, and later served in the supply department, holding the rank of colonel.

The family returned to West Virginia after the war, living in Clay, Parkersburg, Weston, Wheeling, and Charleston. In 1867, Benjamin was employed by Samuel Price of Lewisburg, Allen T. Caperton of Monroe County, and William H. Edwards of Kanawha County as their attorney in perfecting the title to a 93,000 acre tract on Elk that in 1903 became famously known as the Elk River Coal and Lumber Company land.

Bill Byrne's first occupation was as a civil engineer, or surveyor. He was one of the two members of the first graduating class at Charleston High School in 1879, but left just prior to graduation to join a crew that was surveying for a railroad up Elk.

In 1884 he spent ten months in Lewisburg "reading" law under the tutelage of his uncle, Homer A. Holt, a circuit judge and State Supreme Court justice. Holt was the grandfather of future governor Homer A. (Rocky) Holt, his namesake.

Byrne was licensed to practice law in October 1884, and began his career at Sutton in April 1885. He lived across Elk from the Courthouse on what is now South Stonewall Street. He remained in Sutton until 1897, when he moved to Charleston and practiced for another forty years. His office was in the Security Building at the corner of Capitol and Virginia Streets.

Granddaughter Sandy Brown doesn't remember him writing at home, or even having a typewriter there. The likelihood then is that he wrote from his Charleston office the series of articles that became *Tale of the Elk*.

Although an avid trout fisherman, Byrne was not a cold weather trout fisherman. His trips to the headwaters of Elk were usually made in August. He was quoted in *the Webster Echo* that he had visited Webster Springs every year in August from 1885 to 1911.

The *Echo* carried a story about Byrne conversing with Henry Gassaway Davis following breakfast at the Webster Springs Hotel. Davis told about camping on a tributary of Cheat River, and he said the trout were so thick that he had to scoop them out on the bank with his hands to get a bucket of water, and then return them to the stream.

"I can readily understand how that could occur," Byrne replied. "But I never had just such an experience, because in the good old days to which I have referred we never used water in camp."

Byrne had an abiding interest in politics, starting when he was elected prosecuting attorney in Braxton County. He later served as clerk of both the State Senate and House of Delegates, was elected to the House in 1922, and became Speaker of the House in 1923. At the time of his death he was clerk of the State Supreme Court.

There was never any mistaking Byrne's political allegiance. "He was a Yellow Dog Democrat," said grandson Bill Mohler, a Republican. I'd never heard the term, and thought perhaps it had something to do with one of my favorite movies, *Adventures of Yellow Dog*. But Mohler explained that it meant someone who would vote for a yellow dog if the dog was running on the Democratic ticket.

In 1901, Byrne bought *the Daily Gazette* for his brother, George Byrne, who became the editor. The name was changed to *the Charleston Gazette* in 1907. Senator W.E. Chilton bought the paper in 1912, and the Chilton family is still the majority owner.

Byrne and Amanda Austin of Lewisburg were married on June 12, 1889. They had five children, all of whom are now deceased. The last one, Charlotte Byrne Mesmer, died in 2002 in Orlando, Florida. Preceding her in death were George Byrne, who is buried in Staunton, Virginia; Barbara Byrne Mohler, who is buried in South Charleston; Marie Byrne Sheets, who is buried in Charleston; and W.E.R Byrne Jr., who is buried in Yuma, Arizona.

Amanda Austin Byrne died in 1959. She was well known in her own right, having been active in civic affairs for decades. Her obituary in *the Charleston Daily Mail* said that in 1931 she was president general of the United Daughters of the Confederacy, the highest honor given in that organization. She was one of the organizers of the Charleston YWCA, charter member of the Community Music Association, member of the Kanawha Players, Kanawha Literary Club, and Charleston Woman's Club, and a Sunday School teacher at First Presbyterian Church.

- - -

In one of life's ironies, Elk River cost Bill Byrne his life, at least indirectly. He was at his camp in late fall, and developed pneumonia from wading in the cold water, whether fishing or not isn't known. He returned to Charleston and died at home a week later on December 11, 1937. His funeral was held at his home, and he was buried in the Spring Hill Cemetery on Charleston's East End on a bitterly cold December 13.

His obituary in *the Charleston Gazette* was page one news under the heading "Supreme Court Clerk Is Dead." The lengthy story included his picture and a tribute by Governor Rocky Holt, who referred to him as "Cousin Will." The story noted that Byrne was "the author of Tale of the Elk, a collection of his remembrances and historical facts of Central West Virginia."

The most memorable lines in his book were the last two. He wrote a paean to the river and his camp that concluded with these words:

"Let me sleep - let me dream - by the murmuring stream,

"In my Camp at The End of the World."

Twenty Five

Clendenin and Elkview

The Towns Up Elk

Twenty miles above Charleston, Elk comes to Clendenin, which is where Union Carbide, the giant petrochemical firm, got its start in 1921. The only visible evidence today of the Carbide presence is a historical marker on West Virginia 119, and a chunk or two of concrete where a portion of the plant stood in the lower end of town.

When I visited Clendenin on a warm, sunny day in October 2004, my host, appropriately, was Jim Clendenin, the former mayor. He is a descendant of George Clendenin, the founder of Charleston and the probable namesake of the town of Clendenin.

Clendenin was first called Chilton for William Chilton, who laid out the town in 1877. An early post office name was Mouth of Sandy for Big Sandy Creek. The town became Clendenin when it was incorporated in 1904.

It isn't known whether George Clendenin ever visited in the area of present Clendenin. The West Virginia Blue Book doesn't specify him as the namesake. It says only that the town of Clendenin "was named for the Clendenins, pioneer citizens of the Kanawha Valley."

But Jim Clendenin believes that George Clendenin *was* the namesake, and when we set out to enjoy the golden October sun and walk around town, he told me that one of his goals in retirement is to have a marker placed at City Hall telling the historical significance of the town's name.

In its heyday, Clendenin was a thriving shopping center Up Elk

The 1932 Flood at Clendenin
Photo courtesy of Jim Clendenin

that boasted three large department stores in its downtown. Daltons stood on the corner of Main Street and Maywood Avenue, and A.W. Cox and Robertson-Parris were located on Main Street. The Cox building is now the Clendenin Pharmacy, owned by Bill Ore.

Bill's father, Clarence 'Cry Baby' Ore, went to work for Union Carbide when it started in Clendenin, and moved with the firm to the Kanawha Valley in 1929. He was with Carbide for a total of forty-seven years. "Everybody knew my father as Cry Baby," said Bill. "When he was young, he would go fishing in Elk, and if he didn't catch anything he would come home and cry."

Jim and I walked to the end of Main Street where the old Clendenin Bridge once entered the downtown. Now there is simply a blank space over the river. The bridge, built in 1923, came crashing down in three puffs of dynamite in 1997. "Big Boom Drops Elk River Bridge," proclaimed the Clendenin Herald. Downtown Clendenin is so close to the river that a former barber, Harley Gallion, would fish from the window of his shop.

Clendenin, like all towns along Elk, has seen its share of floods, including the 1932 flood pictured in this chapter that reached almost to the deck of the old bridge. The flow of Elk at Queen Shoals, four miles upstream, reached 72,000 cubic feet per second on July 5, 1932, an alltime record at any gauge on Elk. Years ago, Bonner Gillespie, a Clendenin resident, described floods best. "There are two things you can't control," he would say, "and those are ignorance and high water."

We viewed with nostalgia the Roxy, the vacant movie theater on Maywood Avenue that opened soon after World War II and closed in 2002. Don Moore, owner of Moore Theater Equipment in Charleston and son of Roxy proprietor Harold Moore, recalled the stage performances that drew big crowds. Among the headliners were country music pioneers Flatt and Scruggs, and Lash LaRue, movie cowboy whose trademark was expert use of a whip. "One of his crowd pleasers," said Don, was flicking a cigarette out of the lips of sidekick Fuzzy Knight."

- - -

I remember Clendenin as a hotbed of high school basketball. In their heyday, the Cardinals could compete with the best in the Kanawha Valley, and their coach, Paul 'Pop' Workman, became a local sports legend.

"Workman and his assistant, Marvin Lee, were disciplinarians," recalled Buck Geary, the Sage of Big Sandy who played in 1941-44. In Geary's senior year, the team won the Kanawha Valley Conference title, and Geary was named co-captain of the all-conference team with Clyde 'Hard Times' Green of East Bank. Geary became a lawyer, and is still practicing in Petersburg, Grant County.

Clendenin teams won KVC titles in 1944, 1945, and 1950. Jack Matheny, a member of the 1944 team, remembers Hard Times Green, who went on to play at West Virginia University. "It seemed to me his hands were a foot long when he launched shots from outside," said Matheny.

There was always an ample supply of Clendenin kids who could play basketball well. One of the reasons was a vacant lot on Koontz Avenue near the high school where someone nailed a wooden backboard and basket to a sycamore tree. Clendenin kids would spend endless hours there "shooting hoops" and playing pickup games.

"I imagine that at one time or another, we all 'graduated' from that vacant lot," said Andy Settle, who is retired from Bank One and lives on Elk Avenue, a stone's throw from the river. Andy's brother, Bill, is remembered for scoring a goal in the final seconds of a 32-30 win over Stonewall Jackson that gave Clendenin the KVC title in 1945.

Bob Gandee was a senior on the 1950 KVC title-winning team. "We won our sectional that season," Bob recalled, "but I don't remember about the regional. We must not have won it." Bob played college basketball at Glenville State, and became a teacher and coach.

Pete White, who later played three years at WVU, was a junior on the 1950 team. In his senior year in 1951, the Cardinals rolled to a 15-0 record and appeared headed for another title, but White became sick and missed the remaining games, and the team fell short of the title.

White was co-captain of the 1955 WVU team with Frank Spadafore, and was its rebounding leader with an average of 12 per game. That team included sophomore Hot Rod Hundley, a future All-American. In one of White's memorable games in 1955, he scored 29 points and pulled down 27 rebounds against Pitt, the traditional WVU rival.

The team advanced to the NCAA tournament, but lost to LaSalle at Madison Square Garden in New York. White, a 6-4 center, scored nineteen points, although guarded by 6-7 LaSalle All-American Tom Gola. "I never had a hook shot blocked in my career," said White, "but I felt Gola's fingers graze my hand often in that game."

White was drafted by the St. Louis Hawks of the National Basketball Association, but had a three-year ROTC commitment to fulfill, and didn't play pro ball. He became an electronic counter-measure operator on a B-52 bomber.

White lives in Charleston and heads White Planning Group, an insurance firm. He still plays basketball in the West Virginia Senior Olympics, and is an avid tennis player. "I always tell people I'm going to take up golf when I get old," he said, "and they always ask, What are you waiting for?"

- - -

Since Day One, it seems, there have been Gandees involved in sports at Clendenin and Herbert Hoover. The best known of them, because he coached as well as played, is Carlton Gandee. He also had the distinction of coaching his four sons at Hoover in basketball, football, or baseball.

There are many pictures available of Carlton playing or coaching, but the picture chosen for this book, for a special reason, shows him in his Navy flight uniform. After graduating from Glenville State College in 1953, he joined the Navy and became a pilot. He flew the Cutlass, a twin-tailed fighter plane, and therein lies the story.

Carlton helped make history with the Cutlass. His air group was assigned to the shakedown cruise of the USS Forrestal, the first nuclear powered carrier, and on this cruise the first computer guided carrier landings were performed. They replaced the traditional signalman waving wands to bring a plane onto the deck safely.

As a basketball player at Clendenin, Carlton developed a reputation for "seeing things" as the game unfolded that gave his team a competitive edge. His coach, Pop Workman, said it was "like having a second coach on the floor."

Carlton had an out-standing basketball career at Glenville State. In his sopho-more year in 1951, the Pioneers won the West Virginia Confer-ence and played in the NAIA Tournament in Kansas City. He was captain of the Glenville team in his senior year. After his Navy days, he "followed his

Carlton Gandee as a Navy pilot

dream" and became a coach. He coached at Clendenin Junior High, Clen-denin High School, and Herbert Hoover High School before retiring in 1986.

His 1960 team at Clendenin High advanced to the state tourney at Morgantown, where it lost to Romney. Bill Maphis, an outstanding player who would later become a standout at West Virginia University, scored the game-winning goal on a drive to the basket that the Clendenin contingent thought should have resulted in a charging call.

Carlton coached football as well as basketball, and he was a "film fanatic" when big football games were coming up, said his wife, Dottie Lanham Gandee, a Harrison County native who met Carlton when they were attending Glenville State.

"He would bring film home, and I would help him watch it," she said. "He couldn't watch all eleven players, so he'd ask me to watch a particular player on certain plays. He'd say something like, Watch No. 61 for me."

One of the football highlights came in a 1977 game against George Washington in Charleston when both were unbeaten late in the season. "You probably could have robbed a bank up Elk that night and gotten away with it, because everybody was at the game," Dottie recalled. Hoover won and went on to finish the regular season unbeaten, but lost to Fairmont in the state playoffs.

Carlton coached his sons, David, Jeff, Tim, and Terry, at various times at Hoover. In 1975, son David averaged 22.3 points as a guard in basketball.

David lives at Slatyfork, near the Snowshoe entrance, where he and his wife, Jo Debra Galford Gandee, operate four businesses. Jeff is a partner in Superior Windows of Charleston, and lives at Pinch. Tim lives on Cooper's Creek and is a heavy equipment operator for Arch Coal. He coached basketball at Charleston Catholic High School, where his 2000 team won the state Class A title. Terry lives at Clendenin and is a superintendent for S and T Pipeline Company. Their sister, Kelly Jo Evans, lives at St. Albans and is a nurse at CAMC. Carlton and Dottie live on Thorofare Road near Clendenin.

All of the Gandees have pleasant memories of summer days at the Union Carbide boys' camp at Blue Creek, which Carlton directed from 1968 to 1978. He directed the combined boys' and girls' camps the final three years.

- - -

By February 2005, I had long since satisfied a desire to swim at the Big Falls of the Back Fork of Elk, and had transferred my obsessive tendencies to finding the "view" in Elkview, although any of the high ground near the river would seem to fit.

Elkview lies ten miles above Charleston and is the largest town on the river with the exception of the capital city (see Elk by the Numbers). Dana Campbell, a Pennzoil retiree, suggested two "view" possibilities when I visited him at his home and posed the question. One, he said, is the hill above the Tobacco and More Store, and the other, on the opposite side of the river, is the ridge above Hafer Funeral Home.

Dana has an almost encyclopedic knowledge of Elk from its headwaters to Charleston. He produced a copy of River on the Rocks, my 2001 book, and pointed to where I had autographed it at a book signing. At the suggestion of his wife, Rose, I had inscribed it "To Dana, an Elk River fisherman." Until Dana and I talked at his home, I hadn't realized how prescient I had been.

He has fished Old Field and Big Spring Forks, which combine to form Elk; the Slaty section at the start of the river; Whittaker Falls; the canyon area below Webster Springs to Centralia; and the river through Braxton, Clay, and Kanawha Counties. We discussed the long gone community of Samp below Whittaker Falls, the almost gone community of Skelt where Sugar Creek enters the Back Fork, and other byways that only someone with an intimate knowledge of Elk would know about.

Closer to home, he told me about the time Elk ran backwards, and became filled with big carp. Around 1940, when the river was extremely low, a fourteen-foot raise in the Kanawha River pushed Elk upstream to the Walgrove Shoal, fourteen miles above Charleston. "It created a lake," he said, "and in the process 'loaded' Elk with carp from the Kanawha."

From a fishing standpoint, lower Elk doesn't receive the attention that the up-river fishing does, but it may be Elk's best kept secret. Chris Ellis, then with the State Tourism Division, and J.R. Oliver hosted freelance writer Bruce Ingram on a day's outing in the Elkview area in 2004, and Ingram caught and released a twenty-three and one-half inch smallmouth. J.R. told me that the fishing for Kentucky spotted bass is particularly good.

Elkview was first known as Pricedale, a community on the highway side of the river named for early resident James A. Price. At another time, it was known as Jarrett's Ford for Levi and Owen Jarrett, who lived on the south side of the river.

Jarrett's Ford once had a visitor who was to become famous in a way. He was George Ferris, who built the first Ferris wheel. It was twenty-five stories tall, carried 1,400 passengers, and was a prominent part of the World's Columbian Exposition at Chicago in 1893. The far shore of Lake Michigan could be seen from the top of the wheel. Ferris was part of a crew that was surveying for a railroad up Elk in 1881 and camped at Jarrett's Ford for three weeks.

The Carpenters of Elk (see Elk in the Center) were known for building large canoes and johnboats, but they had competition from Mel Cart, who lived on Buffalo Lick Run at Elkview. He once scooped out a canoe from a sycamore tree that, according to legend, was so long that he had to back it up into Blue Creek to turn it around.

Blue Creek is renowned for its oil strike of the early 1900s. A headline in the March 1912 Charleston Gazette proclaimed that "And Still the Gushers Come; Three Yesterday." A few of those early wells are still producing.

The largest island on lower Elk is the one at Blue Creek, where, prior to the oil boom, there was a gambling resort called Island Inn. It is said that Ben Hall won the island in a poker game and started the resort. People would ride the train up from Charleston to stay there. With the oil gushers, it became a boarding house for oilfield workers. Now it is home to the Mount Pleasant Baptist Church Camp, and the Elk Valley Christian School's soccer and softball fields.

Prior to the coming of the railroad, steamboats plied Elk between Charleston and Clendenin. One of them, the Old Bob Henry, exploded in the late 1800s at the Blue Creek shoal, killing three people and injuring several others.

- - -

At one time, Elkview and local Golden Gloves boxing were synonymous. If Clendenin was the hotbed of basketball, Elkview was the hotbed of boxing. It began in the mid 1930s, and blossomed in 1939 when Toby Jarrett, son of the janitor at Elkview High School, trained a group of about seven boys in the downstairs gymnasium. At one time, Jarrett, who fought professionally under the name Toby Mack, was one of the top welterweights in the country.

His assistant at Elkview was Rex Crouser, a chemistry teacher and assistant football coach. Toby Jarrett, a.k.a. Toby Mack, died in 1941, and Crouser took over and became most closely identified in public print with the Golden Glovers that came out of the school. These included Cletus Morris, Junior Kee, and Noble Holt, although there were others, including Junior's brothers, Dean and John.

Junior Kee retired from the Carbide Tech Center in 1982, and lives near Clendenin. In his boxing days, he was a lightweight and welterweight. "I always wanted to be a heavyweight," he said, "and I finally made it. In retirement, I weigh 185 pounds."

He was one of the Elkview boxers who went to the national Golden Gloves tourney at New York's Madison Square Garden. He fought there twice, and lost split decisions both times. "But," he said, "just going to New York was a highlight for an old country boy."

Once the Elkview team went to Virginia to box against Staunton Military Academy. "They seated us opposite the person we were going to fight," Junior recalled. "My opponent was unbeaten, and he kept smiling at me as if I was going to be the next victim. I sort of thought so too, to be honest. But I won the fight on a decision, and he cried. In a way, I felt bad about that."

- - -

The downriver community of Big Chimney was named for a sixty-foot stone chimney that was part of the salt manufacturing process. It stood on the river where Mike O'Neil, an engineer for the Department of Highways, now lives. An 1850 picture of it preserves, in a photographic sense, a part of lower Elk history.

The stone was quarried at Indian Creek near Pinch, hand-cut into blocks of two feet by two feet by six feet, and transported to the Big

Chimney site. "Those blocks weighed an estimated 3,600 pounds," said Mike, a geologist. "I don't know how they got them here, except maybe by flatboat."

Even though the business closed during the Civil War, and the chimney no longer exists, most of the stones do. Approximately eighty percent of them were sold by a previous owner, and were used to build a retaining wall on Hillsdale Drive in Charleston.

Jim and Bill Smith, who were to become well known businessmen in the Elk Valley, farmed the river bottom in the vicinity of the chimney when they were teenagers. The only part of the chimney that remained then, Jim recalled, was the base.

Big Chimney
Photo courtesy of Jim Smith

Their parents, Roane County natives O.V. and Beulah Caldwell Smith, came to Big Chimney in 1928. O.V. Smith got his business start following military service in World War I when he bought a team of horses on credit and hauled casing to the oil wells at Blue Creek. He opened a grocery store in Big Chimney in 1928, and ran it until 1945, when he retired.

Upon retirement, he leased the building for ten years. Meantime, his sons, while still in high school, engaged in the cattle business. They grew corn and put up hay along the river at Big Chimney, and raised cattle there and on two family farms in Roane County, selling the cattle at the stock market in Spencer.

After the lease expired on their father's building, they opened the O.V. Smith and Sons Grocery. "It's was an easy event to remember," said Jim. "We built a fifty-five foot by fifty-five foot building in '55."

It was also the start of a remarkable business story.

Although the grocery store was known for many years as O.V.

Smith and Sons, they were never actually in business with their father, but used his name to borrow money. "He had credit, but Bill and I didn't," Jim explained, "so we used the name O.V. Smith and Sons to satisfy the bank."

Today, the store is known as Smith's Foodfair, as is another of their stores located in the Elk Shopping Plaza at Elkview, a property they bought in 1975. When I visited Jim in March 2005, a third Smith's Foodfair was planned for the former Kroger Store at Clendenin. The brothers also own a carpet business, called Smith's Carpet One, a True Value Hardware, and a furniture, appliance and mattress store.

They began buying real estate in 1965, and today it is almost impossible to be out of sight of Smith property between Big Chimney and Clendenin. The brothers own and lease numerous business properties across the state of West Virginia. Among their tenants are Verizon, Rite Aid, Sears, General Electric, Exxon, Pittsburgh Plate Glass, Napa Auto Parts, Appalachian Power Company, Family Dollar, the state and federal governments, Kroger's, etc.

Big Rock at Big Chimney

One of the buildings they own is the former Big Chimney Elementary School, which they attended. They bought it following school consolidation, and converted it to offices. Jim was one of the organizers of the Elk Valley Public Library. "I heard the community could get a library," he said, "so I bought a building that was formerly a church. I renovated it, and donated it to the Kanawha County Public Library System."

He was among the founders of the Elk National Bank, now United National Bank, and is still a shareholder. "I've never sold a share of the stock in my life," he said. "Neither have I ever drawn a paycheck from a private sector employer."

Jim still lives in Big Chimney near where the old chimney stood, and near where he and Bill caught large catfish as boys and swam at the Big Rock, one of the few large rocks on lower Elk. Bill divides his time between Big Chimney and Naples, Florida.

Jim and his son, George, are avid hunters and fishermen, including hunting for elk in the Western United States, and fishing in Alaska, while Bill enjoys boating and fishing in Florida.

- - -

St. Patrick's Day 2005 was close at hand when I visited the Earl of Elkview, lawyer, entertainer, and ambassador at large to the world. Naturally, he was wearing green. His love of Ireland and the Irish is well known. His great grandfather came to America from Donegal County in the northernmost part of Ireland, and the Earl, a.k.a. George Daugherty, has made many trips to the Old Sod. To listen to him sing or play Danny Boy is to almost forgive him for not fishing Elk River, which flows past his door.

No, I'm not a fisherman," he said with a note of apology creeping into his voice as I stood in his kitchen and looked at the river.

But he is a West Virginia icon. He calls himself a psychoneuroimmunologist, which he defines as a person who studies the art of living, or, expressed another way, a Doctor of Perpetual Celebration. In a 1996 interview, he told Roger Bryant, the West Virginia guitar maestro and country music writer, that "festive living will let your brain cure illnesses that you don't even know you have."

The pseudonym, Earl of Elkview, dates back to 1970 and the Capital City Jamboree at the Custer Theater on Charleston's West Side. "Mom was afraid people wouldn't come to me as a lawyer if I became well known as an entertainer," he said, "so I took it as a stage name." He has been practicing law for forty-six years, first in Charleston and now at his home, so the stratagem must have worked.

Not accidentally, Elkview has gotten a lot of "press" because of his stage name. He chose the name in part as a tribute to the community where he lives. "I'm very grateful to the people of Elkview," he said. "It's a wonderful place." He and his

The Earl of Elkview. Photo by Suzanne Daugherty

wife, Suzanne, live in a familiar two-story house on Reynolds Avenue, near the intersection known as the "Elkview Four-Way."

He was born in Mannington, West Virginia, on the second floor of the Masonic Building, and came to Elkview with his parents at age five. His musical inclination may have taken root shortly after birth, because their apartment at Mannington was located above the Idle Hour Theater, where a woman named Georgie Moore played the piano for silent movies.

Buddy Griffin, director of cultural events at Glenville State College and regarded by many as West Virginia's best musician, or at least its best fiddler, has performed many times with Daugherty. He believes his primary appeal lies in his warmth. "He plays and sings from the heart, and not from the book," said Griffin.

Buddy played the guitar and George the "saw" on an instrumental rendition of Danny Boy that was part of a CD they recorded in 2004 as a tribute to Irish playwright John Keane. My meager musical background did not include any knowledge of a saw as a musical instrument. "It's a regular bow saw played with a fiddle bow," George explained.

The saw has been part of his musical repertoire for forty years. "I sent my son to WVU for eight years," his father, Al Daugherty, once said, "and I ended up with a damn saw player." George learned to play the saw while a freshman at WVU under the tutelage of Jarvey Eldred, a Morgantown businessman whom he'd heard perform at Reynolds Hall.

The walls of George's office at his home are adorned with pictures or drawings of presidents and other luminaries. The "other luminaries" include Sam Chilton, a raconteur and eight-time unsuccessful candidate for West Virginia Secretary of State. Sam and Riley Wilson, two habitués of the old Charleston Press Club, are George's "godfathers of story telling."

His "godfather of song titles" must surely be the late Charleston lawyer, Jack Savage, who suggested a title and George wrote the song: It Takes a Snuff-Dippin' Woman for a Baccer Chewin' Man. He performs it often, and he once sang it, at the groom's request, at a wedding.

Twenty Six

Elk Enters Charleston

George Clendenin's Town

In the 2100 block of Pennsylvania Avenue, which in pre-interstate days was the primary street leading north out of Charleston, Elk River enters the Big City. For the river, it is the completion, or almost, of a journey that begins one hundred and seventy two miles away in the mountains of Pocahontas County.

On a pleasant day in June 2005, Rob and I slid his canoe into the water near the Charleston City Limits sign on Pennsylvania Avenue, and paddled the remainder of the way to where Elk enters Kanawha. The line delineating the city limits is approximately where Terminix International is located at 2120 Pennsylvania.

Although our canoe trip was short, it had history on its side. Charleston is the capital of West Virginia. It was first laid out barely thirteen years after the Revolutionary War had ended, and Daniel Boone had the good sense to live there for several years.

I admire Boone, not just because he was the prototype frontier adventurer and a celebrity equal to George Washington, but also because the story is told that he walked all the way from Charleston to Richmond to attend the 1791 session of the Virginia General Assembly. Asked why he didn't ride horseback, he explained that horses were too much trouble and that it was easier to walk. He may have been right, because, the story continues, fellow traveler and delegate George Clendenin's horse died on the return trip.

In my newspaper days, photographer Larry Pierce and I rode horseback ten miles into the Otter Creek Wilderness of Randolph and

Tucker Counties for a story on drilling being done by Island Creek Coal Company to determine the worth of its minerals. A court order had blocked the company from transporting drilling equipment by motorized vehicle. Ten miles *into* also meant ten miles *out of*, and I determined, as Boone had done two hundred years earlier, that walking was easier.

A footnote to the history of Charleston, which I concede and hereby acknowledge in print, is that its original name has a tenuous connection to a horse. Fort Lee, which Charleston was called for a brief time, was named for Henry 'Light *Horse* Harry' Lee, an American cavalry officer of the Revolutionary War whose daring equestrian maneuvers earned him the rank "Captain of Horse," and who moved for the adoption of the Declaration of Independence in the Continental Congress. He later became governor of Virginia, and the father of Robert E. Lee of Civil War fame.

The founder of Charleston in 1794 was George Clendenin, a Scottish emigrant who in 1787 bought 1,040 acres from Cuthbert Bullitt, brother of Thomas Bullitt. Clendenin, a colonel in the post-Revolutionary War militia, decided to establish a fort on his land, and Fort Lee was built in April 1788 as part of Virginia's system of frontier defense to protect settlers against Indians. It remained a fort until 1795 when the Indian threat had waned and it then became simply a residence.

Thomas Bullitt was a militiaman, French and Indian War veteran, and surveyor. He was the earliest known landowner at the mouth of Elk. A native of Prince William County, Virginia, he headed a surveying party that came to the present site of Charleston in the spring of 1773, and later that year surveyed the city that is now Louisville, Kentucky.

He is believed to have made a "Tomahawk" land claim, which was the term given to staking out land through hack marks on trees. It included all of what is presently Charleston's East End. His claim was said to have never been fully settled, but in any event, prior to his death in 1778, he bequeathed the land to his brother, Cuthbert Bullitt, who sold it to Clendenin.

The frontispiece drawing of Fort Lee in Roy Bird Cook's 1935 *The Annals of Fort Lee* shows a two-story main cabin, several smaller cabins, a stockade, and the fledgling U.S. flag. Whether this represented simply the artist's conception or was based on an early description is not known, although it was probably the former.

The fort stood on Kanawha River at the foot of present day Brooks Street in an area known then as Brooks Landing. Brooks Street is located several blocks east of the mouth of Elk, and three blocks east of the Charleston Newspapers building. In the latter years of my employment at *the Gazette*, Brooks Street was my route out of town, leading as it does to

Interstate 79.

On a hot day in late August 2004, I parked on Virginia Street East and walked to the supposed site of Fort Lee. A stone monument, erected in 1930, marks the spot, or at least is close. The marker sits on the edge of Kanawha Boulevard in front of The Town House Apartments. Across the Boulevard on the high bank above the river is a historical marker that also tells of Fort Lee.

As I crossed Charleston's marvelous riverfront boulevard to read the marker, boaters were swishing up and down the Kanawha, creating waves of seemingly tidal basin proportions, and a towboat pushed a string of barges loaded with coal to feed hungry power plants downriver.

Fort Lee was intermittently known as Fort Clendenin, or Clendenin's Settlement, for its builder. There are other references to it as the Mansion House, meaning the house where Clendenin lived in the fort enclosure, or just behind it.

The Brooks Street location for Fort Lee may have been considered of more strategic value for reasons that are not apparent now, although the mouth of Elk with its commanding view of both rivers would have seemed a more likely site. But the possibility exists that two hundred years ago the Elk bottomland was deemed too swampy to build on, or was lower than it is now and therefore didn't have a commanding view.

Swampy or not, Indians were known to have spent time there, most likely on hunting forays, which was their primary use of Western Virginia when they were being pushed west from their ancestral lands by white settlers. During excavation for the Sears store in Charleston Town Center, artifacts were discovered buried several feet under the loamy soil. They were on display for a time at the Lee Street entrance to the store, and provided a tantalizing glimpse into the world of Charleston's early visitors, or residents, whichever the case may have been.

When George Clendenin laid out the tract that became Charleston, he called it Charles Town in honor of his father, Charles Clendenin. It became simply Charleston in 1819. The change was made because there was already a Charles Town in existence. Charles Town in Jefferson County, named for Charles Washington, brother of the first president, was chartered in 1786.

There are several references, also, to Charleston as "The Town at the Mouth of Elk," starting with the plat label for the Clendenin survey.

There is an excellent description of the birth of Charleston in the book, *John Young: Lieutenant at Elk*, by Roane County lawyer and former state senator Orton Jones, who writes about a surveyor "laying off 40 acres into streets and lots." This includes most, if not all, of the present downtown. The original survey was believed to have been made by Alexander Welch, Greenbrier County surveyor, but it was not put on record. However, a second survey, made by Reuben Slaughter, Kanawha County surveyor, was recorded. (Kanawha was formed in 1788 from parts of Greenbrier and Montgomery Counties, Virginia).

The title of Jones's book is derived from a letter that Daniel Boone wrote to Virginia Governor Henry Lee seeking money for military needs in Kanawha County. In the letter, Boone referred to Young as "Leut at Elk."

Young, a native of Lancaster County, Pennsylvania, came to the Kanawha Valley in 1783 and was one of the builders of Fort Lee, a lieutenant in the Kanawha County militia, a scout, and one of the nine founding trustees of Charleston. He was also a foot soldier for a brief period of time in the Revolutionary War.

Jones tells a remarkable story of Young, his wife, Keziah Tackett Townsend, and their one-day old son, Jacob, escaping from Tackett's Fort near the mouth of Coal River when it was under siege by Indians in 1790. They ran in the pitch darkness, Young clutching his infant son. The Indians discovered them and began shooting, but with bullets zinging around them, they reached a canoe at the edge of the Kanawha, paddled to the north side, and, in a pouring rain, continued twelve miles upstream to Fort Lee, where they took up residence.

In 1801, John and Keziah Young moved "up Elk" and settled at what is now called Young's Bottom, an unincorporated community near Elkview, where they raised a large family and began a Young presence in the Elk and Kanawha Valleys that continues to this day. They both died in 1850 and are buried in the Sand Run Cemetery near the Sand Run Gospel Tabernacle Church.

I visited the cemetery on a mild but overcast day in late September 2004 and appreciated the solitude and the view of the hills of the Elk River Valley. There are many houses nearby, but none are visible from the Young graves. The inscription on the tombstone reads: "*John Young and wife 1758-1850. Commissioned by George Washington as an Indian spy. They were among the first settlers that came down the Kanawha Valley.*"

John Young is said to have moved up Elk from Charleston to find more "elbow room." If he were to return today, he would probably move again.

- ~ -

The presence of Daniel Boone in Charleston during the 1790s gives the city great historical luster, although very little is known about that period of his life, or even why he came there. But, once there, he did have his duties as a lieutenant colonel in the Kanawha County militia. A stone marker in front of the Kanawha County Courthouse tells us that. George Clendenin, the town's founder, headed the militia as "county lieutenant."

Part of the reason for the move may have simply been Boone's restless nature. Or maybe it was because he was a hunter and trapper. Certainly he was already a legend. "He had heard," wrote Norva Balser Warner in her 2004 book, *The Strength of Our People*, "that one could still find buffalo and elk in the Kanawha Valley." Indeed, the last buffalo known to have been killed there was in 1815, and the last elk in 1820 (see End of the Line).

Warner is a native of Kelly's Creek in Eastern Kanawha County who now lives in Tucker County near Parsons. Her ancestors, primarily the Morris and Young families, were among the early settlers in the valley. She wrote that seven of the thirty men who built Fort Lee were her ancestors.

John P. Hale, a Charleston physician, said in his 1886 book, *Trans-Allegheny Pioneers*, that Boone surveyed in the Kanawha Valley, but mainly hunted and trapped, including on the Kanawha and Gauley Rivers. He wrote about Boone trapping on Kanawha a few miles below Kanawha Falls with Paddy Huddlestone, a resident of upper Kanawha.

A June 14, 1791, survey of ten acres at Point Pleasant in Boone's handwriting is on proud display in Charleston's Cultural Center, proving that he did some surveying during his time in the Kanawha Valley.

Charles T. Dodrill, a Huntington lawyer, said in his family history, *Heritage of a Pioneer*, that Boone and William (English Bill) Dodrill "trapped for beaver on the waters of Elk and its tributaries, including the waters of Birch River." In 1799, English Bill settled on the head of Birch in present day Webster County. He was the first recorded white settler on Birch.

A Dodrill family tradition holds that English Bill accompanied Boone to Richmond, not as a delegate to the Virginia Assembly but to sell ginseng and furs. Nathan Boone, Daniel's son, indicated in what became known as the Draper interviews that Boone made two trips to the Virginia Assembly, so it is possible that English Bill accompanied him on one of them.

There is a question mark hanging over the year of Boone's arrival in Charleston. He is said to have left Boonesboro in Kentucky after learning that he didn't have a valid deed to the thousands of acres he thought he had acquired, and legal proceedings had deprived him of the land.

From Boonesboro, he went to Point Pleasant, arriving there as early as 1786, or not long afterward. It was there that he met English Bill Dodrill.

In *Trans-Allegheny Pioneers*, Hale stated that Boone came to Charleston in 1788 or 1789, although other accounts aren't sure. One account says he was "off trapping" in 1789. But he definitely was in Charleston in 1791 when he and George Clendenin went to Richmond as delegates to the Virginia Assembly.

Where he lived in Charleston is also unclear, although Roy Bird Cook wrote that he took up residence "a short distance above Fort Lee," perhaps in the upper end of what is now Kanawha City, within sight of the present capitol building and across the river from the mouth of Campbell's Creek.

Likewise, there is not total agreement on when he left Charleston. The earliest date mentioned is 1795. But Hale said he was still there in 1798 when he made a survey. Hale said the Boone party, including his wife, Rebecca, and son, Nathan, embarked from the mouth of Elk, no doubt to a rousing farewell, given Boone's celebrity status.

The legendary frontiersman never returned to the Kanawha Valley. He went west to Missouri, where he died in 1820 either at Nathan's home, or at the home of a neighbor as he was returning to Nathan's. He was eighty six years old, and no doubt was still looking westward.

- - -

Ironically, George Clendenin didn't finish out his years in the town he founded. According to Roy Bird Cook, he went to Marietta, Ohio, in 1796 to visit his daughter, and died there in April 1797. Marietta was the first organized American settlement in what was then the Northwest Territory (now the state of Ohio). Clendenin is believed to be buried in the historic Mound Cemetery on Marietta's Fifth Street. The cemetery, named for the presence of an Indian mound, contains over four thousand graves.

Whether Clendenin's grave is one of them isn't known for a certainty, because there is no marker. But Ernie Thode of the history and genealogy department at the Washington County Library told me that Clendenin is supposedly buried there in the Meigs family plot. John Meigs, for whom the plot is named, was Clendenin's son in law. Noel Steorts, a Newton, West Virginia, native and a descendant of George Clendenin, also believes that Clendenin is buried at the Mound Cemetery. Steorts now lives in Waterford, Ohio.

Clendenin's primary legacy in Charleston is, of course, as founding father, but he also has a prominent street named for him. Clendenin

Street, which parallels Elk, bisects the Charleston Civic Center and Charleston Town Center, two of the city's showcase structures.

Charles Clendenin, the town's namesake, died in 1790 and is said to have been buried at Fort Lee. One account says his burial spot is on a grassy strip between the Boulevard and the sidewalk near present day 1210 Kanawha Boulevard.

Thomas Bullitt and his brother, Cuthbert, the latter a distinguished judge of his day and president of the Court of Appeals of Virginia, also have a street named for them. Bullitt Street is a short street on the north end of downtown near the West Virginia-American Water Company plant and Elk River.

Daniel Boone's legacy in Charleston is, first and foremost, the historical fact that he was there, but he also had a hotel named for him. The Daniel Boone, an elegant hostelry in its day, was opened in 1929 and was a city landmark until it closed in 1981. During those five decades, many famous people entered its doors, including presidents Truman, Eisenhower, and Kennedy. Equally renowned was the hotel's 1791 Tavern with its authentic period décor, food, and service.

- - -

It is almost two miles from where Elk enters Charleston to its merger with the Kanawha River under the Boulevard Bridge. On the day Rob and I canoed it, we began where Pat Legg and her son, Alan, and their next door neighbor, Bob Williams, live on Arlington Avenue, just downstream from Terminix International.

Our hour-long journey was uneventful, which is the way I prefer canoe trips. A slight headwind buffeted my Albuquerque Isotopes baseball cap, which became a close friend during the three years I worked on *Upper River*. It was given to me by Neil Boggs, the Clay County native who lives in New Mexico forty miles from Albuquerque.

I'd never previously seen Charleston from Elk, but everything gradually came into focus as we proceeded downriver: The mouth of Magazine Hollow, the last tributary to enter Elk from the north side and one that was the scene of a devastating flood in July 1961; the West Virginia-American Water Company office building; Pfaff and Smith, the venerable concrete firm at Spring and Bullitt Streets; the Spring Street Bridge, first of seven vehicular bridges over Elk in Charleston; two railroad bridges immediately below it, one in use, one not.

Farther along came the Interstate 64-77 Bridge, which is crossed by an average of 84,000 vehicles daily; Martin-Marietta Aggregates, where the towboat Earl Martin and its string of barges were docked; the Washington Manor Apartments and the Donnally Street softball field; a glimpse of the Charleston Marriott Town Center Hotel; the Charleston Civic Center, one of the city's showcase buildings; the City Center West Building; the CAMC Women's and Children's Hospital; the Washington Street Bridge; the Elk River Park, completed in 2003; and four more bridges: Lee Street, Quarrier Street, Virginia Street, and, last, the Boulevard Bridge. Elk had come to the Kanawha.

Rob and I turned downriver on the Kanawha, which was ruffled by breezes that kicked up modest whitecaps, and paddled the final one hundred yards to Magic Island, a city park that has been built up over the years by floodwaters from both Elk and Kanawha. Our canoe touched the upper end of the park, thus completing our brief journey in the city, and, symbolically, completing our work on this book.

I thought of the Crooked Fork Basin, one hundred and eighty four miles away, where I had stood with Ed Maguire and his yellow lab, Abby, three years earlier and viewed the headwaters of Elk. Then I turned carefully in the canoe and looked toward the mouth of Elk, which we had just passed, where the river of West Virginia's heartland had ended its own journey.

Elk enters the Kanawha

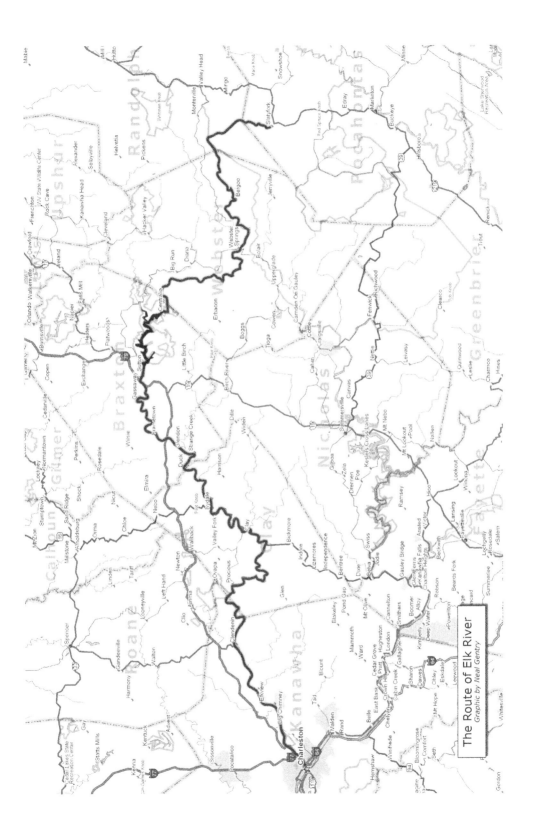

The Route of Elk River

Graphic by Neal Gentry

Elk by the Numbers

Headwater elevations

Thorny triangulation point	4,848 feet
Thorny Flat	4,735 feet
Red Spruce Knob	4,703 feet
Red Lick Mountain	4,686 feet
Gauley Mountain	4,571 feet
Gay Knob	4,542 feet
Sharp's Knob	4,520 feet
Gibson Knob	4,440 feet
Middle Mountain	4,400 feet
Elk Mountain (Randolph)	4,345 feet
Barlow Top	4,313 feet
Moffett Knob	4,160 feet
Slaty Ridge	4,152 feet
Mingo Knob	4,080 feet
Tallow Knob	4,052 feet

River or town elevations

Slatyfork	2,671 feet
Blackhole Run	2,520 feet
Whittaker Falls	2,192 feet
Bergoo	1,880 feet
Webster Springs	1,480 feet
Centralia	1,040 feet
Sutton	940 feet
Gassaway	841 feet
Clay	708 feet
Clendenin	629 feet
Elkview	604 feet
Charleston	568 feet

Rate of descent

Slatyfork to Bergoo	791 feet
Bergoo to Webster Springs	400 feet
Webster Springs to Centralia	440 feet
Sutton to Charleston	372 feet
Average fall per mile	12 feet

Mileages (head to mouth)

Slatyfork to Blackhole Run	4.7 miles
Blackhole Run to *Elk Springs	5.2 miles
Elk Springs to Whittaker Falls	2.6 miles
Whittaker Falls to Bergoo	9.4 miles
Bergoo to Webster Springs	10.5 miles
Webster Springs to Centralia	22.8 miles
Centralia to Sutton Dam	14.9 miles
Sutton Dam to Charleston	101.1 miles
Total	171.2 miles

* Elk Springs is also known as Cowger's Mill

Mileposts (going upstream)

Charleston	0
Queen Shoals	26.8
Clay	53.5
Mouth of Birch	8l.7
Sutton Dam	101.1
Centralia	116.0
Webster Springs	139.0
Bergoo	149.5
Whittaker Falls	158.9
Cowger's Mill	161.5
Slatyfork	171.2

Mileage by counties

Pocahontas	5 miles
Randolph	8 miles
Webster	43 miles
Braxton	40 miles
Clay	49 miles
Kanawha	27 miles

Drainage area

Above Sutton Dam	537 square miles
Below Sutton Dam	1,013 square miles
Total	1,550 square miles

Principal Tributaries (size of watershed)

Holly River (Randolph, Webster, Braxton)	148.4 square miles
Birch River (Webster, Nicholas, Braxton)	143.0 square miles
Big Sandy Creek (Roane, Kanawha)	133.5 square miles
Buffalo Creek (Nicholas, Clay)	113.4 square miles
Blue Creek (Clay, Kanawha)	79.8 square miles
Back Fork (Randolph, Webster)	69.7 square miles
Laurel Creek (Webster, Braxton)	66.8 square miles
Little Sandy Creek (Roane, Kanawha)	50.6 square miles

(The Elk River Basin represents 6.5 percent of the total area of West Virginia. Its drainage area includes approximately 730 direct or secondary tributaries).

Populations of principal towns (2000 census)

Webster Springs	818
Sutton	1,011
Gassaway	901
Clay	593*
Clendenin	1,116
Elkview	1,182
Charleston	53,421

* Clay's population was a model of consistency, rising from 592 in 1990 to 593 in 2000.

Sources: West Virginia State Archives, West Virginia Geological and Economic Survey, U.S. Army Corps of Engineers, Water Resources Section of the State Division of Environmental Protection, U.S. Forest Service, Division of Natural Resources, and U.S. Geological Survey.

Fishes of Elk River

American brook lamprey
American eel
Banded darter
Bigeye chub
Bigmouth buffalo
Black buffalo
Black crappie
Black red horse
Blacknose dace
Blackside darter
Bluebreast darter
Bluegill sunfish
Bluntnose minnow
Bowfin
Brindled madtom
Brook silverside
Brook trout
Brown bullhead
Brown trout
Carp
Channel catfish
Channel darter
Channel shiner
Creek chub
Crystal darter
Dusky darter
Eastern sand darter
Emerald shiner
Fantail darter
Fathead minnow
Flathead catfish
Freshwater drum
Ghost shiner
Gilt darter
Gizzard shad
Golden red horse
Golden shiner
Goldfish

Green sunfish
Greenside darter
Highfin carpsucker
Hogsucker
Johnny darter
Largemouth bass
Least brook lamprey
Logperch
Longear sunfish
Longhead darter
Longnose dace
Longnose gar
Mimic shiner
Mooneye
Mottled sculpin
Mountain madtom
Muskellunge
Northern brook lamprey
Northern madtom
Ohio lamprey
Paddlefish
Popeye shiner
Quillback
Rainbow darter
Rainbow trout
Redbreast sunfish
Redfin shiner
River carpsucker
River chub
River red horse
Rock bass
Rosyface shiner
Rosyside dace
Sand shiner
Sauger
Sharpnose darter
Shorthead red horse
Silver chub

Silver lamprey
Silver red horse
Silver shiner
Silverjaw minnow
Skipjack
Smallmouth bass
Smallmouth buffalo
Speckled chub
Spotfin shiner
Spottail shiner
Spotted bass
Spotted darter
Spotted sucker
Steelcolor shiner
Stonecat
Stoneroller
Streamline chub
Striped shiner
Telescope shiner
Threadfin shad
Tippecanoe darter
Troutperch
Variegate darter
Walleye
Warmouth sunfish
White bass
White crappie
White sucker
Whitetail shiner
Yellow bullhead

(This list was furnished by Stuart Welsh of the West Virginia Cooperative Fish and Wildlife Research Unit at Morgantown. The unit is a joint effort of the U.S. Geological Survey's biological resources division and the West Virginia University Division of Forestry).

Bibliography

Braxton County Historical Society Journals.

Brooks, Maurice, *The Appalachians*, Seneca Books, Inc.

Brooks, Noah, *First Across the Continent: Lewis & Clark*, Mead-Westvaco.

Byrne, J. Holt, *Sutton…a Good Place to Call Home*, Byrne Printing Company.

Byrne, W.E.R, *Tale of the Elk*, Mountain State Press.

Carpenter, Harold, and Carpenter, Richard, family genealogies.

Chapman, Berlin B., *Education in Central West Virginia: 1910-1975*.

Cincotta, Dan, *West Virginia Wildlife*.

Clarkson, Roy B., *On Beyond Leatherbark: The Cass Saga*, McClain Printing Company.

Clay County High School Art Department, *Hickory & Lady Slippers series*.

Clayton, Janet, *Freshwater Mussels in Elk River*, WV Division of Natural Resources.

Clendenin Woman's Club, *History of the Town of Clendenin*.

Cohen, Stan, and Andre, Richard, *Capitols of West Virginia: A Pictorial History*, Pictorial Histories Publishing Company.

Cohen, Stan, and Andre, Richard, *Kanawha County Images*, Pictorial Histories Publishing Company and Kanawha Bicentennial Inc.

Comstock, Jim, *West Virginia Heritage Encyclopedia*.

Cook, Roy Bird, *The Annals of Fort Lee*, West Virginia Press Review.

Dasher, George, *The Caves of East-Central West Virginia*, West Virginia Speleological Survey.

Davenport, H.B., *Tales of the Elk and Other Stories*.

Debord, Mary Jane Dodrill, *A Pictorial History of Point Mountain*

Then and Now.

Deike, George H. III, *Logging South Cheat: The History of the Snowshoe Lands.*

Dodrill, Charles T., *Heritage of a Pioneer.*

Dodrill, William Christian, *Moccasin Tracks and Other Imprints,* McClain Printing Company.

Dulaney, Annie Harvey, *History of Gassaway.*

Gillespie, William H. and Betty, *A Brief Genealogy of Elijah Hedding Gillespie: His Ancestors, Descendents and Their Families.*

Gillespie, Bill, *A Stroll Through Webster Springs.*

Gillespie, Bill, *Letters From the Hills,* West Virginia Hillbilly.

Green, N. Bayard, and Pauley, Thomas, *Amphibians & Reptiles in West Virginia,* University of Pittsburgh Press in cooperation with the WV Division of Natural Resources nongame wildlife program.

Hale, John P., *Trans-Allegheny Pioneers,* The Graphic Press.

Hammon, Neal, Ed., *My Father, Daniel Boone,* the Draper interviews with Nathan Boone, The University Press of Kentucky.

Hamrick, L.W. Jr., *Roots & Wings: The Family Record of Benjamin Hamrick,* Headline Books, Inc.

Hamrick, Mayme, *The Hamrick and Other Families,* Mennonite Publishing House; additional printings by McClain Printing Company.

Hamrick, Ray, *The Blue Hills of West Virginia.*

Hardway, Ronald, *The Hamrick Family and the Beginning of Methodism in the Upper Elk Valley,* the Elk Valley Review of History and Genealogy.

Hopkins, Marian Carpenter, *Braxton County Heritage,* the Carpenter family.

Jarvinen, Larry, *Cultural Resources Inventory, Marlinton Ranger District, Monongahela National Forest.*

Jones, Orton, *John Young: Lieutenant at Elk,* Mountain State Press.

Kelly, R.G., *More Trails On Six Continents,* Charleston Printing Company.

Lesser, Hunter, *Rebels At the Gate,* Sourcebooks, Inc.

Lofaro, Michael A., *The Life and Adventures of Daniel Boone,* The University Press of Kentucky.

Mace, Raymond, *Sketches of Elk.*

Miller, Sampson N., *Annals of Webster County: Before and Since*

Organization, Golden Rule Press.

Milnes, Gerald, *Play of a Fiddle: Traditional Music, Dance, and Folklore in West Virginia*, The University Press of Kentucky.

Morgan, John G., *West Virginia Governors*, Charleston Newspapers.

Nelson, Arnold, *Haven in the Hardwood*, McClain Printing Company.

Newell, Clayton R., *Lee vs. McClellan*, Regnery Publishing, Inc.

Price, William, *Historical Sketches of Pocahontas County*.

Rice, Otis K., *The Allegheny Frontier*, University Press of Kentucky.

Riggleman, Homer, *A West Virginia Mountaineer Remembers*, McClain Printing Company.

Roeder, Fred, *Benchmarks*, New Mexico State Surveyors Association.

Romano, Mark, *Webster: A Pictorial History of Webster County*, Walsworth, Inc.

Shawkey, M.P., *West Virginia In History, Life, Literature and Industry*, Lewis Publishing Company.

Sturm, Harry P. and Rhawn, H.G., *Rimfire:West Viginia's Typical Mountaineer*, McClain Printing Company.

Sutton, John D., *History of Braxton County and Central West Virginia*, McClain Printing Company.

Warner, Norva Balser, *The Strength of Our People*, McClain Printing Company.

West Virginia Writers' Projects, *Gassaway and Community*, and *Sutton on the Elk*, Works Progress Administration.

Williams, John Alexander, *West Virginia and the Captains of Industry*, West Virginia University Foundation.

Young, Henry F., *Tall Tales II*, Jalamap Publications.

Index

SKIP JOHNSON was born on Birch River at Herold, WV, and lived there till shortly before his death in 2011. He retired in 1992 as outdoor columnist and reporter for *The Charleston Gazette.* In 1993, he wrote *Woods and Waters*, a collection of outdoor stories, and prior to that *The Quicker the Sooner* and *The Braxton Connection.*

ROB JOHNSON, the author's nephew, is a native of Charleston, WV, where he works for American Electric Power Company. He more or less grew up on Birch, and his love of the river is evident in his pictures, including the color pictures inside, and the black and white river pictures.

Made in the USA
Monee, IL
01 July 2023

37093307R00175